W9-CMB-904

The Politics of Education

Routledge Research in Education

For a full list of titles in this series please visit www.routledge.com

The Politics of Education

Challenging Multiculturalism

**Edited by Christos Kassimeris
and Marios Vryonides**

Routledge
Taylor & Francis Group
NEW YORK   LONDON

First published 2012
by Routledge
711 Third Avenue, New York, NY 10017

Simultaneously published in the UK
by Routledge
2 Park Square, Milton Park, Abingdon, Oxon OX14 4RN

*Routledge is an imprint of the Taylor & Francis Group,
an informa business*

Typeset in Sabon by IBT Global.
Printed and bound in the United States of America on acid-free paper by
IBT Global.

Library of Congress Cataloging-in-Publication Data
  The politics of education : challenging multiculturalism / edited by
Christos Kassimeris and Marios Vryonides.
    p. cm. — (Routledge research in education)
    Includes bibliographical references and index.
  1. Multiculturalism.   I. Kassimeris, Christos, 1974–   II. Vryonides,
Marios.
    LC1099.P635 2011
    370.117—dc22
    2011016305

ISBN: 978-0-415-88514-0 (hbk)
ISBN: 978-0-203-80251-9 (ebk)

Contents

Figures

Tables

1 Introduction

Christos Kassimeris and Marios Vryonides

Among academic circles there is a belief that education and politics are, or at least should be, separate. Yet education is a thoroughly political enterprise. For the most part, formal education is under direct state control. While education is expected, though in a much perverted manner, to cultivate moral individuals, convert immigrants into patriotic citizens and supply competent workers for a growing economy, it has also been expected to promote fundamental democratic ideals such as justice, equality, freedom and prosperity. It is precisely this controversy over the nature and scope of education that has generated disagreement over the definition of highly cherished social values, not to mention conflicts over individual and group interests. As a result, the process of determining the purpose of education has been a highly political one. It has resulted in battles that have not only divided people philosophically, but also on the basis of religion, region, class, race and ethnicity. Hence, education provides us with a spectacular arena in which to explore the tensions inherent in European and North American societies, as well as an understanding of how politics shapes education policy.

This book assesses the ways in which state institutions, political ideologies and competing interests, both within and outside the education community, influence the content, form and functioning of education. Moreover, it has historically been used as an ideological agency to promote national and ethnic identities which have been essential in the notion of ethnocentric states. As a result it has always been heavily financed by nation states. The notion of state, however, has been eroded over the past few decades. Since the 1970s at least three interconnected social phenomena have come about which had direct effects on the functioning and powers of the state; globalization and its overall impact on states, the emergence of post-modern societies and mass migration. While recognizing that the promotion of national and ethnic identities often seems to emanate primarily from the political right, there is a competing tendency from the left which tends to promote transnational allegiances and global perspectives, thus encouraging individuals to think of themselves as 'world citizens.' As a collection of studies focusing on the political aspects of education and educational policy-making in a number of western countries, this book reaffirms that educational phenomena reflect and inevitably serve political agendas. On the whole, this book offers a comparative examination of how politics influence education that should appeal to scholars in a variety of academic disciplines. The transatlantic character of this volume is, in particular, very instructive for comprehending how North American educational policy differs from Europe. Thus, we hope that these differences will indeed become quite illuminating for the readers.

As far as the opening chapter is concerned, it suffices to say that its main purpose is to set the tone of the book and to provide the general theoretical framework. Chapter 3 assesses education in the now ethnically diverse Britain. Even though there are certain policies and legislative acts in place designed to improve 'race' relations, Britain is not racism-free. Education, in particular, remains a field characterized by racial inequalities given the noticeably poor performance of Black and Minority Ethnic children in schools. This chapter delves into the historical and sociological background of certain education policies that have failed to address this discrepancy. Multiculturalism has been overshadowed by notions pertaining to diversity, citizenship and nation-building. The apparent radicalization of young Muslims in Britain, community cohesion and those educational policies set by the recent Labor governments are central to this chapter, as is the significance of 'whiteness' and the role that White and middle-class culture plays in modern Britain.

The following chapter examines education in the Netherlands. Commencing with a historical assessment of policies arguably designed to tackle racial inequalities, Chapter 4 focuses more on issues denoting to citizenship education. While multiculturalism was once the main objective regarding the future of the Dutch society, it is nowadays apparent that assimilation weighs far more heavily. Evidently, policies designed to combat educational disadvantage in the Netherlands are often dictated by the political ideology of whatever political party is in power with the main differences between left-wing and right-wing parties expanding over the field of education. The role of the extreme right, in particular, reveals interesting findings with regard to immigration.

Education in the US is a rather intriguing topic. A key issue dominating education at national level was Civil Rights and the lack of equality of educational opportunities. The expansion of Civil Rights, the arrival of new immigrant groups, and globalization have revamped the US education system to an extent where what was once considered the domain of state and local authorities nowadays includes the federal government. Still, both schools and states have resisted federal interference in educational policies. In this respect, Chapter 5 assesses the role of the federal government and those structural forces that shaped public education. Central to this chapter are the hypotheses that the increased educational opportunities available to disadvantaged groups and immigrants alike have lessened the career prospects of those pupils coming from the native-born middle class and the growing fears expressed by the business sector concerning a lack of competitiveness of the American labor force in the midst of the worldwide financial crisis and the overall impact of economic globalization.

Chapter 6 examines the relationship between education and the construction of identity in Spain. By way of assessing Catalan, Basque and Galician nationalisms, this chapter makes evident that secessionist nationalism is as manipulative a force as the past unionist, Spanish nationalism was during Franco's era. The use of different languages in schools and the instruction of the different histories and nationalist symbols of Catalonia, Galicia and the Basque Country underline the significance of education and its political dimension in Spain.

The chapter on education in Germany focuses on matters pertaining to citizenship, Europeaness and interculturalism. Comparing the citizenship, geography and history curricula of Berlin and Baden-Württemberg, this chapter makes evident that government policy and ideology helped promote a 'Europeanized national identity' so as to promote the needs of a multicultural society. Germany continues to struggle with shifting its educational policies from maintaining a Europeanized identity to a novel dimension of multicultural citizenship. Tracing the historical background of educational polices in Germany from the times of the Weimar Republic, through Nazism, to the post-war division of the country, it becomes clear that citizenship education has always been instrumental in shaping society.

As with the chapter on US education, Chapter 8 assesses yet another North American education system. This chapter produces an analysis of multicultural education in Canada at provincial level. Changes in textbook content, educational achievement rates of minority students and the ethnic composition and practices of teachers dominate the discussion, while also indicating that despite whatever education strategies inequalities continue to persist in Canadian education. The case of Canada is unique, however, for its manifold cultural identities engage the First Nations peoples, the British and French communities, as well as the immigrant population. As one might expect, the pertinent cultural differences are often reflected in Canada's understanding of multiculturalism and education. Interestingly, education in Canada is a provincial matter rather than a federal issue, thus affecting much the federal government's initiatives to defend multiculturalism.

Chapter 9 demonstrates how highly politicized education is in Greece. This chapter assesses three very interesting cases studies all mirroring the significance of nationalism in Greece. More precisely, it becomes apparent that educational policies intended to facilitate the integration of migrant children are likely to suffer at the hands of extreme right formations, just as the impact of Greek–Turkish affairs may dictate Greek educational policies with reference to the Turkish minority in Thrace. To this end, the heated debate surrounding the proposed new history textbook is, of course, hardly surprising, thus indicating that politics and ethnocentrism complement one another in designing school curricula in Greece.

The final chapter of this book employs ethnographic data from one Flemish school in order to explore the nature of interaction between instructors and students. Taking into account the school's ethnic composition, senior management policies and national educational policies, all examined against the background of multiculturalism, the teachers' stereotyping of ethnic minority students of Turkish origins is assessed.

As a collection of studies that reveal the politicized nature of education in contemporary western societies, this book reaffirms that educational phenomena reflect and inevitably serve certain political agendas that do not necessarily coincide with the all-pervading notion of multiculturalism. Yet amidst the rabid social changes brought about by globalization and post-modernity, states and governments try to reaffirm their power to promote policies that reflect the needs and the priorities set out by those in power. Hence, this book aims at situating education in a political setting and should, therefore, appeal to political scientists, sociologists and educationalists with an interest in the political aspects of education.

2 Politics and Education

Christos Kassimeris and Marios Vryonides

Since the time of the emergence of the post-Westphalia ethnocentric states, national governments in their effort to build nation states have used an array of ideological tools in order to cultivate national identities of shared cultures, histories, languages, religion, traditions, etc. Education, especially after it has become a mass social phenomenon post-World War II, has often been used as an ideological tool for implementing such national policies for cultivating and strengthening a uniform cultural and national identity. In this effort they often resorted to the suppression or eradication of competing identities and peripheral nationalisms. The examples are numerous and can be found all around the world.

The process of nation-building and the use of education as a tool towards this end has been particularly true in states that emerged after the post-colonial era from the time of the independence of the US until today; for example, in the case of the newly independent Balkan states or those that emerged after the collapse of the Soviet Union. The way with which this has often been promoted was through national curricula that usually prescribe common histories, memories and cultures. However, much of sociological research tended to focus not only on the content of the official national curriculum but at times it was thought that such policies were more efficiently implemented through the workings of the "hidden curriculum" (Meighan and Siraj-Blatchford 1997). Meighan and Siraj-Blatchford offer a working definition of the hidden curriculum which is "all the things that are learnt during schooling in addition to the official curriculum" (1997, 65) and express the idea that schools do more than simply transmit knowledge, as laid down in the official curricula, but also pass on norms, values and beliefs.

Education as one of the primary institutions of an individual's socialization transmits those cultural values that are regarded by many as necessary for the preservation of social solidarity and order. The institution of education, however, has not operated without criticism stemming from ideological, political and philosophical debates. In terms of political debates, education has always been regarded as a thoroughly political enterprise and powerful stakeholders, particularly those with political influence, have always aspired and worked towards creating and maintaining control over the contents, the goals and the way it is implemented. This has often resulted in social divisions and an ongoing debate about the winners and losers of this enterprise in a number of areas; social class, gender and ethnicity to name a few. Social class tensions in education have attracted quite a lot of interest, so much so that, as we will examine later on, Marxist sociologists, for example, have characterized education as an arena where the capitalist ideology is been promoted at the expense of the working classes (Bowles and Gintis 1976). Others, too, following the eminent work of French sociologist P. Bourdieu, have seen education as a mechanism of cultural reproduction which leads to the reproduction of social advantages of those middle classes that are better positioned within the educational market.

In our analysis, while recognizing these discourses concerning education, we will not go into them but rather focus on the ways national policies in education become politics of national continuity amidst an environment which operates in an eroding fashion for the nation-state. This has been the outcome of what has come to be known as the Globalization phenomenon which has created unparallel social conditions for individuals and societies in a way that the pace with which they occur (because of advances in Information and Communication Technologies) is often very difficult to track and examined in all of their dimensions. One of the consequences of the Globalized era is the creation of the notion of multicultural societies and the need of education to respond to this new reality. Recently, however, the political goal of cultivating multicultural policies has suffered significant blows by an emerging changing attitude towards multiculturalism exemplified by the realization of many European leaders mostly from the political right, such as German Chancellor Merkell, French president Sarkozy and Italian premier Berlusconi, that the multiculturalism project has in fact been unsuccessful in Europe. This realization would likely point to shifts in national policies and specifically in changes in the direction of educational policies that for so long promoted the goal of multicultural societies. Many interpret these political leaders' stand as a response to the new realities posed by the so called "international terrorism" (especially post-9/11) and by national discourses about the consequences of the global economic crisis. There are also voices that connect the latter with migration and its consequences in domestic social, cultural, economic and political agendas.

Our chapter will start with an examination of the goal of education in societies and the relationship of education and the state. We will then go on to examine the development of education in a globalized world and the changing discourse that emerges in Europe about the promotion of multiculturalism as a political objective. What we would like to argue in this chapter is that even though up until now education was seen as a vehicle for promoting multiculturalism and that such a rhetoric is still present and visible in many countries it is also evident that national countries still treat education as an ideological tool for promoting nationalist specific goals of national unity, identity and cohesion.

THE GOAL OF EDUCATION IN SOCIETY

In any approach one adopts to examine the role of education in society regardless of the outcomes and its consequences it is probably an undisputed fact that education is expected to perform some functions. These include cultivating individuals in the norms and social values of the time, integrating migrants into the host society and supplying competent workers for the economy. As most national curricula would have it, education is also expected to promote fundamental democratic ideals such as justice, equality, freedom and prosperity. It is precisely this controversy over the nature and scope of education that has generated disagreement over the definition of highly cherished social values, not to mention conflicts over individual and group interests. As a result, the process of determining the purpose of education has been a highly political one. It has resulted in battles that have not only divided people philosophically, but also on the basis of religion, region, class, race and ethnicity. Hence, education provides us with a spectacular arena in which to explore the tensions inherent in European and North American societies, as well as an understanding of how politics shapes education policy.

There are at least two ways of examining the role education in societies. From a structuralist perspective, education functions in such a way so as to promote society's need to achieve equilibrium and social order. Structural functionalists believe that the primary aim of key institutions, such as education, is to socialize the new generations in such a way (directly through the formal curriculum, but also indirectly through "the hidden curriculum") so as to internalize the knowledge, attitudes, norms and values that they will need as future citizens. Apart from socialization education performs another function, that of sorting individuals in the labor market. Those who achieve higher are given better opportunities for training and get the most important jobs and by extension the highest social rewards. Those who do not achieve as high are directed to the least demanding jobs, which entail fewer social rewards. This, in many ways unproblematic, view of education does not take into account power relations and the unequal distribution of material and symbolic resources in society, part of which are regulated and safeguarded by the various functions of education. There are of course serious objections to such an approach to education put forward by theorists who adopt either conflict, critical and neo-Marxist perspectives. The common ground of these approaches is that education is a means of social reproduction of those social groups (or classes) who are better socially positioned, have different aspirations, have access to better life opportunities through their material and symbolic resources and generally end up with gaining better social rewards. Thus, education in essence is a field of social antagonism whereby it is characterized by symbolic (and real) domination and subordination.

A key advocate of this perspective has been the French sociologists Pierre Bourdieu whose theoretical framework on the role of education in cultural and social reproduction is built around the concepts of habitus, field, social and cultural capital. For Bourbieu the cultural capital of the dominant (usually middle and upper class) groups, in the form of practices and relation to culture, is assumed to be the legitimated form of knowledge and therefore it is rewarded by the school by giving access to educational capital and prestigious qualifications. Lower-class students are disadvantaged in this process because their social and cultural capitals are not of the currency that the school recognizes as having value. This usually means that these children find success harder in school due to the fact that they must learn the proper and acceptable way of behaving in schools in terms of language, culture, preferences, etc. In this process only a small number of less-privileged students achieve success but according to Bourdieu this success only serve as a way to make the whole system legitimate and thus unchallenged. The previous perspective and others influenced by the critical school of thought and neo-Marxist approaches regard the whole education system as being shaped by an ideology provided by the dominant group which stipulates that a major goal of schooling is to strengthen equality while, in reality, schools reflect society's intention to maintain the previous unequal distribution of status and power. This inevitably leads to social reproduction.

THE ROLE OF EDUCATION IN THE ECONOMY IN A GLOBALIZED WORLD

The move towards globalization and its interconnected consequences in almost all spheres of social life has inevitably brought about changes in education. These changes can be found in the influences of neo-liberal ideologies in economy and the commodification of education and changes in the relationship between the state and education. As commended previously, education has historically been used as an ideological agency to promote national and ethnicity identities which have been essential in the notion of ethnocentric states. As a result, it has always been heavily financed by nation-states. The notion of state, however, has been eroded over the past three of four decades due to globalization effects. Since the 1970s at least three interconnected social phenomena have come about which have had direct effects on the notion of the state: (a) The first change is that of globalization and its subsequent changes in the nature and powers of the state; (b) second, is the emergence of the post-modern world and the domination of ICTs which often transcend the boarders and the boundaries of the state; and (c) thirdly, the unprecedented phenomenon of mass migration towards Europe and the US. These changes inevitably brought about changes in the political aspects of education and educational policy making in many countries. In this book we focus on European countries and the US, and it will be shown, we hope, that educational phenomena reflect and inevitably serve political agendas.

According to Burbules and Torres (2000, 2) in this new environment within which education has to operate new concepts and vocabularies being used in the debates that are taking place about the role of education such as "neoliberalism", "the state", "reform", "restructuring", "identity", "citizenship", "multiculturalism", etc.

PROMOTING POLICIES OF MULTICULTURALISM

In promoting policies of multiculturalism, language plays a key role in promoting integration for the use of a single language across any given nation-state certainly has the potential to produce the necessary grounds to further develop the idea of national identity, as well as to create a distinct political community. Within this context, Ernest Gellner stressed that "modern loyalties are centred on political units whose boundaries are defined by the language (in the wider or in the literal sense) of an educational system" (Gellner 1994, 59). In contrast, regional dialects may just as easily bring about sociopolitical fragmentation. Describing the decision of the First French Republic to make use of one national language, Pierre Bourdieu said that "[t]he imposition of the legitimate language in opposition to the dialects and patois was an integral part of the political strategies aimed at perpetuating the gains of the Revolution through the production and the reproduction of the 'new man'. Condillac's theory, which saw language as a method, made it possible to identify revolutionary language with revolutionary thought. To reform language, to purge it of the usages linked to old society and impose it in its purified form, was to impose a thought that would itself be purged and purified" (Bourdieu 1999, 47). Once purged and purified, the communication tool that is language will make itself available to help shape society, if suitably employed, in a manner that would at least ensure its continued existence. Mary McGroaty argued that "[l]anguage policies in education represent a critical arena in which a society's expectations for the success of its future members are simultaneously expressed, enacted, and constrained" (McGroarty 2002, 17). It should be noted, nonetheless, that the success of a society's members is merely a reflection of the success of society itself, thus the need for obligatory education. If educated, the political animal that man is will become better equipped for participating in all things societal, or else Gellner would have no reason to support that "[t]he minimal requirement for full citizenship, for effective moral membership of a modern community, is literacy" (Gellner 1994, 55). To defend the prominence of education Gellner needed only recruit history to remind the reader that "[t]ime was, when the minimal political unit [the nation] was determined by the preconditions of defence or economy: it is now determined by the preconditions of education" (Gellner

1994, 56). Perhaps education became obligatory to accomplish no more than increasing literacy levels for the sole purpose of producing socially acceptable citizens, for the political elite would otherwise struggle to command attention.

Indeed, research findings suggest that high levels of education are associated with participation in political affairs, particularly voting in elections and campaigning (Hillygus 2005). Demonstrating the prominence of education in society is the staggering number of students, given that "[i]n 2007, about 1.4 billion students were enrolled in schools around the world. Of these students, 694 million were in elementary-level programs, 519 million were in secondary programs, and 151 million were in postsecondary programs" (Snyder and Dillow 2010, 577). Obviously employing similar evidence, Sidney Verba, Kay Lehman Schlozman and Henry Brady (1995) suggest that better educated citizens seek for increased participation in politics as a means of communication with politicians. From a similar perspective, Michel Foucault argued that "power and knowledge directly imply one another; there is no power relation without the corrective correlation of a field of knowledge, nor any knowledge that does not presuppose and constitute power relations" (Foucault 1980, 27). A case in point is the very use of books, for they play a key role in shaping school curricula, while also dictating the core principles of civic education and the knowledge available to pupils and teachers alike. Benedict Anderson underlines the significance of books in his *Imagined Communities* (1991) in an attempt to support that nations are products of the modern era aiming to fulfill certain social, political and economic objectives. Emphasizing the role of education in sustaining a sense of belongingness to the nation, as well as making available the necessary means for the elite to maintain control over a population, are Eric Hobsbawm in *Nations and Nationalism Since 1780* (1992) and Anthony Smith in *National Identity* (1991). Just as Hobsbawm underlined the significance of education in perpetuating national heritage within the well defined boundaries of a nation-state, Smith argued that "[c]ivic education . . . is potentially the most significant feature of territorial nationalism and the identity it seeks to create" (Smith 1991, 118). Richard Mole concurs stressing that the ultimate purpose of education is "to create loyal members of society whose ability to function as such would not be hampered by attachments to subgroups within or beyond state boundaries" (Mole 2007, 5). The European Union's approach to integration differs little given the emphasis put on the apparent link between assimilation and education when considering not only the content of curricular across member states, in terms of what is perceived as European culture and history, but also the well established mobility of teachers and students alike on account of the exchange programs available.

Yet developing a successful recipe to support European integration continues to burden all pertinent actors. In terms of employing education to facilitate European integration Paul Connolly (1994), Gill Crozier (1989),

Ghassan Hage (1998) and Herne Varenne and Ray McDermott (1998) all concur that intercultural education has not only failed to fulfill its predetermined goals but has paradoxically achieved to reproduce racist stereotypes. Rather than eliminating racial discrimination and strengthening diversity, or at least helping educate pupils, intercultural education policies and practices have actually reinforced segregation. Hage appears adamant that the kind of multiculturalism states endorse today only contributes to perpetuating society's current power relationships. Already defined to serve the dominant white, intercultural education appears to perform a political function in that it masks intolerance while maintaining resistance to all things foreign. Supporting a similar view is the European Commission against Racism and Intolerance (ECRI) stressing that "EU Member States have responded to the increasing ethnic diversity by implementing curricula changes that not only target minority groups but the entire school population. [. . .] While intercultural education is said to foster a better understanding of one's own and other cultures, multicultural education is often seen as an appropriate response by the education systems to prepare pupils for life in a multicultural society" (ECRI 2004, 87). A more recent, diametrically-opposed assessment of the likely prospects of intercultural education, however, maintains a markedly distinct view for the Guidelines on Intercultural Education, as endorsed by the United Nations Educational, Scientific and Cultural Organization to celebrate the more dynamic character of interculturalism, argues that "[m]ulticultural education uses learning about other cultures in order to produce acceptance, or at least tolerance, of these cultures whereas intercultural education aims to go beyond passive coexistence, to achieve a developing and sustainable way of living together in multicultural societies through the creation of respect for and dialogue between the different cultural groups" (UNESCO 2006, 18). The efficacy of the previous evaluations notwithstanding, it becomes apparent that while education is usually perceived as quite an appropriate tool for combating racial discrimination and intolerance, the empirical evidence available supports the exact opposite.

Given that government-sponsored education encompasses the all-important attributes for strengthening one's sense of belongingness to a predetermined group (Bush and Saltarelli 2000), the construction of a distinct identity naturally presupposes that multiculturalism threatens the cohesion of any given community. Institutionalized education is more often than not designed to produce civically-oriented citizens suitably 'educated' in what best promotes society's norms and values. Likewise, where interculturalism is preferred, the instruction of the native language for example, may allow room for assimilation, however, the mere reproduction of inequalities through intercultural education will almost certainly maintain segregation. The sheer categorization of pupils based on their nationality or citizenship status, their subdivision into non-nationals and aliens, as well as the likely distinction between refugees and asylum seekers, for example, essentially render education susceptible to discrimination. When pupils from a distinct background are all together placed into special, minority classes, the racialization of these groups is inevitable, thus ensuring the dominance of the host culture. Limiting their achievement and advancement in such an environment, pupils from different ethnic backgrounds are condemned to lower educational attainments. Furthermore, the placement of pupils in such classes also has a severe demoralizing effect when considering that local culture may become as dominant as to suppress the customs and traditions of ethnic communities. While neither approach appears to be convincingly more prudent, multiculturalism and interculturalism both deserve a thorough examination against the background of education in the countries assessed herein. To avoid any premature conclusions, therefore, a succinct country-by-country overview is imperative.

In Belgium, pupils are separated between Flemish and Walloons and then subdivided into groups according to citizenship, with most migrants usually originating from France, Italy, Morocco, the Netherlands and Turkey. Despite an increase of immigration in the past, there has been a considerable decrease of the foreign population since many migrants have become naturalized. Given the country's diverse population, Belgium adopted an intercultural approach to education that focuses precisely on diversity with half of the Flemish primary schools and some 10 percent of secondary schools offering relevant curricula. What's worth, statistically more foreign pupils attend French-speaking schools (10 percent) than Flemish schools (4–6 percent).

Canada's multicultural approach to education clearly reflects the country's ethnic diversity, which may also account for the fact that there is "no federal department of education and no integrated national system of education" (Council of Ministers of Education 2008, 7). The degree of ethnic diversity in Canada becomes evident when considering that at the dawn of the twenty-first century more than a quarter of the school population in the wider areas of Toronto and Vancouver, for instance, were immigrants, while some 20 percent of the pupils had a home language other than English or French. Also significant, in terms of numbers, is the Aboriginal school population, particularly in Canada's Census Metropolitan Areas.

The education system in Germany differentiates nationals from foreigners with the data available indicating a further subdivision between nationals on one hand and European Union (EU) and non-EU citizens, and various other ethnic groups on the other. The great influx of 'guest workers' from the 1960s to the 1980s and the reunification of Germany have been translated into a considerably high number of pupils of foreign descent, particularly from the former Yugoslavia and Turkey, accounting for 9 percent of the total school population. As with Belgium, German education, too, has adopted an intercultural approach that:

> was initially introduced within the framework of the so-called 'foreigners pedagogy' (*Ausländerpädagogik*) and was restricted to classes

with a high percentage of migrant children. Today it is increasingly seen as an across-the-board duty of schools, which is relevant to all subjects and to all children. However, this task can be undertaken in a wide variety of curricular approaches, the implementation of which is still dependent on the initiative of the individual teachers. Therefore, demands have repeatedly been made to include intercultural education within teacher training. It is also asked that school textbooks focusing on various foreign cultures from different perspectives should be used in teaching in order to follow the principle of intercultural education. Even though some progress has been made in this area, there is still repeated criticism that school textbooks support prejudices about certain ethnic groups. (ECRI 2004, 89)

Statistical data on pupils in Greece indicate the existence of two groups, nationals and immigrants; however, the latter also includes ethnic Greek immigrants. Ever since the collapse of communism in Eastern Europe, the number of immigrant pupils in primary schools has increased to more than 10 percent, their majority originating from Albania and the former Soviet Union. Even though Law 2413 of 1996 stresses that immigrant pupils shall be assisted accordingly so as to facilitate their integration in Greek society, the ECRI report on Migrants, minorities and education has brought to light disturbing evidence regarding the Greek perception of interculturalism (ECRI 2004, 90).

Categorizing pupils in the Netherlands appears less elaborate, yet the terms selected to describe those pupils command attention for

[a]n ethnic minority pupil is defined as someone who was born in one of the so-called target group countries or someone who has at least one parent born in a target group country. The definition of target groups is part of the policy on disadvantaged peoples, for whom an extra school budget is made available for overcoming learning lags. Since not all countries of origin are regarded as criteria for disadvantage, certain countries have been selected as 'target' countries. Target countries include Turkey, Morocco, Surinam, Netherlands Antilles, Aruba, Greece, Italy, former Yugoslavia, Portugal, Spain, Cape Verde Islands, and Tunisia. (ECRI 2004, 6)

All in all, some 15 percent of pupils in primary schools are of foreign descent, the majority originating from Aruba, the Dutch Antilles, Morocco, Surinam and Turkey. Worthy of note is the fact that the Netherlands first employed intercultural education in 1984.

Foreign pupils in Portugal are categorized, as per the relevant data, in 'cultural groups and nationalities' with the majority originating from Angola, Cape Verde and Guinea, even though statistics also distinguish EU nationals from non-EU citizens. Their number amounts to no more than 7 percent in primary schools, yet what is interesting is the decision of the Portuguese to convert from multicultural to intercultural education in the 1980s due to the former approach placing "minority groups in a 'ghetto-situation'" (ECRI 2004, 92). Intercultural education, as dictated in a number of legislative measures, was initially supported by the Coordinating Secreteriat for Multicultural Education Programs. It was designed "'to coordinate, foster and promote, within the education system, the programmes aiming to teach the values of conviviality, tolerance, dialogue and solidarity between different peoples, ethnicities and cultures'. This institution, currently called Intercultural Secretariat, was the most important political measure taken to this date dealing with the education of minority communities. Since 1996, however, the Intercultural Secretariat's budget has been reduced and its effective action has diminished accordingly" (ECRI 2004, 92).

Pupils in Spain are also distinguished according to citizenship. Accounting for less than 5 percent, the majority of foreign pupils come from Africa and South America. Like Portugal, Spain, too, has experimented with education ever since

> the drafting of the new Basic Law 10/2002 on the Quality of Education (LOCE), stirred a debate on two very different education models. On the one hand, there are advocates of cultural assimilation who claim that pupils of foreign origin must assimilate to Spanish cultural values and that the education system must not suffer any curricular variation from what has been traditionally taught in the country. On the other hand, there are those who push for intercultural education and think that integration must be a concern based on the respect for cultural differences, which are a fundamental characteristic of the current society (ECRI 2004, 92)

Much unlike those European states mentioned previously, the United Kingdom "distinguishes groups according to race rather than according to citizenship", but until recently "the categories used for recording data relating to minority ethnic communities in education were inconsistent", not to mention that the "effectiveness of broad use of racial categories has been debated" (ECRI 2004, 7). Regardless, pupils from different ethnic communities in England amount to some 12 percent in primary and secondary schools, but those whose mother tongue is not English account for 10 percent of the school population. English education, however, combines the need to promote integration and diversity with eliminating discrimination from society. To this end,

> the Home Secretary's Action Plan in response to the MacPherson Report has identified and prioritised the need to amend the curriculum in order to better reflect the needs of a diverse society. The inclusion statement—introduced as part of the revised national curriculum in 1999—provides a statutory requirement on schools to meet pupil's

diverse learning needs. This can be interpreted as to include promoting cultural diversity. The Race Relations (Amendment) Act 2000 also places a positive duty on the local education authorities (LEAs) and on schools to eliminate unlawful racial discrimination. This can be interpreted as a basis for developing multicultural and antiracist approaches in education. (ECRI 2004, 93)

Nevertheless, the inclusion statement and the Amendment Act both failed to fully endorse multiculturalism.

Finally, the United States, too, employs a multicultural model of education that echoes all-important notions such as 'diversity' and 'inclusion' so as to convey a rather strong statement on culture and integration. Classifying elementary and secondary level pupils into White (57 percent), Black (14.2 percent), Hispanic (21 percent), Asian (4 percent), Pacific Islander (0.2 percent), American Indian/Alaska native (0.9 percent) and what is without doubt a peculiar category comprising pupils of two or more races (2.7 percent), multiculturalism in the United States is evidently well reflected all through its school population (National Center for Education Statistics 2010). Its multicultural education, nevertheless, should be examined against the historical background of racial segregation that characterized education in the United States up until the early 1970s.

While the majority of the countries mentioned previously employ interculturalism as far as education is concerned, multicultural education constitutes a more efficient tool for combating racial and cultural stereotypes. Given that the content of any given curriculum is more often than not dictated by society's supreme cultural norms, usually reflecting core characteristics of a dominant White group, multicultural education aims to dissociate pupils from those conventional structures that merely serve to perpetuate stereotypical representations of all things alien. Multicultural education is designed in such a fashion so as to make good use of concepts pertaining to race and culture, thus engaging pupils in learning processes that will envelop a positive view of diversity. Irrespective of the acutely interactive prefix that precedes the very noun that denotes society's qualitative properties, the kind of interaction that interculturalism allows among pupils from distinct backgrounds contributes little to promoting diversity, since it merely masks segregation.

REFERENCES

Anderson, Smith D. 1991. *National Identity*. London: Penguin.

Bourdieu, Pierre. 1999. *Language and Symbolic Power*. Translated by Gino Raymond and Matthew Adamson, edited by John Thompson. Cambridge: Harvard University Press.

Bowles, Samuel, and Herbert Gintis. 1976. *Schooling in Capitalist America*. London: Routledge and Kegal Paul.

Burbules, Nicholas, and Carlos A. Torres. (Eds.). 2000. *Globalization and Education: Critical Perspectives*. London: Routledge.

Bush, Kenneth, and Diana Saltarelli. 2000. *The Two Faces of Education in Ethnic Conflict*. Florence: UNICEF Innocenti Research Centre.

Connolly, Paul. 1994. "All Lads Together? Racism, Masculinity and Multicultural/Anti-Racist Strategies in a Primary School," *International Studies in Sociology of Education* 4(2): 191–211.

Council of Ministers of Education (Canada). 2008. *The Development of Education, Reports for Canada, Report One: The Education Systems in Canada—Facing the Challenges of the Twenty First Century*. Toronto: Ontario.

Crozier, Gill. 1989. "Multicultural Education: Some Unintended Consequences". In *Politics and the Processes of Schooling*, edited by Stephen Walker and Len Barton, 58–81. Philadelphia: Open University Press.

European Commission against Racism and Intolerance (ECRI). 2004. *Migrants, Minorities and Education: Documenting Discrimination and Integration in 15 Member States of the European Union*. Report submitted by Dr. Mikael Luciak on EUMC. Luxembourg: Office for Official Publications of the European Communities.

Foucault, Michel. 1980. *Power/Knowledge: Selected Interviews and Other Writings 1972–1977*. Translated by Colin Gordon, Leo Marshall, John Mepham and Kate Soper, edited by Colin Gordon. New York: Pantheon.

Gellner, Ernest. 1994. "Nationalism and Modernization". In *Nationalism*, edited by John Hutchinson and Anthony D. Smith, 55–63. Oxford and New York: Oxford University Press.

Hage, Ghassan. 1998. *White Nation: Fantasies of White Supremacy in a Multicultural Society*. West Wickham: Pluto Press.

Hillygus, D. Sunshine. 2005. "The Missing Link: Exploring the Relationship between Higher Education and Political Behavior". *Political Behavior* 27, 1: 25–47.

Hobsbawn, Eric. 1992. *Nation and Nationalism since 1780: Programme, Myth, Reality*. Cambridge: Cambridge University Press.

McGroarty, Mary. 2002. "Evolving Influences on Educational Language Policies". In *Language Policies in Education: Critical Issues*, edited by James Tollefson, 17–36. Mahwah, NJ: Lawrence Erlbaum Associates.

Meighan, Roland, and Iram Siraj-Blatchford. 1997. *A Sociology of Educating*. London: Cassell.

Mole, Richard. 2007. "Discursive Identities/Identity Discourses and Political Power". In *Discursive Constructions of Identity in European Politics*, edited by Richard C. M. Mole, 1–24. New York: Palgrave Macmillan.

National Center for Education Statistics. 2010. Estimates of Resident Population, By Race/Ethnicity and Age Group: Selected Years, 1980 Through 2009. http://nces.ed.gov/programs/digest/d09/tables/dt09_016.asp?referrer=list

Smith, Anthony D. 1991. *National Identity*. London: Penguin.

Snyder, Thomas D., and Sally A. Dillow. 2010. *Digest of Education Statistics 2009*. Washington, DC: National Center for Education Statistics, Institute of Education Sciences, US Department of Education.

United Nations Educational, Scientific and Cultural Organization (UNESCO). 2006. *Guidelines on Intercultural Education*. Paris: UNESCO.

Varenne, Herne, and Ray McDermott. 1998. *Successful Failure: The School America Builds*. Boulder: Westview Press.

Verba, Sidney, Kay Lehmann Schlozman, and Henry Brady. 1995. *Voice and Equality: Civic Voluntarism in American Politics*. Cambridge: Harvard University Press.

3   The Politics of Education
Challenging Racial Discrimination and Disadvantage in Education in the British Context

Gill Crozier

In Britain[1] the development of policies on 'race'[2] and education and equality of opportunity in general has taken place in relation to social issues and grassroots struggles as well as political expediency. Britain has been an ethnically diverse country in an acknowledged way since the arrival of HMS Windrush from Jamaica in 1948, although Black African-Caribbean people and people from other parts of the former British colonised world, not to mention since the slave trade, have lived in this country for hundreds of years. Since those post-war years 'Race' Relations in England and Britain as a whole have improved in a range of ways. In 1976 racial discrimination was made illegal by the introduction of the Race Relations Act and anti-racist legislation was later strengthened by the Race Relations Amendment Act (RRAA) 2000. Since the RRAA not only is it illegal to overtly discriminate against Black and Minority Ethnic people but if institutions seem to be organised in a racist way or have policies that appear to discriminate then they can be prosecuted. Moreover racism can now be defined by those who experience this behaviour. All publicly run organisations, including schools, are also required to devise and implement race equality policies.

It was frequently claimed by the New Labour Government prior to the May 2010 Parliamentary elections that Britain is now a more tolerant and fairer society than it was when it first came in to office in 1997. In some respects Britain does 'feel' a more positive place now than for example in the 1990s and certainly the 1970s when it was not uncommon for Black people to be gratuitously attacked in the street by gangs of white racists and prior to the Race Relations Act 1976 racial discrimination, racist jokes, stereotyping and imagery was unashamedly explicit (for example, this kind of notice was openly displayed in the windows of Bed and Breakfast establishments and public houses: "SORRY NO COLOUREDS, NO IRISH, NO

DOGS"). However, a recent report from the Equalities and Human Rights Commission (2010) on how fair Britain has become shows that it is not as fair as many seem to have thought. The report states that one-quarter of people in prison are from an ethnic minority; Muslims now make up 12 percent of the prison population and the proportion of people of African-Caribbean heritage is almost seven times greater in relation to their share of the population. Black people constitute 3 percent of the population and yet 15 percent of this group were stopped by the police in 2008. Moreover, the now well known (in Britain) but nevertheless obdurate education achievement statistics show that Black Caribbean, Black African and Pakistani heritage children are the lowest achieving in Mathematics and English at 16 years when they take their GCSE examinations. Furthermore, social mobility has ground to a halt.

During the period of 13 years of the New Labour Government a raft of education policies in general but also specifically targeting 'race' and education were initiated. The aim of the chapter is to examine discursively why these policy initiatives have apparently failed to address fundamental inequalities of educational opportunity and achievement. In order to do this I take a historical as well as sociological perspective and discuss the policy shifts, the socio-political contextual influences on these and the ideological implications for race equality and education. During the past 30 years we have seen the rise and fall of multiculturalism as a policy strategy which more recently has been superseded by the more favoured notions of 'diversity and difference', together with nation-building and citizenship education. These developments are seemingly contradicted if not directly, then certainly by the insinuation and ramifications of policies on immigration and even the community cohesion initiatives which have been associated with government anxieties about the putative radicalization of young British Muslims.

'Race' and education policy and practice is often discussed in isolation from education policy and the analysis of the education system in general. Just as multicultural and anti-racist education practice is marginalized so, too, is the analysis of the roots of racism within education. As Gilroy (1999, 243) has argued " . . . just as racism itself views black settlers as an external, alien visitation, anti-racism can itself appear to be tangential to the main business of the political system as a whole". This attitude gives rise for example to the "bad apple" syndrome argument and the 'quick fix' approach to dealing with racism. Racism is not the only disadvantaging and discriminating experience that impacts on black people's lives and life chances. However, 'race' and racism are a central part, intertwined with class and gender, of structural oppression: "[they are not] fringe questions but [are a] volatile presence at the very centre of British politics actively shaping and determining the history not simply of blacks but of this country as a whole . . ." (Gilroy 1999, 243–244). Following Solomos, Finlay,

Jones and Gilroy (1982) and Gilroy (1999) I take the view that 'race' is not 'a unitary fixed principle ' but changes in different historical periods; it is "a contradictory phenomenon which is constantly transformed along with wider political-economic structures and relations of the social formation" (Solomos et al. 1982, 11). 'Race' along with other structural inequalities is thus embedded in the very fabric of a basically unequal society which in turn are reproduced by the State, within State apparatuses such as school/ing (see, for example, Althusser 1972).

The work of Bernstein, Bourdieu, Apple, Young and Whitty, to name but a few, made clear this relationship between Education and the socio-political, economic and historical context more than three decades ago. Since then studies of knowledge and the curriculum have diminished with the rise of neo-liberal policies and the technicist approach to teaching but the salience of this work not only remains but is of increasing importance. The nub of the argument is that there is a strong link between the desires of the State and the provision of education. From this perspective the role of school is manifold: its purpose, for example, is to reproduce a differentiated workforce (Apple 1995), social status and classed relations (Bourdieu and Passeron 1977), the creation and recreation of a dominant culture (Apple 1995; Bourdieu and Passeron 1977). As Apple (1995, 38) explains: "[Schools] teach norms, values, dispositions and culture that contribute to the ideological hegemony of dominant groups". Education is not value-free and all who are engaged in it whether they realize this or not are engaged in a political act (ibid.). One of the central points here for my purposes, is the reference to the reproduction of the dominant culture that is both White and middle class. Schooling, therefore, it is argued, is a means through which dominant ideology is perpetrated and interpellated by the students. This process of hegemony of White superiority serves to mediate all efforts to engage with 'race' and racism but also cultural diversity and difference. This process is reinforced by immigration policies indicating that migrants are unwanted, the rise of Islamophobia including the perpetration of the view that all Muslims are terrorists, the demonization of Black people as gang members, drug pushers and/or benefit scroungers.

Social and ideological reproduction operates through the overt and the covert curricula; the organisation and management of the school and fundamental to this are power relationships between the State, the economy and schools and teachers, teachers and pupils, teachers/schools and parents and so on.

In the rest of the chapter 'race' and education policy development over the past 15 years or so is analysed in relation to this perspective just outlined, concluding that the superficiality of the policy approach, rooting out 'bad apples' or 'painting over the cracks' could not succeed in dealing with racism itself nor adequately address educational under achievement.

'RACE', POLITICS AND EDUCATION

Britain like the rest of Europe and the so-called Western world is faced with the impact of the globalisation phenomenon, worldwide social upheavals through war, famine and other natural disasters. The global interrelationships have never been clearer and with that, growing recognition of 'developed world' moral responsibilities. Alongside this of course lie fears of change, threats to national identities and anxieties about the Other. In Britain, as in all of the countries represented in this volume, the Other includes those constructed or identified as Black or South and East Asian, or from another minority ethnic group such as Gypsies, Roma or Travellers or people coming from Central or Eastern Europe.

In a recent publication Sally Tomlinson (2008) traces and analyses the policy and political responses to this emergent and ever changing multiracial and multi-ethnic society. In her book she identifies the struggles around racist immigration legislation, the rise and fall and rise again of the far right and the hegemonic and residual impact of racism as it has permeated society in general and education in particular. As part of this she traces the ideological and theoretical debates between multiculturalism and anti-racism, debates which have never really been resolved and practices that have never been wholly or effectively implemented (see, for example, Crozier 1989, 1994; Troyna and Williams 1986).

In some respects 'race' and education, somewhat like gender and education, have been widely debated within educational spheres and also within charitable and community organisations (e.g., The Runnymede Trust). The former Commission for Racial Equality represented symbolically a voice on 'race' issues in society. The fact that it was incorporated into the Equality and Human Rights Commission earlier in 2010 may be a worrying sign that 'race' is no longer being taken as seriously. However, up to now over the past 13 years there has been a plethora of 'race' and education related initiatives and reports. One, if not the, most significant was the McPherson Report (1999) following the murder of Stephen Lawrence by white racists which led to the Race Relations Amendment Act (2000) and the duty to act in challenging racism imposed on schools and other educational establishments referred to earlier.

The Race Relations Amendment Act, the struggles around the murder of Stephen Lawrence and the MacPherson Report played a significant role in placing the issues of 'race' back on the educational agenda. There is generally greater recognition of the importance of educating young people for citizenship and to value diversity in society. There is also concern over the academic underachievement of Black and Minority Ethnic pupils. Such concerns have manifested themselves in, for example, the then Department for Education and Skills (DfES; now the Department of Education) Aiming High and Aiming Higher initiatives to support disadvantaged groups in going to university and the inclusion in the

Teacher Development Agency (TDA), Qualified Teacher Status Standards of the importance of diversity, equal opportunities, celebration of cultural diversity, teacher expectations, English as an Additional Language (EAL) and multilingualism. The TDA sponsoring of the online teacher development resource network, which directly addresses 'race' and education as well as a range of other inequalities (www.multiverse.ac.uk), is a further example, as is the incorporation of these issues into the assessment of Initial Teacher Education (ITE) practice by the Office of Standards in Education (Ofsted). However, none of these initiatives is without their problems and challenging racism and developing explicitly anti-racist practice is still not a foregrounded or overt priority in government policy or initial teacher education standards of practice.

In spite of these developments, which arguably represent some positive progress, within the same historical period there has been the tightening of national borders and an increase in immigration controls, together with anxieties about terrorism and the putative indoctrination/radicalisation of young British Muslims. This has led to the PREVENT (2008) initiative whereby funding is invested in counteracting such possibilities but with the implication that South Asian people and Muslims in particular are to be feared and albeit an unintended consequence is that this adds to the rise of Islamophobia (Stone 2004).

In the early part of the decade (2000–2010) Asian youths gave vent to their frustrations and disgruntlement. However rather than view the urban unrest in the multi-ethnic cities of Bradford, Oldham and Burnley in 2001 as an expression of grave concern over poor educational opportunities and job prospects as well as the racism encountered on a daily basis, the subsequent enquiry reported that the riots were a result of dislocated and disaffected, introspective communities (Cantle 2001).The London bombings in 2005 carried out by British-born Pakistani heritage men, were said to add further evidence to this claim of dislocation and alienation. It was said that Asian communities had not integrated and this contributed to the fuelling of radical Islamist attitudes. Schools with predominantly Black, Asian and Muslim populations were cited as further evidence of the lack of integration. In 2006, Trevor Phillips, the Head of the former Commission for Racial Equality and now the Equalities and Human Rights Commission, declared that Britain was a segregated society. The value of multiculturalism was thus questioned. In late summer of 2007, Ruth Kelly, formerly Secretary of State for Education and by then Minister for Communities, announced the setting up of yet another commission entitled The Commission on Integration and Cohesion. In her rationale for this Commission she raised the question as to whether the multicultural project had failed. She asked: "In our attempt to avoid imposing a single British Identity and culture, have we ended up with some communities living in isolation of each other, with no common bonds between them?" (Press Statement, Department for Communities and Local Government August 2006, 2).

The 'multicultural project' was blamed therefore for reinforcing separation rather than bringing communities together. Astonishingly the media made a huge leap from this to linking multiculturalism with terrorism and laying at its door responsibility for leading young British Muslims to turn to terrorism and suicide bombing. The prioritisation of policy was thus given to community cohesion and nation-building through citizenship education and the requirement for new immigrants and anyone who wanted to take out British citizenship to pass an English language test. According to Kundnani (2002, 2): " . . . from the State's point of view the 'multiculturalist settlement' which has dominated race relations thinking for the past two decades, is no longer working. . . . The establishment needs a revised strategy to manage and preserve a racially divided society, as effectively as 'multiculturalism' did in an earlier time . . . The new strategy is 'community cohesion' and the Cantle Report is the blue print".

This marked a shift in the policy discourse taking on the language of 'diversity' and again eschewing the much needed confrontation with racism. Even under the guise of multiculturalism there had been more of a focus on culture and values rather than equality of opportunity and challenging discrimination. In fact multicultural education has been extensively and consistently criticised for its ineffectuality and tokenistic, diversionary gestures. Policy discourse had and has gone little further than promoting tolerance—in itself a patronising notion. But now there was greater emphasis on nation-building (Cheong et al. 2007) and the discourse of diversity became a generic term to cover a range of disadvantage without having to tackle difficult, troubling and controversial issues such as institutional racism.

CHALLENGING RACIAL DISCRIMINATION AND DISADVANTAGE: MULTICULTURAL EDUCATION, DIVERSITY POLITICS AND ANTI-RACIST EDUCATION

Although the politics of difference has enabled some voices to be heard and discrimination based on sexuality, age and religion, as well as 'race', disability and gender (but still not class) is now legislated against, as Safia Mirza (2006) has argued, it is questionable how much these groups have gained by this. British Bangladeshi and Pakistani heritage children continue to be failed by the education system as do the children of African-Caribbean heritage, especially boys; women graduates of African Caribbean heritage are three times as likely as White women to be unemployed on graduating from university (Commission for Equality and Human Rights 2006). Research has shown that British Bangladeshi and Pakistani children experience, at times daily, racist harassment either verbally or physically or in some cases both (Crozier and Davies 2008). And others (e.g. Stone 2004) have shown that since 9/11 and more recently the London bombings of July 2007 (referred to as '7/7') the abuse of South Asian people has intensified.

For example, following the 7/7 London bombings, newspapers reported an incident that took place on a plane from Manchester bound for Ibiza. Two unsuspecting holiday-makers were ejected from the plane after protests by White passengers in a vigilante/lynch-mob style simply because they were thought to be speaking the language of the putative 'terrorist'. In fact they were speaking Urdu, not Arabic as it was thought, but of course that makes no difference. To the majority of white people on that plane the two Pakistani heritage men were alien, different and threatening.

Diversity politics and multiculturalism has done little to avert these stereotypical and taken for granted assumptions. Rather the evidence demonstrates that diversity politics was never about challenging discrimination, or as Kenan Malik (2003) argued, in discussing diversity training:

> . . . diversity training is not and never has been about combating racism. . . . Diversity training is really a PR exercise, a way of projecting a positive public image. "Diversity" has become a brand, a kind of Benetton shorthand for cool, liberal modernity. And any organisation that wants to brush up its image signs up. When the BBC wanted to shake off its fuddy-duddy image, it replaced its big globe balloon logo with shots of wheelchair-bound dreadlocked basketball players and Indian classical dancers. When the Arts Council wanted to become more relevant it launched its Year of Diversity. When Ford motor company was revealed to be "whiting out" black faces on its posters, it instituted a glossy, multi-million-pound diversity programme.

This is a similar argument that Paul Gilroy (1987) made about municipal anti-racism. On the face of it—with buses, the underground, the corridors of schools and other public institutions festooned with anti-racist posters, anti-racist badges, rock against racism and so on—it seemed a radical stance was being taken, but little actually changed in terms of challenging structural racism.

The discourse of 'diversity', as well as projecting a more positive public image, tends to focus on differences to deal with putative 'problems'; so, for example, South Asian parents who don't attend their children's school events are told they must learn English; African Caribbean boys who don't do well in school, fail because it is said their mothers are lone parents and are either not to be able to cope or else boys don't have appropriate role models and so have to have separate classes taught by African Caribbean male teachers and so on. Heidi SafiaMirza (2006) dubs this the 'new cultural racism' which she argues is little more than the previous 'sari, samosa and steelband' incarnation. But this is not quite the same as the cultural racism Tariq Modood (2005) talks of which is more related to the concept of symbolic violence (Bourdieu 1993) and ethnocentricism; this is a new form of cultural racism more like the cultural racism that Martin Barker (1981) discussed in his seminal work 'The New Racism' 30 years ago, which marks out difference as inadequacies, as deficiency, as reasons for 'their'—'the Other's'—own failure. It is turning the celebration of culture back on itself almost like a stigma. As SafiaMirza also says, this argument is the old argument around self-concept/self-esteem deficiency. But it is even more complex than that. In many schools in Britain outside of the major cities, there is limited practice of the 'three Ss'. By my argument this should be a good thing, except that it also signifies a lack of regard for anything other than a dominant White culture.

Certainly from my research with Bangladeshi and Pakistani families in the North of England referred to earlier, although not intentionally looking at school curriculum provision, it was clear that the schools had either no or virtually no understanding of diversity in any broad sense. In some primary schools they celebrated in a somewhat tokenistic fashion, for example, Diwali but not Eid or had a 'multicultural' theme to the school fete; in the secondary schools there was variable but limited recognition of 'diversity' in any form. In the schools with between 8–12 percent of visible minority ethnic children, the refrain often heard was that there wasn't "a problem here"; in the few schools with slightly higher percentages of minority ethnic children, there was English as an Additional Language (EAL) provision, and in one school where there was an issue of extended absences by the British Bangladeshi children, some teachers went on a visit to Sylhet to see what their country of origin was like: reminiscences here of a similar Department of Education initiatives circa 1974 and Roy Hattersley's 'integration' speech (1965).The emphasis here is on White teachers becoming 'informed' about 'difference' and instigating initiatives to make these children 'feel better' about themselves. In another secondary school where the children of British Pakistani heritage were said not to take part in the classical Western traditional school concerts or plays, the Head, with all good intentions, bought in an "Asian dance teacher" for lunch time classes as a form of compensation. So on the one hand we have what Troyna and Hatcher referred to as cultural pluralism—another term in my view for 'diversity', which they argued is given primacy over anti-racism and the focus is on: "the lifestyles not life chances of black children" (1992, 10). Such initiatives were directed at the Black and Minority Ethnic children. And on the other, we have a complete lack of regard for difference and a pedagogy that in effect is a form of symbolic violence.

The focus on diversity and difference has led to a neglect of structural and political issues and power relations (Sarup 1991, 61). As Madan Sarup asked "Is a society based on the principle of difference without hierarchy possible?" (1991, 130). Therefore, the focus on culture, or indeed 'cultural racism', can hide or be used to hide the existence and significance of structural and institutional racism. Moreover, as Darder and Torres (2003, 247) argue, "capitalist social relations and the existence of class divisions within racialized subordinate populations" are not addressed. Nevertheless, it is clear that organising around collective identities such as the historic Black

Power movement and subsequently Black identity throughout the West, has been necessary in the struggle against racism. In spite of the recognition of multiple and fluid identities as Stuart Hall developed in New Ethnicities (Hall 1992), there is also what Hall has called the need for a politics that is composed of 'unities within difference'" (cited in Back 1996, 4) or/ and at times what Spivak (1987) referred to as 'strategic essentialism'.

Moreover, it is also important to recognise difference, for if not, therein lies the danger of homogenisation which in turn acts as a control mechanism. As Miles and Phizacklea (1984, 168) wrote over 25 years ago:

> In a society where racism takes the form of demanding that 'they' become like 'us', the wearing of 'traditional' dress becomes laden with political significance.

We have already seen examples of this in France and in some comprehensive schools in the UK there have been struggles over dress conformity. It may have been useful for the State to keep minority groups on the margins but as these groups have raised more demands—for better schooling, services and the right to be heard, such as in the Bradford and Oldham riots (in 2001), then this can be seen by the State as threatening. More young South Asian women wear the hijab or shalwar kamiz or niqab now in the UK than hitherto: their assertion of their identity. Not surprising then State anxieties about integration/assimilation or lack of it.

Manifestations of this nation-building shift in policy in Britain are, as already indicated, represented by the Community Cohesion strategy involving citizenship courses and ceremonies for newer immigrants and English language classes in, as Cheong, Edwards, Goulborne and Solomos (2007, 27) argue "a bid to promote the learning of a 'common' language and supposedly 'core' values and culture". This in itself has had limited overt implications for schools. Its impact on education is more covert, such as in relation to the inference of South Asian communities and Black and Minority Ethnic groups more widely, as problematic and troublesome together with the rise of Islamophobia and stereotyping all Muslims as potential terrorists, as discussed earlier. A further manifestation of greater import for schooling, is the Citizenship Curriculum which is compulsory for lower secondary education (11–14 years) and optional for other age groups. Underpinning this curriculum development is the desire for the strengthening and development of a sense of Britishness: a 'British identity' also in keeping with the desire for the building of nationhood (Cheong et al. 2007). In spite of this narrow rationale for the Citizenship Curriculum, the schemes of work guidance provided by the Qualifications and Curriculum Authority potentially provide an opportunity to address race inequalities and racism. However, its efficacy in this respect is very dependent on how the individual teacher interprets and subsequently delivers this. Given that a survey of initial teacher education providers

(Davies and Crozier 2005) showed that only limited attention was given to 'race' and education for pre-service teachers and there was virtually no critical engagement with these complex issues, then it is doubtful that the Citizenship Curriculum has or will be implemented in a radical transformative way other than by a minority.

WHITE HEGEMONY AND RACISM

The cultural, social and political landscape of contemporary Britain has changed, and is changing, in radical ways from the mid-1980s, often cited as the time when 'race' and education politics stopped. Likewise racism (or racism*s*) in contemporary society is manifested in different ways and some argue, goes beyond colour racism (e.g., Modood 2005; Darder and Torres 2003). In this interrelated world where national boundaries are porous and culture is increasingly fluid, culture is both a hopeful feature as well as a source of racism in itself. This importance of culture is one which Paul Gilroy (2004) has identified as indicative of hope in the form of 'conviviality'. As he says,

> Given the extent of Britain's deepening economic and social divisions, it is perhaps surprising that the convivial metropolitan cultures of the country's young people are still a bulwark against the machinations of racial politics. (Gilroy 2004, 132)

Although he cites the fusion of youth cultures as an example of people getting along together and the willingness to 'harmonise', there still remains a dominant White culture, a White hegemony, which allows or might allow those who *fit in*, in and keeps out those who don't or can't, or don't want to.

Whiteness frequently goes as an unmarked identity: White people tend not to recognise their own racialized position. White people are seemingly not raced. 'Race' apparently is only about being 'Black'. Whiteness tends to be defined in relation to 'none White'. However, Whiteness is not always what it may seem. Leonardo (2002, 128) talks of 'flexible Whiteness'; he cites the Irish immigrants to the US (but could also apply to the UK) as an example, whereby in the nineteenth century they were regarded as he says: "black niggers". Irish people eventually 'became white' as a means of social mobility and were 'allowed' to do so, Leonardo argues, as a device for subverting social class solidarity with Black workers.

Moreover, there are *shades* of whiteness (Reay et al. 2007) that denote acceptability and signify social class stratification. Historically, Irish people in Britain and the US had to lose their Irishness to become 'white' and arguably only recently in the UK are the Irish tentatively accepted. But social class adds to the murkiness of racial dynamics. Multiculturalism in its focus on ethnicity and self-esteem issues contributed to the polarisation between black and white working class. The murder, by a white working class boy, of a British Pakistani boy in the school playground at Burnage School in 1988 (MacDonald et al. 1989) is a clear example of how destructive such polarised policies can be. Moreover, within the discourse of multicultural-ism the alterity of the White working class is underlined by their absence. A further twist to this argument is revealed in the research project on White middle-class families and school choice (Reay, Crozier and James 2007). The research identified the abjection of the White working-class denoted by White middle-class parents as: "the Chavs" and "White Trash" and the deployment of apparently acceptable minorities—"the model-minority" (Leonardo 2002) of, frequently, East Asian students who espouse seem-ingly White middle-class values, as a buffer against these abject Whites.

As Robert Young has argued: "White culture was regarded (and remains) the basis for ideas of legitimate government, law, economics, science, lan-guage, music, art, literature—in a word, civilization" (Young 2003, 3). Whiteness as a focus for study is therefore central to understanding racial dynamics and discriminatory practice. But Whiteness studies are as prob-lematic as any other aspect of racialised discourse, with regard for instance, to essentialism and reification; dualism and the privileging and foreground-ing of Whiteness when Whiteness is already a source of privilege. There is a danger of Whiteness studies making the same mistakes as Racism Awareness Training of the 1980s whose effect seemed to antagonise White people, make them feel guilty and retrench them in any negative, racist or whatever position they formerly held. Mac an Ghaill (1999) argues that social theorists have focused too much on those positioned as subaltern. What we now need, he says, is the development of frameworks that explore the changing collective self-representations and material and symbolic sys-tems that produce this, of the White majority (41). There is a clear need to address the invisibility of White privilege and White normalisation but this needs to become part of a critical challenge to racism and a challenge to hegemonic culture and values.

CONCLUSION

As we have seen the political and economic context impacts on or indeed provides the conditions for the changing nature and manifestations of rac-ism. Racism works differently in different contexts. The challenge to racism therefore must recognize and adapt to this complexity (Solomon, Portelli, Daniel and Campbell 2005). Within Educational Studies in Britain we have tended to fall back on soft options. Although campaigns and political struggle brought about anti-racist legislation and a swathe of initiatives which gave some recognition to the multi-ethnic and multicultural soci-ety that Britain is, it can be seen that they have in many respects largely acted as a diversion to the crucial task of dismantling racism and challenging White hegemony. As Gilroy (2004, 249) has argued reducing 'race' to issues of culture and identity, as important as these maybe in themselves, "obscures the inherently political character of the term". At the same time we need to be aware of the changing political landscape and balance of forces. In mid-2010 Britain once again has a right of Centre government and in Britain together with the rest of Europe, we are seeing a resurgence of ultra-right wing groups (such as the English Defence League and the British National Party in Britain). Multiculturalism may be inadequate in the face of the challenges for social justice and equality but it has helped to maintain these issues on the political and educational agendas. Moreover as Fortier (2008, 105) concludes, what is particularly concerning: " . . . is the replacement of multiculturalism with a fiercer and more adamant assertion of the Nation Thing . . . which clears a space for more rather than less inequality, resentment and hostility against those whose 'cultural identity' and 'cultural ways' are marked as hindering national unity and disturbing national comfort".

In the US and more recently and modestly in Britain, Critical Race Theory (CRT; see, for example, Tate 1995) has developed as a framework for trying to address the obfuscation of 'race' in educational and legal discourses. The key feature of CRT is the centrality given to 'race'. However, Darder and Torres (2003) question the credibility of CRT raising amongst others the focus on the non-concept of 'race' and the inherent dangers of pathologising black people rather than foregrounding racism itself. They also argue for a plurality of racisms, the importance of multiple identities and the need to move away from the essentialising notions of White supremacy. Critical Race Theorists have also been criticised in particular for ignoring or diminishing the salience of social class analysis (Cole 2009). Bearing these concerns in mind, engagement with Critical Race Theory and Whiteness issues can shift the focus of debate onto specific discriminatory practices and Othering and away from the obfuscation and safe or safer space of cultural exoticism. Primarily though it is essential to engage, as Mac an Ghaill (1999, 13) has asserted, with "both materialist and differentialist approaches", in order, as he says, "to make sense of the interconnectedness between multiple relations of power . . . and the making of subjective identities" and thus to generate more relational and contemporaneously appropriate understandings of 'race', racism and ethnicity. Such an approach has to include a class and also gender analysis.

NOTES

1. Although I will refer to Britain in this chapter it should be said that Britain does not have a common education system across all of its domains.
2. The term 'race' is placed in inverted commas in order to denote the problematic nature of 'race'. That is to say that 'race' is a social construct with

no scientific basis. It is nevertheless used here as it clearly represents certain forms of discrimination and oppression.

REFERENCES

Althusser, Louis. 1972. "Ideology and the Ideological State Apparatuses". In *Education, Structure and Society*, edited by B. Cosin, 242–280. Harmondsworth: Penguin Books.

Apple, Michael. 1995. *Education and Power* (2nd edition). New York and London: Routledge.

Back, Les. 1996. *New Ethnicities and Urban Culture*. Abingdon, Oxfordshire: Routledge.

Barker, Martin. 1981. *The New Racism*. London: Junction Books.

Bourdieu, Pierre. 1993. *Sociology in Question*. London: Sage.

Bourdieu, Pierre, and Jean-Claude Passeron. 1977. *Reproduction in Education, Society and Culture*. London: Sage.

Cantle, Ted. 2001. *The Community Cohesion Report*. London: The Stationery Office.

Cheong, Pauline Hope, Rios Edwards, Harry Goulborne, and John Solomos. 2007. "Immigration, Social Cohesion and Social Capital: A Critical Review". *Critical Social Policy* 27(1): 24–49.

Cole, Mike. 2009. *Critical Race Theory and Education: A Marxist Response*. London: Palgrave MacMillan.

Commission for Equality and Human Rights. 2006. http://www.equalityhumanrights.com

Crozier, Gill. 1989. "Multicultural Education: Some Unintended Consequences". In *Politics and the Process of Schooling*, edited by L. Barton and S. Walker, 59–81. Milton Keynes and Philadelphia: Open University Press.

Crozier, Gill. 1994. "Teachers' Power, Anti-racist Education and the Need for Pupil Involvement". *International Studies in Sociology of Education Journal*. 2(4): 213–228.

Crozier, Gill. 2004. Parents, Children and Schools: Asian Families' Perspectives. *ESRC End of Award Report (R000239671) www.societytoday.ac.uk*

Crozier, Gill, and Jane Davies. 2008. "'The Trouble is They Don't Mix': Self-Segregation or Enforced Exclusion? Teachers' Constructions of South Asian Students". *Race, Ethnicity and Education 11(3):* 285–301.

Darder, Anotnia, and Rodolfo Torres. 2003. "Shattering the 'Race' Lens: Toward a Critical Theory of Racism". In *The Critical Pedagogy Reader*, edited by A. Darder, M. Baltodano and R. D. Torres, 245–261. New York and London: Routledge.

Davies, J., and G. Crozier. 2005. Diversity and Teacher Education: Research into Training Provision in England. March–November 2005. *Research Report. www.multiverse.ac.uk*

Equalities and Human Rights Commission. 2006. Accessed August 2010. http://www.equalityhumanrights.com

Equalities and Human Rights Commission. 2010. *How Fair Is Britain?* http://www.equalityhumanrights.com

Fortier, Anne-Marie. 2008. *Multicultural Horizons*. London and New York: Routledge.

Gilroy, Paul. 1987. *There Ain't No Black in the Union Jack*. London: Hutchinson.

Gilroy, Paul. 1999. "The End of Antiracism". in *Racism*. Edited by Martin Bulmer and John Solomos, 242–250. Oxford: Oxford University Press.

Gilroy, Paul. 2004. *After Empire. Melancholia or Convivial Culture?* Abingdon, Oxfordshire: Routledge.

Hall, Stuart. 1992. "New Ethnicities". In *'Race', Culture and Difference*, edited by James Donald and Ali Rattansi, 252–259. London, California and New Delhi: Sage Publications with the Open University.

Kundnani, Aarun. 2002. "The Death of Multiculturalism". www.irr.org.uk/2002/april/ak00000.1.html

Leonardo, Zeus. 2002. "The Souls of White Folk. Critical Pedagogy, Whiteness Studies and Globalization Discourse". *Race, Ethnicity and Education* 5(1): 29–50.

Mac an Ghaill, Martin. 1999. *Contemporary Racisms and Ethnicities*. Buckingham: Open University Press.

MacDonald, Ian. 1989. *Murder in the Playground*. London: Longsight Press.

MacPherson, William. 1999. *The Stephen Lawrence Inquiry*. London: The Stationery Office Cm 4262-

Malik, Kenan. 2003. "The Dirty D Word". *The Guardian*, October.

Miles, Robert, and Anna Phizacklea. 1984. *A White Man's Country: Racism in British Politics*. London: Pluto Press.

Modood, Tariq. 2005. *Multicultural Politics. Racism, Ethnicity and Muslims in Britain*. Minnesota: University of Minnesota Press and Edinburgh: Edinburgh University Press.

PREVENTStrategy2008. August. [Press Statement.]. Department for Communities and Local Government. *http://www.communities.gov.uk/publications/communities/preventstrategy*

Race Relations Amendment Act. 2000. London: Her Majesty's Stationery Office.

Reay, Diane, Gill Crozier, and David James. 2007. White Middle Class Parents and Identities and the Urban Comprehensive School. *ESRC End of Award Report* (RES-148-25-0023) *www.societytoday.ac.uk*

Reay, Diane, Sumi Hollingworth, Katya Williams, Gill Crozier, D. James, Fiona Jamieson, and Phoebe Beedell. 2007. "'A Darker Shade of Pale?' Whiteness, the Middle Classes and Multi-Ethnic Inner City Schooling." *Sociology* 41(6): 1041–1060.

Safia Mirza, Heidi. 2005. "The More Things Change the More They Stay the Same: Assessing Black Children's Underachievement". In *Tell it Like it is: How Our Schools Fail Black Children*, edited by B. Richardson, 111–119. Stoke-on-Trent, UK and Sterling, US: Trentham Books.

Sarup, Madan. 1991. *Education and the Ideologies of Racism*. Stoke on Trent: Trentham Books.

Solomon, Patrick, John P. Portelli, Beverly-Jean Daniel, and Arlene Campbell. 2005. "The Discourse of Denial: How White Teacher Candidates Construct Race, Racism and 'White Privilege'". *Race Ethnicity and Education* 8(2): 147–169.

Solomos, John, Bob Finlay, Simon Jones, and Paul Gilroy. 1982. "The Organic Crisis of British Capitalism and Race: The Experience of the Seventies". In *The Empire Strikes Back*, edited by The Centre for Contemporary Cultural Studies, 9–46. London: Hutchinson Publishing Group.

Spivak, Gayatri. 1987. *In Other Worlds: Essays in Cultural Politics*. London: Methuen.

Stone, Richard. 2004. *Islamophobia, Issues, Challenges and Action*. Stoke on Trent and Sterling: Trentham Books.

Tate, William F. 1995. "Critical Race Theory". *Review of Research in Education* 22: 201–247.

Tomlinson, Sally. 2008. *Race and Education. Policy and Politics in Britain*. Berkshire.

Troyna, Barry, and Richard Hatcher. 1992. *Racism in Children's Lives*. London: Routledge.

Troyna, Barry, and Jenny Williams. 1986. *Racism, Education and the State*. London, Sydney: Croom Helm.

Young, Robert J. C. 2003. *Postcolonialism*. Oxford: Oxford University Press.

4 Combating Ethnic Educational Disadvantage in the Netherlands

An Analysis of Policies and Effects

Geert Driessen

Since World War II, the Netherlands has been confronted with an influx of various categories of immigrants. Which category migrates to what countries depends on the historical, political and economic contexts of both the country of departure and the country of receipt. The manner in which the receiving countries react to the arrival of immigrants greatly varies (Banks 2008). And there are also major differences in the manner in which immigrants deal with the expectations and demands of the receiving society.

Based on the criterion of 'country of origin', which indicates that at least one of the parents was born abroad, more than 20 percent of the total Dutch population (16.5 million) in 2010 were immigrants (Centraal Bureau voor de Statistiek 2010). Four main categories can be discerned:

- Western immigrants (N = 1,501,000), from such countries as Belgium and Germany, who often came to work in the Netherlands.
- Immigrants from former colonies, with the main countries being Indonesia (N = 382,000), the Antilles (N = 138,000) and Surinam (N = 342,000). They came for political and economic reasons and to study.
- Labor immigrants ('guest workers') from the Mediterranean area arriving in the 1960s and subsequent waves of immigration for purposes of family reunification and formation. The main countries of origin are Turkey (N = 384,000) and Morocco (N = 349,000).
- Asylum-seekers/refugees, lately mainly from countries such as Somalia, Iraq and Afghanistan (requests for asylum in 2009 N = 16,000).

In this chapter the focus is on the three categories of non-Western immigrants, of which most reside in the poorer parts of the major cities. Immigration from non-Western countries is increasingly being viewed as a problem in the Netherlands for a number of reasons. To begin with, immigrants have become much more visible, as a result of not only their increasing numbers but also because of their external characteristics (e.g., color of skin, language and dress code) and behavior (e.g., overrepresentation in crime statistics). Equally important is the fact that the Dutch welfare state cannot be maintained for reasons pertaining to the extensive use of social services from immigrants because of their low levels of education, poor command of the Dutch language and the kind of discrimination they suffer from.

The 9/11 events were a catalyst for the increasingly negative view on immigration and the shift of attention from ethnicity to religion (Driessen and Merry 2006). While it was taboo to say anything negative about immigrants in the Netherlands prior to 9/11, the populist right-wing Dutch politician Pim Fortuyn articulated the feelings of dissatisfaction shared by so many people after the 9/11 attacks and particularly the native Dutch population living in deprived urban areas who were confronted with the consequences of immigration on a daily basis. As a result of Fortuyn's political efforts, which were predominantly aimed at immigration and integration, politics has seen a remarkable shift towards the extreme right (Van der Brug, Fennema, Van Heerden and De Lange 2009). The murder of Dutch filmmaker Theo van Gogh by a fanatic young Muslim served as another catalyst for this development. The main protagonist of this new right faction now is the extremely successful populist anti-Islam Member of Parliament Geert Wilders and his Party for Freedom [Partij voor de Vrijheid].

This negative view of immigration and its impact upon integration is not entirely new. It is noteworthy that left-wing politicians (i.e., the Labor Party) until very recently kept to their ideal of a multicultural society while it was in particular their own native-Dutch working-class constituency in the big cities who had already been living and dealing with its problematic consequences for some decades. The dissatisfaction in society especially pertained to the use of general and specific provisions by immigrants and the slow pace of integration. This discontent has until recently been interpreted as imperfect societal acceptance and a matter of time. Nevertheless, this does not take away the fact that already in the 1970s the government received serious signals that immigration also had negative sides to it and deemed it necessary to formulate specific policies to counteract these developments. One of these signals pertained to the problems and disadvantage immigrant children were encountering in education.

In the remainder of this chapter, a general overview of Dutch policies aimed at combating educational disadvantage of immigrant children will be presented. Following this, attention will be paid to the results of evaluations of specific elements of these policies. Then, in a similar approach, the focus will be on a recent element, viz., citizenship education. This policy has less of a cognitive goal and mainly a social goal; it is specifically aimed at two-sided integration and functioning in society. The chapter will be concluded with an evaluation of the various policies. The leading questions then are: What policies have been implemented? What were the underlying goals? Have the goals been achieved? And if not, why not?

POLICIES ON ETHNIC INEQUALITY IN EDUCATION

In the Netherlands, policies aimed at combating educational disadvantage have strongly been guided by the political ideologies of the governments in power, with the political left having distinctly different perspectives, aims and approaches than the political right. In addition, social, economic, demographic, cultural and political developments both nationally and internationally have been of importance (Karsten and Meijnen 2005). In the 1960s, the unfavorable position of working-class children stood central. Under the influence of democratization processes, a society with more egalitarian and meritocratic principles was being striven for. It was argued that one's position in society should only be acquired on the basis of personal competences and one's socioeconomic background should play no role in this. In the process of acquiring such competences education was assigned a central selection and allocation function. Starting in the 1980s, large numbers of immigrant[1] children entered the Dutch schools. It soon became apparent that they lagged greatly behind their native Dutch peers. And although their position has improved somewhat over the past decades, immigrant students still significantly underachieve when compared to native Dutch middle-class students. As a result of this, the policy's focus for some time almost exclusively turned to minority children. Meanwhile the position of working class children is still very worrisome and even deteriorating relative to that of the immigrant children (Driessen 2009).

Two perspectives thus stand central in Dutch educational disadvantage policy, viz., social milieu and ethnic background. The distinction between the two is rather analytic, however, as they are strongly intertwined: most ethnic minorities are from lower social milieus. In the following historical overview of policies the focus is on the primary and secondary education of 4- to 18-year-olds as this age group has been the policy's principal target. In primary education, a total of 13 percent of the 1,597,000 students was of non-Western origin in 2008. In the four big cities (Amsterdam, Rotterdam, The Hague and Utrecht) this percentage varies from 33 to 54, however. In addition, 8 percent of the 7,108 primary schools have more than 50 percent non-Western students and 4 percent have more than 80 percent. In secondary education, also 14 percent of the 943,000 students were of non-Western origin in 2006; in the four big cities the percentage varies from 36 to 51. And, also, 8 percent of the 664 schools catered for more than 50 percent of non-Western students and 4 percent for more than 80 percent of such students (Centraal Bureau voor de Statistiek 2009).

A HISTORICAL OVERVIEW

Categorical Policies

In the 1960s and 1970s compensation programs were developed in a few big cities targeting native Dutch working class children. The objective was to improve the educational opportunities via specific programs, teacher training, parental involvement and stronger relations between neighborhood and school. Theoretically, these programs were based on the cultural deprivation and deficiency paradigms, which state that working-class children grow up in families and communities that show deficits in terms of formal language use, cultural capital and pedagogical style. The homes and environments of these children do not transmit the right cultural attitudes and skills necessary for learning in schools that in their approach depart from a middle-class perspective (Banks 1993).

Although evaluations of these local programs showed disappointing results they still laid the basis for a national Educational Stimulation Policy (Onderwijsstimuleringsbeleid). In 1974 a start was made on the centralization of policy intended to combat the disadvantages of working class children by providing schools with additional resources. Cooperative relations were established between schools, school advisory services and welfare institutions (e.g., libraries, child care services). From the evaluation of this policy it was concluded that the instruction was of a fairly traditional nature with an emphasis on socioemotional objectives and lowered aspirations for language and mathematics achievement. Parental participation was given little priority, just as cooperation with welfare services (Mulder 1996).

In the 1980s, the number of immigrants grew rapidly, particularly in the big cities. Despite this the government maintained that the Netherlands was not an immigrant country and thus no official immigration policy was needed. Because many of the immigrant children were experiencing major problems, the government still made additional resources available to schools as part of the Cultural Minority Policy (Culturele Minderhedenbeleid). This policy was characterized by an ambiguous two-track strategy. It was expected that many of the immigrants would return to their country of origin while others would stay. As a consequence the government strove for remigration and integration at the same time. One instrument to achieve these objectives was Mother Tongue Instruction (Onderwijs in Eigen Taal en Cultuur). The relevant students were taught in Turkish or Arabic, for example (Driessen 2005), but also Dutch as a Second Language (Nederlands als Tweede Taal). Another instrument was Intercultural Education (Intercultureel Onderwijs), which was intended to teach both minority and native Dutch children to handle the similarities and differences associated with ethnic and cultural background. Intercultural Education in part was a reaction to the earlier mentioned deficiency hypothesis. Critics of this hypothesis formulated the difference hypothesis which states that low-income and immigrant children experience cultural conflicts in school, but these are rich and varied cultural differences and not deficiencies as such.

Integrated Policies

Meanwhile, the conviction grew that the problems of immigrant students were essentially the same as those of the native Dutch working class children. In 1985, this led to the integration of the Educational Stimulation Policy and the Cultural Minority Policy into the Educational Priority Policy (Onderwijsvoorrangsbeleid). To reduce educational delays arising from economic, social and cultural factors two components were distinguished (Driessen and Dekkers 1997). Under the Educational Priority Areas component, primary and secondary schools and welfare institutions worked together, e.g., in preschool activities, reading promotion, homework assistance and guidance projects for truant students. Under the staffing component, primary schools were given additional teachers depending on the number of disadvantaged students they catered for. For this, every student was assigned a weighting factor: ethnic minority children counted as 1.90, Dutch working class children as 1.25 and non-disadvantaged children as 1.00. Thus, a school with predominantly ethnic minority students had nearly twice as many teachers as a school with mostly non-disadvantaged children. This staffing component in essence thus boiled down to an ethnic minority policy. The schools were free to determine the use of the allocated resources, but most of them formed smaller classes. In secondary education, minority children were temporarily allocated resources aimed at the facilitation of their entry into the education system. Examples were Dutch as a Second Language classes and International Transition Classes (Internationale Schakelklassen), which were special classes to prepare recently immigrated children for participation in Dutch education.

At the beginning of the 1990s, concern about the educational problems of native Dutch working class children disappeared even further into the background. All attention was now focused on minority children. It was clear that thus far the policies were not producing the desired effects. While some progression could be observed, the ethnic minority children's performance nevertheless lagged far behind that of native Dutch children. Therefore, with the aid of the National Policy Framework (Landelijk Beleidskader), the general Educational Priority Policy objectives were crystallized into more specific goals of which the most important was to improve the language and mathematics achievements. Other goals were to improve the initial reception at school, reduce absenteeism and prevent unqualified school leaving. Also, there now was a call for attention to the preschool and early school periods.

From an administrative and organizational point of view, the idea was that the central government would no longer carry responsibility for the details of how to tackle the educational disadvantages and that the municipalities would take over. The school was also assumed to be better equipped to fulfill its primary task when closer links to the broader societal context were established. And at a local level there would be more possibilities for education to be given a place in an integrated policy. The keywords underlying the new approach were: decentralization, deregulation and increased autonomy. The government provides only the policy framework with responsibility for the further planning, implementation and evaluation of the policy lying with the local municipalities. In 1998, the Educational Priority Policy was replaced by the Municipal Educational Disadvantages Policy (Gemeentelijk Onderwijsachterstandenbeleid). Financial resources were distributed to municipalities in one lump sum. The municipalities had to use them in accordance with a local plan which elaborated upon the objectives formulated within the National Policy Framework and indicate just how the schools were going to deploy the resources.

In 2000, a critical evaluation of the educational disadvantages policy appeared (Tweede Kamer 2000). There was concern about the effectiveness of the policy. A new trajectory was introduced and referred to as the Educational Opportunity Policy (Onderwijskansenbeleid). The focus was on a select group of some 400 disadvantaged schools. A central element in the new policy was customization. The Municipal Educational Disadvantaged Policy was aimed primarily at projects initiated by the community with very few connections to the core activities of the schools themselves. In contrast, the Educational Opportunity Policy required the school to first present a problem analysis based on the specific situation of the school and the particular needs of the students and parents. Given this information, the school then determined which sustainable changes were desired, preferably using an integrated approach. This development forms another step towards even further decentralization of policy and responsibilities concerning educational disadvantages.

In 2004, a policy note entitled 'Education, integration and citizenship' (Onderwijs, integratie en burgerschap; Ministerie van Onderwijs, Cultuur en Wetenschap 2004b) appeared. It was announced that the roles of the schools, communities and national government in the combat of educational disadvantage were going to be revised. In fact, the trend towards decentralization was continued, with increased autonomy and scaling-up accompanying this. Responsibility for the combat of disadvantage in primary and secondary education was placed mainly with the school administrations, without interference of the municipality. The municipality nevertheless continued to play an important role in the provision of preschool education and the staffing component has been revised. Up until this point, primary schools were allocated extra teachers on the basis of the parents' education, profession and country of birth. As of 2006, the allocation of extra resources on the basis of ethnicity gradually disappeared and was solely based on parental education. In addition, a ceiling value of 80 percent of disadvantaged students was introduced which implies that no extra funding will be awarded beyond this percentage. Schools in deprived areas receive a further extra funding for each disadvantaged child, which can be interpreted as a return to the former areas approach (Ledoux and Veen 2009). This also applies to the introduction of the Community school (Brede school) which focuses on the collaboration of various parties in the neighborhood, such as education, care, culture and sports. Transition classes (Schakelklassen) were, again, introduced with a focus on proficiency in the Dutch language of immigrant children. The policy for the allocation of extra resources for secondary schools with numerous minority students has also been adapted in such a manner that the resources go to schools in deprived neighborhoods based on income. These developments thus imply a remarkable shift from specific policy for ethnic minorities to a general policy for all disadvantaged children. Attention was also paid in the aforementioned policy note to integration, segregation and citizenship. The negative effects of so-called black schools (i.e., schools with a high concentration of minority students) from both cognitive and societal perspectives (Driessen 2002) and the problems of Islamic schools (Merry and Driessen 2005) are mentioned in particular. And it is further indicated that greater attention should be paid to the establishment of citizenship and social cohesion in the future.

THE EFFECTIVENESS OF THE POLICIES

In 2000, the General Audit Office drew up the balance with regard to the results of policy aimed at the reduction of educational disadvantage (Algemene Rekenkamer 2001). With an expenditure of more than half a billion Euros annually,[2] the conclusions were downright negative. According to the Audit Office, no lasting results had been achieved; educational disadvantages had not declined noticeably. This may be due in part to the fact that the objectives of the policy had only been rarely operationalized into measurable terms. Furthermore, the connections between the educational disadvantage policy and other policy tracks (e.g., reduction of class sizes, restructuring of secondary education) were not at all clear. As a result, observed effects could not be attributed unambiguously to specific policy operations (Rijkschroeff, Dam, Duyvendak, De Gruijter and Pels 2005).

In the following, an attempt is made to determine the effectiveness of the educational disadvantaged policy, i.e., whether the policy has contributed to the achievement of the objectives which have been set. This will be done first with regard to the policy in general and then with regard to a few concrete components of the policy.

Educational Priority Policy

Studies in both primary and secondary education for the period 1988–1992 show the poor language and mathematics performance of Dutch working class and ethnic minority children to not improve, in general, with the performance of Turkish and Moroccan children lagging far behind, in particular. Minority students were also more likely to shift to a lower level of secondary education, repeat a year or leave school without a qualification. From a theoretical point of view it can be concluded that the EPP in general turned out to be more of a macro factor approach (with an accent on structure and budget) than an approach concerning factors closer to the educational process. The failure of the EPP was in part attributed to the fact that the extra budget had not been earmarked and was often deployed to compensate for earlier cuts in spending or simply for class size reduction.

Mother Tongue Instruction

Under the EPP, all children of guest workers were entitled to receive Mother Tongue Instruction (MTI) in the official language of their parents' native country. MTI has seen many changes in goals and practice. Initially, MTI involved both a linguistic and a cultural component, but later the cultural component was dropped. In the 1970s the official objective was based on the assumption of temporariness and it was intended to help immigrant children reintegrate back into their native countries upon their return there. Around 1980, the government acknowledged the permanent presence of such immigrants in the Netherlands. MTI then had the following functions: to help develop a positive self-concept; diminish the gap between school and home environment; and contribute to intercultural education. MTI was now aimed at acculturation into Dutch society. MTI was increasingly viewed as a means to improve the educational success of immigrant children. After 9/11, the political climate in the Netherlands changed dramatically. Calls for assimilation as opposed to the maintenance of minority languages and cultures became influential and included the abolition of MTI as of 2004. According to the Ministry of Education, evaluations of MTI had shown no clear effects, not in terms of their mother tongue, nor in terms of facilitating mastery of the Dutch language (Driessen 2005). Priority should therefore be given to the learning of Dutch.

Intercultural Education

Intercultural Education (ICE) was seen as an important tool for acculturation or the two-way process of getting to know each other, being open to each other's cultures and accepting and appreciating each other. The underlying assumption was that children grow up in a multicultural society. Over the years, the knowledge aspect of ICE has received increased emphasis. This involved not only acquisition of knowledge of each other's backgrounds, circumstances and cultures but also insight into the manner in which values, norms, customs and circumstances influence the behavior of people. Such affective and sociopsychological objectives as respect, acceptance and self-image have been incorporated into the relevant policy along with a number of cognitive objects. And ICE was also considered useful to combat the structural inequality fuelled by ethnic prejudice and discrimination.

Evaluations showed ICE to be given low priority at primary and secondary schools (Fase, Kole, Van Paridon and Vlug 1990). Furthermore, there was just as much prejudice and discriminatory behavior in schools working with ICE as in schools not working with ICE. Not only operational objectives and concrete suggestions for everyday practice were lacking but also quality requirements. Only 10 percent of the schools reported putting ICE into practice. This was very surprising in view of the fact that ICE had been a compulsory component of primary education for a number of years already. There was a widespread lack of clarity with respect to the exact nature of ICE. When ICE efforts actually got off the ground, this was primarily in schools involving considerable numbers of immigrant children. Leeman and Reid (2006) evaluated an attempt by the Ministry of Education to revitalize ICE. Their study showed that teachers have moved away from culturalism and focused more on individual differences of age, religion and lifestyle than on ethnic differences. Teachers see ICE mainly as education of tolerance, and promoting empathy and communication skills. This emphasis on the individual does not take account of the political aspects and power imbalances in society.

Preschool and Early School Education

Disadvantaged students and particularly ethnic minority students often lag considerably behind their peers already when they start primary school and hardly catch up over the years. For this reason, the focus of attempts to combat educational disadvantages is increasingly being placed upon the preschool and early years of school. The underlying assumption is that many of the elements which prepare children for middle and upper socioeconomic backgrounds for school are missing in the family situations of ethnic minority and working class children. From a theoretical point of view this focus on shortcomings in the child's home milieu means a remarkable return to the earlier mentioned deficiency hypothesis. All kinds of home- and center-based intervention programs have thus emerged for children between the ages of 0 and 7 years. The emphasis is on the linguistic and cognitive development of the children, and this may be combined with the provision of educational support for the parents. Recently, a major impulse has been provided in the areas of preschool and early school education. One objective is to reach 100 percent of the disadvantaged children to participate in an intervention program in 2011.

Considerable controversy surrounds the effects of various provisions, including day-care attendance, preschool attendance and specific programs (Driessen 2004). The main conclusion up until now has been that any effects are very limited and often fade away. However, there are some signs that the situation is changing and that some positive effects in the long run may occur. Such positive effects may depend on a particular set of conditions including the duration and intensity of the care, the quality and efforts of the caregivers and the continuity of the service or program with the children's later care and education.

Transition Classes

In the 2005/2006 school year, the concept of Transition classes has been re-introduced, this time in primary schools. These classes are meant for both immigrant and native Dutch students who, because of their language delays, underachieve and of whom it is expected that after an intensive language training trajectory they will be able to continue successfully in regular education. The language training takes 1 year and during that year the relevant students are put in separate classes. Different options exist: a transition class parallel to Grades 1 through 8, an extra class before Grade 1, between grades (e.g., between Grade 3 and 4), and after the last grade. Transition classes thus can take the form of full-time classes, part-time classes or as extra lessons after regular school hours. The results of studies into the effects of these classes show to be promising (Mulder, Van Der Hoeven-Van Doornum, Vierke, Van Der Veen and Elshof 2009).

POLICIES OF INTEGRATION AND CITIZENSHIP

From Integration to Assimilation

Despite a long tradition of receiving immigrants, the concept of 'integration' was only used in the formulation of policy with respect to ethnic minorities in the Netherlands at the beginning of the 1980s. The relevant policy was aimed for quite some time at 'integration with maintenance of own culture', which meant that immigrants were expected to adapt to some extent to Dutch society, but at the same time could keep to their own culture. However, a recent shift has occurred towards policy with clear assimilatory characteristics. Whereas immigrants were previously accepted into the Dutch welfare state with little or no discussion, an undeniable problematization of immigration and hardening of policy has occurred during the last decade under the motto 'compulsory integration, own responsibility' (Ministerie van Volkshuisvesting, Ruimtelijke Ordening en Milieu/Wonen, Wijken en Integratie 2007; Stevens, Clycq, Timmerman and Van Houtte 2011).

Shared Citizenship

The recent government standpoint is that too much emphasis has traditionally been placed upon acceptance of the differences between immigrants and the native Dutch population. The presence of immigrants has typically been viewed as a 'value' and as enriching the society in which we live. But, according to the government, everything that is different need not always be of value. In other words, cultural gaps cannot be bridged via the cultivation of own cultural identities. The unity of a society must be found in what citizens have in common, which is being citizens of one and the same society. The objective of current integration policy is thus shared citizenship for immigrants and native Dutch inhabitants alike. Such shared citizenship presupposes proficiency in the Dutch language and adherence to basic Dutch norms and values, with the latter including democracy, efforts to provide for oneself, law abidance, recognition of the right of each individual to say what he or she thinks, respect for the sexual preferences of others and equality for men and women. Citizenship thus means a willingness to actively contribute to society and participate in all its facets (Ministerie van Volkshuisvesting, Ruimtelijke Ordening en Milieu/Wonen, Wijken en Integratie 2007).

Compulsory Integration, Own Responsibility

The present government's emphasis on compulsory integration and the responsibility of each individual immigrant to integrate (i.e., assimilate) has also led to a shift in policy away from categorical provisions for specific groups towards general provisions. As a consequence, many subsidies for immigrant organizations that were not aimed at integration have been discontinued.

Another radical change from the past is that as of 2006 those from non-Western countries who wish to immigrate to the Netherlands have to take a civic integration examination in their native country. This oral examination which takes 30 minutes includes both a test of basic knowledge of the Dutch language and the Dutch society. If the applicants fail this test they are not allowed to immigrate to the Netherlands. The government does not prescribe ways as to how candidates should acquire the desired competencies; that is their own responsibility and they have to pay for it themselves. As of 2007, the obligation to take a civic integration examination also applies to a number of categories of immigrants who already reside in the Netherlands. This is, too, the own responsibility of the immigrants (Ministerie van Volkshuisvesting, Ruimtelijke Ordening en Milieu/Wonen, Wijken en Integratie 2007). In 2009 the Government decided to tighten up the entry criteria for marriage and family migration by adding a written component to the oral examination, raising the level of the language component and laying more responsibility for the integration and education of the new immigrant with the immigrant already residing in the Netherlands (Ministerie van Wonen, Wijken en Integratie 2009).

Active Participation

When conceptualized in such a manner, integration, and in line with this citizenship, is operationalized as the individual obligation to actively participate in a variety of societal domains (Wetenschappelijke Raad voor het

---

Regeringsbeleid 2001). The following domains have been distinguished: political-judicial, social-economic, ethnic-cultural and religious. A division frequently used is that between structural integration, measured as the level of education attained and position on the job market, and social-cultural integration, measured in terms of social contacts and participation in cultural institutions. For the Dutch government, participation in education and the job market stand central. In addition, the importance of social participation (e.g., membership in associations and clubs), political participation (e.g., voting), cultural participation (e.g., visiting museums), societal participation (e.g., volunteer work) and athletic participation as different means to achieve citizenship is also often mentioned.

POLICY ON CITIZENSHIP EDUCATION

In a certain sense, citizenship is a rather recent topic in Dutch education. That is not to say that no attention has been paid to it at all, but insofar that was the case it mostly was as part of other subjects, such as history, social studies and religious and ideological movements. Depending on how citizenship education is being operationalized, however, it is also true to say that elements of the already mentioned Intercultural Education can be considered as a precursor (Leeman and Pels 2006).

The Policy Document

In 2004, the policy document 'Education, integration and citizenship' (Onderwijs, integratie en burgerschap; Ministerie van Onderwijs, Cultuur en Wetenschap 2004b) was published. Attention was focused on integration, segregation and citizenship in primary and secondary schools. The Minister of Education observed that in recent years Dutch society had been confronted with important new issues relating to the changing ethnic composition of the Dutch population. Effects of this development could also be felt at the school level. Problems related to the slow integration of some categories of immigrants and the growing ethnic segregation in society and in education are urgent and beg for solutions. Concerning the latter, the negative effects of so-called black schools (i.e., schools with a high concentration of minority students) and the problems of Islamic schools in particular were mentioned. The government therefore announced that it intended to attack such problems actively. Promoting citizenship education in primary and secondary education was seen as an important means. To this, the government added the goal of social integration. For both ethnic minority and native Dutch youth active citizenship was considered to be important, so as to learn from each other to live in a society that is being characterized by ethnic, cultural and religious heterogeneity.

The following measures were suggested in this policy document. All schools will be expected to contribute to the socialization of children of different backgrounds through sports and cultural events, by visiting companies and social institutions, by school linkage and exchange programs, in short by learning in different social environments. City councils and schools can also take specific measures to enhance social integration in local situations where high-risk students are unevenly distributed over the schools. Citizenship education, including social integration will receive a legal basis. Because of the freedom of education, which forms the basis for Dutch education and which entails the freedom of the competent authority to determine the content of teaching and the teaching material, the government's role in this is limited. The Ministry will only facilitate the exchange of good practices and the Inspectorate of Education will have an evaluative and monitoring task. The following examples were mentioned: behavioral codes, bullying protocols and students' statutes.

In primary education and the first years of secondary education, 'citizenship education' will be part of the new attainment targets. 'Social studies' will remain a compulsory subject for all students in the last years of secondary education. Here, structural elements of citizenship education can be addressed in a coherent historic perspective. In addition, elements of citizenship education will be examined through examination programs in history, economy, geography, philosophy and art. For secondary vocational education, new competencies have been proposed in which citizenship plays an important role. They include normative competencies, such as independent behavior as a citizen, socially involved and responsible, based on socially accepted basic values, as well as cultural competencies, such as the ability to participate in the multiform and multicultural society at the national and at the European level, while respecting the characteristics of each other's cultural communities.

The Revised Education Acts

At the end of 2005, the plans had been put into a law which was accepted in Parliament. As of February 2006, schools are obliged to actively promote citizenship and social integration into Dutch society (Ministerie van Onderwijs, Cultuur en Wetenschap 2005). This obligation means that education also:

- departs from the fact that students grow up in a multiform society;
- aims at contributing to active citizenship and social integration; and
- aims at students having knowledge of and coming into contact with the different backgrounds and cultures of peers (Centrale Financiën Instellingen 2006).

According to the Ministry, active citizenship implies the willingness and preparedness to be part of a community and actively contribute to that community.

This legal task concerns the obligation, but not the form and contents. As a consequence of the freedom of education schools and teachers are free to decide as to how they wish to implement citizenship education. The law includes a presentation of general guidelines and desirable outcomes. In the following overview some of the activities announced by the Ministry are presented (Centrale Financiën Instellingen 2006; Ministerie van Onderwijs, Cultuur en Wetenschap 2004a):

- The publication of information brochures for schools with regard to legislation and the controlling task of the Inspectorate of Education.
- The development of core curricula that will help primary and secondary schools planning and implementing citizenship education in their curriculum.
- The development of a multiyear project 'Citizenship education in primary school'.
- The development of school television programs for primary schools and the lower years of secondary schools.
- The implementation of practical training periods in society (or service learning) in secondary education (e.g., doing volunteer work).
- The development of a website where schools can find information on citizenship education and social integration.
- Stimulating local initiatives by making inventories of good initiatives by schools at the primary and secondary level.

From Law to Practice

Because of the freedom for schools to interpret the concept of citizenship and also because the schools may implement citizenship education geared towards their specific local situation, various and sometimes ambiguous terms are used in relation to citizenship education, for instance, civics, moral education, social competence education, value education and democratic education (De Wit 2007). There is not only variety with regard the definition of citizenship education, but probably even more with respect to the ways citizenship education is being operationalized and put into practice. The reason for this is that schools must consider their denomination, vision and philosophy of life, the local context, the social and ethnic composition of the student population and the wishes of the parents.

In a survey by the European Commission (Eurydice 2005) three approaches were discerned:

- cross-curricular (citizenship education is present throughout the whole curriculum);
- integrated (the topic forms part of one or more other subjects, such as history and social studies); and
- as a separate subject (a subject in its own right which may be compulsory, a core curriculum option or optional).

According to this survey, in the Netherlands citizenship education in primary schools takes the integrated form, while in secondary schools it is taught in a cross-curricular manner. Where it is integrated within other subjects, citizenship education is at all levels most commonly included in history, social studies, geography, religious and moral education, ethics, philosophy, foreign languages and the language of instruction. The number of hours reserved for citizenship education is not prescribed.

In 2004, the Minister of Education had carried out a study into the ways in which in the various EU member states citizenship education was given shape (Ministerie van Onderwijs, Cultuur en Wetenschap 2004a). This study showed that citizenship education was being addressed in very different manners:

- In some countries and schools citizenship education has been introduced a discrete area of enquiry into the curriculum, that is, as a separate subject.
- In many countries and schools a cross-curricular approach is considered most appropriate. This more or less holistic approach reflects a shift in emphasis from teaching to learning. Since experience with a cross-curricular approach is limited and since it is not so easy to codify in rules, guidelines and textbook, the contents should be geared to local needs. Schools therefore develop their own ideas and methods.
- In some countries and schools citizenship education is implemented as an extra-curricular approach. Learning-by-doing and action are an important guiding principles. Some examples include simulating a low court; setting up an animal awareness project; organizing project weeks where children who live in a city go out to the country side to study the ways people live there, and vice versa.
- Not all learning is intentional. The socializing impact of the schooling experience includes much more than what is visible through official explicit curricula. Much is taught through the implicit or hidden curriculum, for instance in the way teachers and students interact in the classroom and through role-modeling.
- It is not only the micro-behavior in the classroom where citizenship education is transmitted. The school can also be seen as a micro-society, a social environment whose social norms and values set the parameters for future behavior in society at large.

To this diversity of approaches should—of course—be added that all sorts of combinations of approaches are also possible. According to the official viewpoint of the Ministry citizenship education is not regarded as a separate subject. It should be a matter-of-fact integral part of the curriculum content (Ministerie van Onderwijs, Cultuur en Wetenschap 2004b, 2005).

IMPLEMENTATION AND EFFECTS

A report of the Inspectorate of Education (Inspectie van het Onderwijs 2007) pertaining to the situation in 2005/2006 describes the results of a representative study into the implementation of citizenship education and social cohesion. The data show that 80 percent of the secondary schools have a view on how to improve citizenship and integration. However, many of these schools have only formulated this view in global wordings and ideas. When asked what forms of cohesion-increasing education they feel important, social competencies, rules for politeness and good manners and basic values are mentioned most. Half to two-thirds of the schools indicate that they only work with very general goals. In addition, more than half of them say they do not use teaching materials; this applies even more to the higher levels of secondary education. These findings reflect that citizenship education is in many places still in an exploratory phase (Ministerie van Onderwijs, Cultuur en Wetenschap 2004a).

Little is known about ways in which citizenship education are implemented (Schuitema, Ten Dam and Veugelers 2007). In the relevant document (Centrale Financiën Instellingen 2006), the Ministry of Education has announced a number of measures. What has come of these measures thus far, that is, three years later, is summed up in the following overview:

- A general information brochure for schools with regard to legislation and information on backgrounds, implementation and evaluation.
- Information on the controlling task of the Inspectorate of Education for schools. The Inspectorate's monitoring system will focus on, for instance, the school's view on citizenship education, risks and conflicts with basic values, social competencies and diversity.
- A core curriculum citizenship education for secondary schools for students with learning and behavioral difficulties.
- An inventory which contains 94 titles, that is, all material where there is any reference to aspects of citizenship education. Most material, mainly from the 1980s and 1990s, is for primary schools and deals with topics such as world religions, voting and elections and the European Union.
- The project 'Citizenship education in primary school'.
- Attention to citizenship in a very few school television programs for primary schools.
- The Ministry of Education website where schools can find information on citizenship education and social integration is in a developmental phase and contains very little practical information for schools.

Data on (any) effects of forms of citizenship education are even more sparse; one reason for this is because there are hardly any adequate instruments available. Some (international) studies have recently been conducted into the effects of citizenship education. However, neither national nor international analyses provide a great deal of evidence on what exactly works in citizenship education, especially as far as acquiring attitudes is concerned, let alone the question of whether these attitudes take root and are practiced in real life situations (Ministerie van Onderwijs, Cultuur en Wetenschap 2004b).

CONCLUSION

The situation with regard to citizenship education can be summarized as follows. Citizenship education is a topic which has been introduced into the Dutch educational system very recently; the relevant law was put into effect in 2006. It is not considered as a separate subject by the Ministry and there are no extra facilities or subsidies provided, there are no specific teachers and there are no specific textbooks prescribed. Rather, the prevailing view is that citizenship education is something which any teacher can incorporate into his or her lessons. Because of the Dutch dominating principle of 'freedom of education' in combination with the Ministry's policy of decentralization and giving more autonomy to individual schools, each school is free to interpret the concept of citizenship as it likes and each school may implement citizenship education geared towards its specific local situation. This freedom has resulted in a diffuse picture of schools, each of which gives its own interpretation and implementation of citizenship education. In practice, citizenship education mostly is given form by the ethos, rules and conventions of a school, the attitude and behavior of the teachers (as role models) and the way certain topics are treated during the regular lessons, but also by incidental lessons or projects on specific citizenship aspects. In addition, it also is incorporated in the subject of social studies. The monitoring study of the Inspection of Education shows that more than half of the secondary schools do not use teaching materials for citizenship education. Insofar as things have been realized, the most has been done for primary education. Citizenship education clearly still finds itself in a developmental and experimental phase and one may wonder whether it is not heading the same way as Intercultural Education did some decades ago.

Equality in education and society has been an ultimate goal of many political parties, especially those of the left. Nowadays, the main objective of policy focusing on ethnic minorities is proportional educational participation. With proportional is meant that immigrant children should occupy a position in education which is comparable to that of children with the same background characteristics such as age, socioeconomic status and sex.

For more than forty years now, the Netherlands has devoted policy to combat educational inequalities, firstly as a categorical approach focusing on disadvantages stemming from the children's social milieu and from their ethnicity, respectively, and then in an integrated approach which combined both perspectives. The various policies developed and implemented were the result of an ongoing struggle between political factions, especially at the left and the right (Karsten and Meijnen 2005). Because of the typical Dutch so-called *poldermodel* (which aims at consensus decision-making) a constant compromising of political views was needed. This is the reason why sometimes little remained of the original outspoken plans and why they ultimately were half-hearted of character. Also of importance is that ministers often are very ideologically driven and ambitious. They are in a hurry to have (if possible positive) results before the end of their term, which puts an immense pressure on the policy makers in the ministry. At the same time they are not always accessible for criticism, for instance from practitioners. As a consequence, implementation of new policies often occurred without adequate preparation and support from educational research and practice (Doolaard and Leseman 2008).

During those forty years, the constant change of political parties and ministers in power was accompanied by a change of goals, target groups and instruments (Ledoux and Veen 2009). More specifically, though there was a lack of consistency in the sociocultural objectives, in some respects there was consistency in the socioeconomic and emancipatory dimensions (Rijkschroeff et al. 2005). Several developments can be discerned. For instance, although in a formal sense there has been a shift in scope from ethnic disadvantage to disadvantage in general, in practice a strong focus on ethnicity has remained. While in the staffing component the criterion of ethnicity was dropped, because most ethnic minority parents have little education they still remain the policy's main target group. At the level of the practitioners the central goal was improving the position of immigrants and much less solving the problems of the native Dutch. There also has been a shift from an accent on emancipation and socioeconomic disadvantage to cultural and religious differences and incompatibility of norms and values. Another important development concerns the level of steering and the division of responsibilities. The policy has gone through an evolution from local policy to central policy and back again to a decentralized level, momentarily from the level of the municipality ('territorial decentralization') down to the level of the school board and—to some extent—the school ('functional decentralization'). The central government more and more limits itself to providing a framework and increasingly offers autonomy to municipalities and school boards with regard to the implementation of the policy.

What is the state of the art regarding the results of all of these efforts? Despite an investment of billions of Euros and hard work of many professionals, the various policies have produced disappointing results. Analysis of the most recent data show the delays of the children with low-educated minority parents to be still quite large while the delays of children with native Dutch working class parents are somewhat smaller but still substantial. The good news is that in recent years the position of some minority groups has improved, but this does apply to a lesser extent to the two largest groups, viz., the Turks and Moroccans (Driessen 2009; Herweijer 2009).

How can this slow pace be explained? Apart from the consequences of the constant change of goals, target groups and instruments, as summarized above, there are a number of other reasons. Mulder (1996) in the evaluation of the Educational Priority Policy concludes that the policy's goals were formulated very ambiguously and contained contradictions. It was not until the introduction of the National Policy Framework in the late 1990s that goals were operationalized in a more specified manner. Still, the policy mostly was one of input financing with little relation to output requirements. Because of the principle of freedom of education extra funding rarely has been earmarked or only in a global manner. Municipalities, school boards and schools may use the extra funding as they see fit. The last decades a process of increasing decentralization and autonomy has been set into motion, which gives municipalities, school boards and schools even more freedom as to how to decide how to spend the extra funding. According to Karsten and Meijnen (2005), the recent developments of giving school boards and schools more autonomy and stimulating market forces in education have in particular led to more ethnically segregated schools.

Doolaard and Leseman (2008) question the assumption that educational disadvantage is the result of social and cultural factors that are typical for a certain social group. Genetic-biological factors probably are more important. This means that the core of the policy's staffing component is based on the wrong premise. In addition, they argue that the indicators used in the staffing component (parental educational level and ethnicity) are very crude measures. As a consequence many children with factual delays do not receive extra funding, but also many children with no delays nevertheless receive extra funding. Furthermore, most schools use the extra funding to create smaller classes (Mulder 1996). In this way all children in a class profit, both the disadvantaged as well as the non-disadvantaged.

In their recent review Doolaard and Leseman (2008) summarize their criticism as follows: the quality of the interventions implemented too often is insufficient, too often they are under the pressure of ambitious politicians and administrators without adequate policy instruments and facilities, too little has been invested in the development and strengthening of quality, and while many administrative changes have taken place, systems of quality care have not been adapted to these changes.

NOTES

1. Although they have different connotations, for the sake of readability in this chapter the terms immigrant, ethnic minority and minority are used interchangeably, as are the terms Dutch and native Dutch.

2. In 2008, this was 612 million Euros, excluding expenses for combating school drop-out (Herweijer 2009).

REFERENCES

Algemene Rekenkamer. 2001. *Bestrijding Onderwijsachterstanden*. Den Haag: Algemene Rekenkamer.

Banks, James. 1993. "Multicultural Education: Historical Development, Dimensions, and Practice". *Review of Research in Education* 19: 3–49.

Banks, James. 2008. "Diversity, Group Identity, and Citizenship Education in a Global Age". *Educational Researcher* 37: 129–139.

Centraal Bureau voor de Statistiek. 2009. "*Onderwijs*". http://statline.cbs.nl

Centraal Bureau voor de Statistiek. 2010. "*Bevolking*". http://statline.cbs.nl

Centrale Financiën Instellingen. 2006. *Voorlichtingspublicatie. Wet van 9 December 2005 (. . .)*. Den Haag: Ministerie van Onderwijs, Cultuur en Wetenschap.

De Wit, Cees. (Ed.). 2007. Maatschappelijk en Pedagogisch bij de Tijd. 's-Hertogenbosch: KPC.

Doolaard, Simone, and Paul Leseman. 2008. *Versterking van het Fundament*. Groningen: GION.

Driessen, Geert. 2002. "School Composition and Achievement in Primary Education: A Large-Scale Multilevel Approach". *Studies in Educational Evaluation* 28: 347–368.

Driessen, Geert. 2004. "A Large-Scale Longitudinal Study of the Utilization and Effects of Early Childhood Education and Care in the Netherlands". *Early Child Development and Care* 174: 667–689.

Driessen, Geert. 2005. "From Cure to Curse: The Rise and Fall of Bilingual Education Programs in the Netherlands". In *The Effectiveness of Bilingual School Programs for Immigrant Children*, edited by Arbeitsstelle Interkulturelle Konflikte und Gesellschaftliche Integration, 77–107. Berlin: Wissenschaftszentrum Berlin für Sozialforschung.

Driessen, Geert. 2009. *Prestaties, Gedrag en Houding van Basisschoolleerlingen. Stand van Zaken in 2008 en Ontwikkelingen sinds 2001*. Nijmegen: ITS.

Driessen, Geert, and Hetty Dekkers. 1997. "Educational Opportunities in the Netherlands. Policy, Students' Performance and Issues". *International Review of Education* 43: 299–315.

Driessen, Geert, and Michael Merry. 2006. "Islamic Schools in the Netherlands: Expansion or Marginalization?" *Interchange* 37: 201–223.

Eurydice. 2005. *Citizenship Education at School in Europe*. Brussels: Eurydice.

Fase, Willem, S. Kole, Carla van Paridon, and Veronica Vlug. 1990. *Vorm Geven aan Intercultureel Onderwijs*. De Lier: ABC.

Herweijer, Lex. 2009. *Making Up the Gap. Migrant Education in the Netherlands*. The Hague: SCP.

Inspectie van het Onderwijs. 2007. *De Staat van het Onderwijs. Onderwijsverslag 2005/2006*. Utrecht: Inspectie van het Onderwijs.

Karsten, Sjoerd, and Wim Meijnen. 2005. *Leergeld. Sociaal-Democratische Onderwijspolitiek in een Tijd van Nieuwe Verschillen*. Amsterdam: Mets & Schilt Uitgevers.

Ledoux, Guuske, and Annemiek Veen. 2009. *Beleidsdoorlichting Onderwijsachterstandenbeleid. Periode 2002–2008*. Amsterdam: SCO-Kohnstamm Instituut.

Leeman, Yvonne, and Trees Pels. 2006. "Citizenship Education in the Dutch Multiethnic Context". *European Education* 38: 64–75.

Leeman, Yvonne, and Carol Reid. 2006. "Multi/Intercultural Education in Australia and the Netherlands". *Compare* 36: 57–72.

Merry, Michael, and Geert Driessen. 2005. "Islamic Schools in Three Western
Countries: Policy and Procedure". *Comparative Education* 41: 411–432.

Ministerie van Onderwijs, Cultuur en Wetenschap. 2004a. *Citizenship—Made in
Europe: Living Together Starts at School.* Den Haag: Ministerie van Onderwijs,
Cultuur & Wetenschap.

Ministerie van Onderwijs, Cultuur en Wetenschap. 2004b. *Onderwijs, Integratie en
Burgerschap.* Den Haag: Ministerie van Onderwijs, Cultuur en Wetenschap.

Ministerie van Onderwijs, Cultuur en Wetenschap. 2005. *Voorstel van Wet en
Memorie van Toelichting.* W2624K-2. Den Haag: Ministerie van Onderwijs,
Cultuur en Wetenschap.

Ministerie van Volkshuisvesting, Ruimtelijke Ordening en Milieu/Wonen, Wijken
en Integratie. 2007. *Integratienota 2007–2011: Zorg dat je erbij Hoort!* Den
Haag: Ministerie van Volkshuisvesting, Ruimtelijke Ordening en Milieu/
Wonen, Wijken en Integratie.

Ministerie van Wonen, Wijken en Integratie. 2009. *Kabinetsaanpak Huwelijks- en
Gezinsmigratie.* Den Haag: Ministerie Wonen, Wijken en Integratie.

Mulder, Lia. 1996. *Meer Voorrang, Minder Achterstand? Het Onderwijsvoorrangsbeleid Getoetst.* Nijmegen: ITS.

Mulder, Lia, Anneke van der Hoeven-Van Doornum, Hermann Vierke, Ineke van
der Veen, and Dorothé Elshof. 2009. *Inrichting en Effecten van Schakelklassen.*
Nijmegen: ITS.

Rijkschroeff, Rally, Geert ten Dam, Jan Willem Duyvendak, Marjan de Gruijter,
and Trees Pels. 2005. "Educational Policies on Migrants and Minorities in the
Netherlands: Success or Failure?" *Journal of Education Policy* 20: 417–435.

Schuitema, Jaap, Geert ten Dam, and Wiel Veugelers. 2008. "Teaching Strategies
for Moral Education: A Review". *Journal of Curriculum Studies* 40: 69–89.

Stevens, Peter, Noel Clycq, Christianne Timmerman, and Mieke Van Houtte. 2011.
"Researching Race/Ethnicity and Educational Inequality in the Netherlands: A
Critical Review of the Research Literature between 1980 and 2008". *British
Educational Research Journal* 37: 5–43.

Tweede Kamer. 2000. *Aanpak Onderwijsachterstanden. Bestrijding van Onderwijsachterstanden.* 's-Gravenhage: Sdu Uitgevers.

Van der Brug, Wouter, Meindert Fennema, Sjoerdje van Heerden, and Sarah de
Lange. 2009. "Hoe Heeft het Integratiedebat Zich in Nederland Ontwikkeld?"
Migrantenstudies 25: 198–220.

Wetenschappelijke Raad voor het Regeringsbeleid. 2001. *Nederland als Immigrat-
iesamenleving.* Den Haag: Sdu Uitgevers.

5 The Expanded Federal Role in US Public Schools
The Structural Forces of Globalization, Immigration and Demographic Change

A. Gary Dworkin and Pamela F. Tobe

The Constitution of the United States does not address public education and provides no specific role for the federal government in promoting education or enhancing educational opportunities. Public education was the near exclusive domain of the individual states, and in turn, the local communities and school boards.

Under the "Due Process" clause of the XIV Amendment (ratified in 1868), the federal government could intervene in issues of education when Constitutional rights of citizens were denied by state law. In fact, it was through the "Due Process" clause that the US Supreme Court abolished school segregation in the landmark Brown v. Board of Education case of 1954. Nevertheless, the principal role of the federal government was to provide technical support for public schools and to protect the civil rights to an education for diverse groups of students. Actual curricular issues and the assessment of academic performances were left to the local schools and state education agencies. By contrast, in the past three decades the federal government has been more proactive in holding states and schools more accountable for the academic achievement of their public school students and the performances of their schools and teachers.

The present chapter examines the interrelated structural forces that changed the participatory role of the federal government in public education. We propose that the expansion of educational opportunities to previously disadvantaged groups and changes in the size and composition of immigrant populations in the country caused the native-born, middle class to believe that public schools were no longer creating educational and career advantages for their children. Further, we suggest that changes in the nature and extent of economic globalization has resulted in concerns by the business sector regarding the competitiveness of the American labor force and fears among the current labor force regarding the exportation of well-paying jobs to the Third World or more competitive nations. Finally, these concerns have culminated in what has been identified as the "Standards-Based School Accountability Movement", which resulted in increased federal involvement in public education, including a mandate for standardized student achievement testing to assess school performance.

It must be recognized that because of the significance of the issue of "States Rights", the increased involvement of the federal government in state and local education has not occurred without objections. Each wave of school reform that was tied to federal mandates has been met with increasing resistance at the state and local levels. In some instances the resistance has taken the form of rejection of the reforms; in others it has resulted in law suits against the federal government; and in still others it has resulted in the states "gaming the system" (Dworkin 2008b). Thus, this chapter must also explore the nature of the resistance to federal involvement in public education.

THE HISTORICAL ROLE OF THE FEDERAL GOVERNMENT IN PUBLIC EDUCATION

A federal department of education was created in 1867, but its role was limited to assisting states with information on schools and teaching. It became an "office" within the Department of Health, Education, and Welfare in 1953 and finally a department, with presidential cabinet status, in 1980. The US Department of Education chronicles legislation[1] that resulted in a federal role in education assisting the land-grant colleges and universities. Later Acts[2] supported vocational education, including home economics, industrial arts and agriculture in the public high schools. In 1944, the G.I. Bill funded post-secondary education for World War II veterans. Following the Soviet Union's launch of the first space satellite, "Sputnik", in 1957, Congress passed the 1958 National Defense Education Act, which funded science, math and foreign language instruction in primary, secondary and tertiary schools.

The Civil Rights Act of 1964, the 1972 Title IX of the Education Amendments and Section 504 of the 1973 Rehabilitation Act resulted in federal protection against discrimination based on race, ethnicity, gender and disabilities. Finally, under the aegis of the Elementary and Secondary Education Act of 1965 (ESEA), broad-ranging programs were established to aid public schools and their students. A special focus on the needs of disadvantaged children was incorporated in the ESEA legislation under Title I. Comparable broad-ranging programs were also funded in the Higher Education Act, including the funding of Pell Grants to allow low-income students to attend college.

Despite the amount of broad-based legislation, the US Department of Education reports that it provides only 10.5 percent of public school funding, with the balance coming from states and local communities. The largest portion of the federal share comes from the US Department of Agriculture, which funds the school lunch program for students from low-income families. Another portion comes from the US Department of Health and Human Services, which funds "Head Start" and similar programs for economically disadvantaged preschool children. The principal role of the federal government in much of the legislation was to provide technical support for public schools and to protect the civil rights to an education for diverse groups of students. Actual curricular issues and the assessment of academic performances were left to the local schools and state education agencies.

A CHANGING PERSPECTIVE

It is possible to date the expanded role of the federal government in mandating performance standards for the public school to the publication of *A Nation at Risk* in 1983, published by the National Commission on Excellence in Education. The report began with the following observation:

> Our nation is at risk. Our once unchallenged preeminence in commerce, industry, science, and technological innovation is being overtaken by competitors throughout the world. This report is concerned with only one of the many causes and dimensions of the problem, but it is the one that undergirds American prosperity, security, and civility. We report to the American people that while we can take justifiable pride in what our schools and colleges have historically accomplished and contributed to the United States and the well-being of its people, the educational foundations of our society are presently being eroded by a rising tide of mediocrity that threatens our very future as a Nation and a people. What was unimaginable a generation ago has begun to occur—others are matching and surpassing our educational attainments (1983).

The corporate sector, social conservatives and later middle-class parents had charged that by placing a greater emphasis on humanistic and multicultural issues, public schools of the 1960s and 1970s had abandoned educational "basics" and caused a decline in student achievement, with a commensurate decline in US economic competitiveness. After the release of the report state legislatures began to adopt school reforms. This first wave of reforms sought " . . . to introduce uniformity and conformity through standardized curricula, rigorous requirements for student performance, promotion and graduation, and teacher evaluation" (Smylie and Denny 1990, 235). The goal of this first wave of school reform was to ensure that only competent teachers were in classrooms and only educated students graduated.

At the time of the establishment of the National Commission on Excellence in Education in 1981, public confidence in public schools had been diminishing. Consequently, a second stage of school reforms was initiated by the administration of the first President Bush when data from the National Assessment of Educational Progress (NAEP), known as the "Nation's Report Card", continued to reveal that a high percentage of the students in the two tested grades (4 and 8) were not proficient or even performing at basic levels in reading and mathematics. Under the aegis of the reauthorization of the *Elementary and Secondary Education Act of 1965*, the first Bush administration called for reforms known as *America 2000* (1991). This legislation called for the development of "world class standards' and the creation of "break the mold school". Decentralization and site-based decision making (decision making made at the community and district level) was the proposed solution.

The Clinton administration in the *Goals 2000* (1994) advocated high-stakes testing, the use of standardized achievement tests taken by students as the principal evaluation instrument to assess students, teachers, school administrators, schools or school districts. Initially, high-stakes testing was aimed at schools and indirectly, teachers, where test passage rates would become public information. Making school academic achievement information public, affected housing values and community attractiveness; neighborhoods whose schools produced high test scores had increased property values while low test scores saw declines (Viadero 2006; Clapp, Nanda and Ross 2007; Sedgley, Williams and Derrick 2008). Community pressure to maintain high property values provided support for employing severe measures to correct low student and school performance.

The third stage of reform efforts expanded the consequences of high-stakes testing to include the students. In this stage, not only could schools be closed and teachers fired, but a student's low standardized test performance could lead to being retained in grade. Many states passed laws eliminating social promotion thereby making test failure high stakes for both students and school personnel. *The No Child Left Behind Act of 2001* (NCLB) represents a national implementation of the high-stakes testing movement begun under *Goals 2000*. NCLB specified a timetable and sequence under which schools could be deemed *In Need Of Improvement* (INOI) and ultimately subject to closing (faculty and staff terminated).

Finally, the Obama administration has ushered in *Race to the Top* (2009) as part of the *American Recovery and Reinvestment Act of 2009*, which was passed by Congress to aid the country in recovering from the worldwide recession that began in 2008. *Race to the Top* maintains many of the elements of NCLB, but stipulates that federal funds for the program are competitive, with states having to adopt successful standards and assessments, create and maintain data systems the measure student achievement and inform teachers and principal on how to improve instruction, recruit and reward effective teachers and principals and raise the achievement in low-performing schools (www2.ed.gov/programs/racetothetop/index.html). The demand for greater uniformity of standards across states, including curricular content, has led at least two state governors (from Alaska and Texas) to refuse to participate in the application process for funding.

Both NCLB and currently Race to the Top have encountered significant resistance from some states, although the magnitude of resistance and even sabotage of NCLB is considerably greater than what has occurred recently with Race to the Top. States have charged that NCLB is an unfunded mandate by the federal government, as no additional funds were allocated to cover the cost of the administration of standardized achievement tests used to assess student progress. Many states did not have a test, while others attempted to use an "off the shelf test". Dworkin (2005) cautions that many of the tests would not satisfy the criteria for test acceptability required to determine if schools were failing to meet their Adequate Yearly Progress goals.

Perceived declines in student academic achievement and concerns regarding the competitiveness of the future American labor force have been instrumental in increasing the federal government's role in public education. Over the course of the country's history education has shifted from exclusively the domain of state and local government and local communities to one that involves a growing role for the federal government. The course of these changes came first in supplying necessary resources for schools, and then to mandating the equality of educational opportunity for disadvantaged groups, and now to requiring states to implement policies that raise student achievement and school effectiveness so that the American labor force can regain its competitiveness.

Changes in Student Achievement Since the Waves of Reforms

Concerns about the academic competency of American students did not begin with *A Nation at Risk* (1983). However, federal involvement and policies relating to the academic competitiveness of American students did gain prominence in the 1980s. The dual concerns that future American labor forces were not being adequately trained and that as a consequence, American industrial dominance would fall continued. Immigration into the US, particularly from developing nations and involving ethnic minorities, has been blamed as a source of declining academic performance. Likewise internal migration of these groups and the general population, including traditional minority groups, have spread declines in achievement across the nation and challenged the school systems.

In a report describing internal migration within the US between 2005 and 2007, Cohn and Morin (2008) reported that the Southern and Western states made substantial gains in population, with the lion's share of movement leaving the Northeastern and Midwestern states. The National Assessment of Educational Progress (NAEP) is a national standardized achievement test, often described as the "nation's report card", has linked the growing populations with lower student achievement. NAEP results are displayed by performance categories from a low of "below basic", to "basic", to "proficient", to "advanced". Proficient and advanced performances indicate that students are competitive. In science in 2005 (www.nationsreportcard.gov), for example, 55 percent of the 4th graders in Mississippi (a Southern state with a large minority population) were below basic and 13 percent were proficient or advanced. Among the 8th graders from Mississippi, 60 percent were below basic in science and 14 percent proficient or advanced. By contrast, in the relatively homogeneous northern states of North and South Dakota and Montana (with few ethnic minorities), 18 to 21 percent of the 4th graders were below basic in science, while 35 to 37 percent were proficient or advanced. Among 8th graders in those three states, 23 to 24 percent were below basic in science while between 41 and 43 percent were proficient or advanced.

What is seen as regional variations in student achievement that disadvantage students in some states is also prevalent in global competitions. Two international tests have been used to compare the academic abilities of students from different nations: the PISA exam (Program for International Student Assessment) administered to 15-year-olds in some 69 countries in 2010 and the TIMSS (Trends in International Math and Science Study). In 2006, US students were lower than the OECD average in science and mathematics and in 2003 they were at the OECD average in reading ability. At the aggregate, US students are not competitive with students from other developed nations and in an era of global economics in which multinational corporations can pick and choose their labor forces, the local variations in student competencies, that are in part a function of localized control of education, perform a disservice for American students.

One educator has suggested several structural and historical factors that can account for past and current concerns about the competitiveness of American students. Ruby Payne (2003) reports that a common set of demographic, structural and technological factors may account for what she had termed a "hundred-year repeat pattern". While it is impossible to draw a trend line from two data points (late-nineteenth century and late-twentieth century) it has been her contention that the current reforms replicate processes present more than a century ago. She notes that there were concerns about public education in the period between 1870 and 1910 that mirror the concerns over the period from about 1970 to the present. Key among the elements of the nineteenth century calls for reform were societal transitions, including economic changes from agrarian to an industrial-based society; a substantial increase in immigration (generally from Eastern and Southern Europe); the emergence of private schools that could tap the supply of elite students; a technological shift from animal power to machine power; the inclusion of traditional minorities into the paid labor force; active involvement of the business community in public schools; and a change in the delivery of education (to larger schools that with age-graded classes). These transitions led business, government and the public to question whether public schools could supply the needed, competitive labor force for the next century, and expressed concern regarding the effect of a less able labor force would have on national competitiveness in the twentieth century.

The period since 1970 also witnessed an equivalent transition according to Payne. The national economy shifted from a industrial base to one that relied on knowledge and enhanced human capital; substantial increases in immigration occurred (although this time from Latin America and Asia); technological changes resulted in decreased use of machines and greater use of computers; an array of federal programs and legislation offered resources and opportunities to disadvantaged groups (racial and ethnic minorities, women, people with disabilities, etc.); a rekindling of business involvement in public education; and the rise of alternative ways of introducing instruction (including the Internet, as well as alternative schools and charter schools). The result has been an array of policies intended to make public schools more competitive, and possibly to discredit the current public schools as not doing enough.

It is Payne's contention that the specific mix of structural changes resulted in calls for school reform in both eras. It is the contention of the present analysis that several of the factors served as indicators that were used by social change agents to press for government intervention into the schools, rather than causes of actual declines in the capacity of schools to meet needs. Our focus is upon perceived threats to the American middle class and to business that we see are most significant. The specific perceived threats are a function of changes in the makeup of student populations occasioned by the expansion of the civil rights of minority groups and the change in the number and demography of immigrant populations, both of which require the use of and redirection of school resources. The second factor is the role of globalization on the local labor markets and the capacity of business to rely on readily available labor forces. That is, it is our contention that changing demographic characteristics of the student and labor force populations were seen as threats to both middle-class privilege and to business interests. Likewise, international economic competition and globalization have challenged the ability of US businesses to compete in a world where the United States no longer has an economic and industrial hegemony.

CHANGES IN THE CONSTITUENCY OF STUDENTS AND WORKERS: IMMIGRATION AND INTERNAL MOBILITY

Immigration

It is an often-quoted maxim in the United States that the country is a nation of immigrants. Early colonization of what became the United States was by immigrants from Northern Europe in the seventeenth and eighteenth centuries. By the fact of being a "settler society" the Europeans often violently displaced the Native American population. According to Stasiulis and Yuval-Davis (1995), the Europeans and their descendants displaced indigenous populations and continue to maintain political dominance over those populations. Over time such societies have increased their heterogeneity and have become increasingly stratified in terms of race, ethnicity and social class (1995, 3). As late as the beginning of the twentieth century, over 90 percent of all immigrants to the US came from Europe (Dworkin and Dworkin 1999; Gibson and Lennon, 1999). In fact, Europeans represented the largest contingent of immigrants to the United States until the end of the 1950s. Since then, Latin America and Asia have supplied the vast majority immigrants to the country. Both in the earlier part of the twentieth century and the present many of the immigrants came without knowledge of English and with limited skills. In the nineteenth, twentieth and now in the twenty-first centuries the native born residents expressed concerns about the influx of immigrants, despite the fact that the country has through much of its history been termed "a nation of immigrants" and immigrants often occupied a necessary economic niche. Between 2000 and 2050 the population in the US is expected to grow by 142 million, reaching an estimated size of 438 million individuals. The highly-respected Pew Research Center forecasts that 82 percent of the population increase in 2050 will be composed of immigrants, their children and grandchildren (Passel and Cohn 2008). This would mean that 60 percent of all Americans in the US would be immigrants or the children and grandchildren of immigrants by 2050.

The US Congress passed the first legislation regulating immigration in 1819, when most immigration came from Northern Europe. After the American Civil War (1861–1865) immigrants from Central and Southern Europe, as well as from Asia became more plentiful (many of whom were brought country to work on the construction of the transcontinental railroad and earlier following the discovery of gold in California in the late 1840s). It was the Asian immigration following the Civil War that led to fears of what was termed "Yellow Peril" and resulted in the Chinese Exclusion Act of 1882. Immigration of the Chinese was severely limited. Immigration of Chinese individuals was suspended for ten years, but the ban was renewed every decade until 1943. Renewals of the act imposed further restrictions on Chinese immigrants, including a ban against naturalization and citizenship. Ironically, it was the ban on Chinese immigration that led to the recruitment of Japanese immigrants to work in the sugar cane fields in Hawaii near the end of the nineteenth century (Fujiwara and Takagi 1999, 300).

Anti-immigrant sentiments among native Protestant White Americans grew as the numbers of immigrants topped 8 million between 1901 and 1910. Most of the new immigrants were not Protestants and their numbers and cultural differences were seen as threats by the dominant population.

During the administration of President Woodrow Wilson Congress passed legislation that included a literacy test for immigrants. In 1921 quotas were established for immigrants from many nations and in 1924, Congress passed the National Origins Act that established set quotas for immigrants for each country. The permissible number of immigrants from each country was set at 2 percent of the count for the country in the 1890 Census. During the post-World War I era through the middle of the 1920s hate groups such as the Ku Klux Klan (KKK) grew in popularity among native White Americans so that in 1924, some 40,000 Klan members in full hooded robes marched in Washington, DC to express opposition to the rights of immigrants, African Americans, Catholics and Jews. There were Klan chapters in virtually every state and many high government officials (senators, congressmen, governors and judges) were affiliated with the Klan during that era. Membership at the time was estimated to number at least 4 million, although that number was likely greatly exaggerated by the press and the Klan itself (Chalmers 1968, 1981).

Following the Great Depression and World War II the restrictive immigration law curtailed the migration of many refugees following the war. It was not until 1965 that the National Origins Act was repealed and replaced by a less restrictive law. Following the large influx of Latin Americans, many of whom were undocumented, following economic collapses and civil wars Congress replaced the 1965 legislation with the Immigration Reform and Control Act of 1986 (IRCA) that granted amnesty to certain undocumented workers and required employers to check the work authorization documents of each employee, including US citizens. As the numbers of the undocumented have increased (although since the economic recession of 2008 the rate has declined), concerns about the control of immigration has become a central issue of US political debate, with each political party promising to control immigration. It will be an important issue in the 2012 Presidential election.

Immigrant access to educational opportunities has been a significant issue from the early years of the United States. However, since World War II the issue has been contested vigorously, as educational opportunity makes accessible better jobs and the ability to compete with citizens. In 1982 the Supreme Court held in the case Plyer v. Doe (457 US 202, 1982) that immigrant children had a Constitutional right to a free public education. Texas had provided free public education to the children of undocumented immigrants until 1975, when the state legislature passes legislation that prohibited the use of state funds for such education. The US Supreme Court struck down the Texas law and all other state laws that had barred immigrant children from a free public school education. This meant that even if the parents were undocumented and were considered to be in the country illegally, their children, even if not born in the US, were entitled to attend and graduate from a public school without having to pay tuition. Federal legislation such as the Bilingual Education Act provided for language training of immigrant children and a transition into English instruction, while the Emergency Immigrant Education Act provided school districts with additional funding to accommodate increases in immigrant enrollments. The logic of the Supreme Court ruling and the legislation was not to punish children for the decisions of their parents and to educate a potential future labor force should the children eventually receive status as permanent residents or citizens.

However, graduation from public school or even from college did not entitle immigrant children the right to secure employment in the US. Currently, once immigrant students have completed their education IRCA (1986) requires them to return to their home countries prior to applying to return to the US. They must have a guarantee of a job or financial support in order to return. Of course, not being able to apply for jobs after graduation means that they will have difficulty meeting the requirement for re-entry into the country. One solution that has been discussed in the US Congress is the Dream Act, which if passed would grant permanent resident status to immigrants who graduated from school or entered the armed forces (currently, undocumented immigrants are not accepted into the military). With such status the individuals could work in the US and eventually seek naturalized citizenship.

Internal Mobility

Migration within the United States represents a further challenge to the effectiveness of schooling in creating a competent labor force. The US Census Bureau reports that on average 14 percent of the US population change residence each year (US Census Bureau 2009). While this percentage is less than it had been during the Great Depression, in which numbers of families left their farms to look for work in other states, the continued amount of mobility has significant educational ramifications. The present analysis will address only two of the many consequences of internal migration and student mobility. One is the effect of mobility of student achievement and an array of negative impacts of depressed student achievement, and the other is the effect of local control of curricula on the competitiveness of a geographically mobile student population.

Student Mobility and Academic Outcomes

In a society with a national curriculum, and especially where migration from state to state or school to school would not result in students falling behind in subject matters, some amount of mobility would not be dysfunctional. However, in the United States each state can determine its own curricula and often each school district or individual school can determine the order in which material are presented to students. Thus, mobility may result in students falling behind academically or never being introduced to some important educational material, either because the material is not presented, or because the student missed the material because it was presented in a different temporal sequence in his or her new school. While federal reform legislation including *The No Child Left Behind Act of 2001* has established some general standards such as proficiency in reading, mathematics, history and science, the details are left up to the states and more specifically to individual school districts, schools and even teachers.

The majority of research has found generally negative consequences for "non-promotional school changes" or the changing of schools for reasons other than that the students have completed all grade levels at their present school and move, usually with their classmates, to the next higher school. Alexander, Entwisle and Dauber (1996); Roderick and Camburn (1996); Rumberger 2003; Rumberger and Larson (1998); and Rumberger, Ream and Palardy (1999) have examined the interplay between mobility and school changing and academic risk. Such non-promotional mobility frequently occurs when families change residences, either because of the demands of employment or because of housing needs and financial pressures. These school transfers are most commonly observed among students who are immigrants, ethnic minorities and from low income families. These students are more likely ultimately to drop out of school (Rumberger et al. 1999).

Under the guidelines prescribed by *The No Child Left Behind Act of 2001*, students attending a low-performing school that fails to meet its Adequate Year Progress goals for two consecutive years must be offered public school choice, or the opportunity to transfer to a higher-performing school. Dworkin and Lorence (2007) found, however, that unless the student transferred to a substantially higher-performing school the academic losses due to mobility were not made up even after several years at the new school. Minority students and those from low-income families (those most likely to have attended a low-performing school) were placed at a greater disadvantage because of the mobility than majority and students from more affluent families. However, the substantially higher performing schools are generally found in the more affluent suburbs and neighborhoods within cities. NCLB permits schools to refuse to accept students from outside their own attendance zones if they certify that they would become overcrowded if such transfers were to occur. Wells (2001) reported in her study of the Cleveland, Ohio, schools that the higher-performing suburban schools refused to admit any children attempting to transfer in from low-performing urban schools.

Societal Outcomes of Student Mobility and Local/State Curricula

One hallmark of American education has been local and state control of public schools. The principle, dating back from the founding of the nation, holds that educational decision-making that is closest to the local community serves that community (and presumably the society) best. Under the aegis of the 1991 reauthorization of the *Elementary and Secondary Education Act* (referred to as *America 2000*) during the administration of the first President Bush states enacted site-based management plans that empowered local councils composed of the school principal, teachers, parents and community stakeholders with the responsibility to develop local school policies. While major school reform legislation following the release of *A Nation at Risk* (1983) has guaranteed a federal role in educational and curricular policies, the principle of "State's Rights", guaranteed under the 10th Amendment to the US Constitution, permits considerable state and even local latitude in curricular details. State boards of education in Texas and Kansas, for example have restructured history and science curricula to favor politically conservative interpretations. Issues ranging from the teaching of Creationism, the banning of sex education classes, and until effectively challenged before the US Supreme Court, prayer in schools have been the purview of local school boards and/or state education agencies.

Local and state control of schools and curricula were functional during a time when citizens rarely left the communities in which they were born and educated. However, a mobile population, especially in an age of global economics, must be competent in more than the locally-relevant subject matter. Imagine if a local community decided that the teaching of science was not relevant to their needs and thus minimized teaching of chemistry, physics, biology and geology. How poorly might their students perform on a college admissions test such as the SAT or ACT? And, how uncompetitive might their graduates be in competing for job in other states or, given a global economy and labor force, competing for jobs in Europe, Asia, Africa or Latin America?

DIVERSITY AND AMERICAN STUDENT COMPETITIVENESS IN A GLOBAL ECONOMY

Two conflicting forces have emerged in US schooling over the past few decades, as it has in other developed nations. Concerns about the competitiveness of American students in light of standardized tests scores suggests that mass education (what Ball [1990, 2003] refers to as the "Fordist" model) should be enhanced and become more rigorous so as to insure that "no child will be left behind". However, pressures from middle-class parents as well as the business sector also stress a "Post-Fordist" model (Ball 1990, 2003) in which specialization, testing and assessment pervade public education in order to strengthen the skills of the most competitive of students. This latter model exaggerates differences among groups of students based on social class, although the differentiation is often expressed in terms of abilities. The use of standardized tests contributes to the "marketization" of education. That is, consumers of education (principally the middle-class parents) use test scores to determine the quality of schools and "shop" around for the best school options for their children. In the US is not uncommon for realty firms to report the test scores of a local school in a neighborhood as a "selling point" to prospective buyers. Thus, the manifestations of the Standards-Based School Accountability Movement have been in terms of calls to narrow the achievement gap between rich and poor, majority and minority. However, the effect of academic specialization, tracking across schools (e.g., magnet schools and other specialized schools) rather than within classrooms where detracking is becoming more acceptable, has been to widen gaps in the actual breadth of knowledge. The focus on basic skills tests, however, tends to make for the appearance of a narrowed gap among groups, while the results of more rigorous tests suggest the opposite. Between 1971 and 2008 the test score gap between Black students and White students on the NAEP has narrowed in reading and mathematics. Likewise, the test score gap between Hispanic and Anglo students has also narrowed. Nevertheless, the gaps, which nearly forty years ago were over 20 percent of the total score, is now somewhat over 10 percent of the total (NCES 2009).

The Scholastic Aptitude Test used by many colleges and universities as a component for admissions shows no significant decrease in the gaps by race and social class (Kobrin, Sathy and Shaw 2007; The College Board 1996, 2009). The verbal and mathematics portions of the test have a score range from 200 to 800. Comparing the 1972 recentered SAT results for college-bound seniors with the 1996 results, and in turn the 1996 results with the 2009 results shows that the Black–White gap remains at more than 100 points, or about a full standard deviation across each time period. Likewise, the gap between students from low and high income families continues to remain at about 130 points, or more than a standard deviation.

While some gaps have been whittled down, other significant differences persist. The dropout rate among high school students remains alarmingly high (Dworkin 2008a), especially among Latinos and African American males (Lewis, Uzzell, Horwitz and Casserly, Council on Great Cities Schools 2010). Heckman and LaFontaine (2007) examined trends in the federal National Center for Education Statistics data base to report that real graduation rates in the US have been declining since 1968. The National Center for Education Statistics of the US Department of Education (2007, 161) reported that 9.4 percent of the population of students between the ages of 16 and 24 lack a high school credential, be it a diploma, a certificate of completion or an equivalent credential such as a General Education Development (GED) certificate. This statistic is referred to as a "status dropout rate". When race/ethnicity is considered the rates become even more worrisome. While the status dropout rate for Whites between the ages of 16 and 24 in 2005 was 6 percent, the status dropout rate for African Americans was 10.4 percent and the Hispanic status dropout rate for 2005 was 22.4 percent. Thus, the African American rate approaches twice that of Whites and the Hispanic rate approaches four times that of

Whites. Further, the status dropout rate for students who are Hispanic immigrants is 36.5 percent.

Balfantz and Legters (2004) of Johns Hopkins University report that the dropout problem is concentrated in high schools that have poor "promoting power", or the schools inability to enable students to make normal progress from eighth grade (middle school) through twelfth grade (the last year of high school). They observed that on average about 80 percent of the freshman class will reach Grade 12 in four years. However, in "schools with weak promoting power, fewer than 60 percent of a freshman class will reach twelfth grade four years later and in true 'Dropout Factories' fewer than 50 percent of freshman reach twelfth grade four years later. Balfantz and Legters (2004) reported that the percentage of high schools with weak promoting power and the number of dropout factories has increased over the period from 1993 to 2002. They further report,

> "In high schools with weak promoting power, the overwhelming majority of students represent racial and ethnic minorities. A school in which more than half of the students come from minority backgrounds is five times as likely to have weak promoting power as a school in which the majority of students are white" (2004:62).

Furthermore, the high schools with weak promoting power

> " . . . are concentrated in about 50 large cities and 15 primarily southern and southwestern states. . . . They are engines driving the low national graduation rate for minority students and the growing number of dispossessed young adults who are neither employed nor in school" (2004:77).

GLOBALIZATION AND THE COMPETITIVENESS OF AMERICAN WORKERS AND AMERICAN COMPANIES

Historically the United States was concerned with its competitiveness in the global marketplace and those who expressed the most concern were educators and the business community. The federal government did not regularly express concerns about the quality of public education in the US because there had not been an expressed role for the federal government. States also rarely expressed concerns prior to World War II. Educators were concerned because the performance of school students reflected on their pedagogical skills. Businesses expressed concerns because labor markets prior to the end of World War II were generally not global and most businesses tended to be anchored in a single country. Thus, the lack of competitiveness of a labor force meant that companies were unable to hire the best and the brightest and the company's economic position suffered.

Globalization meant that multinational corporations were not tied to a single country or region of the world in which to obtain a workforce.

The destruction of industry in Europe and Asia after World War II permitted the US to maintain hegemony over high-skilled jobs and well-paid labor throughout the 1950s and even into the early 1960s. Additionally, the products of war-torn countries were often poorer than those in the US and most of the foreign work was in extractive industries in countries where the raw materials were located and in the production of labor-intensive, inexpensive products. However, as Europe and Asia rebuilt or developed their industries they had more modern plants than those in the US and they needed to train a regional labor force to work in those plants. The relocation of steel making, the auto industry and electronics manufacturing out of the US resulted in crises for American workers and concerns for state and local governments. Initial analyses of the loss of good jobs in the US were explained by those who were critical of public schools. Edward Fiske (1991), the then education editor of the *New York Times* reported New York Life Insurance Company, was shipping its claim processing and accounting to Dublin, Ireland, because they could not find competent workers in New York. In reality, it was not because accountants in New York in the 1980s were incompetent, but that accountants in Dublin were cheaper. When multinational industries can get access to a less expensive, but competent, labor force in another country they will do so.

WHY STATES RESIST SOME FEDERAL INVOLVEMENT IN PUBLIC EDUCATION

There has been considerable resistance among states to school reforms mandated by the federal government under the reauthorizations of the Elementary and Secondary Education Act of 1965, just as there was resistance by states and local school districts to implement the Supreme Court ordered school desegregation. The issue is sometime referred to as one of "States' Rights" and emanates from the "Reserved Powers" clause of the 10th Amendment to the Constitution. The amendment states that powers not granted to the federal government, nor prohibited to the states by the Constitution, are reserved to the states and the people of the United States. Since public education is not specified as a federal right or Constitutional guarantee its implementation becomes the reserved right of the states and local communities.

State and local resistance to school desegregation, especially in the South, was pervasive during the late 1950s and throughout the 1960s and 1970s. Federal troops had to be sent to Little Rock, Arkansas, in 1957 to enforce the desegregation by nine African American students at Central High School. George Wallace, the governor of Alabama, physically stood in front of the auditorium of the University of Alabama to block the admissions of two African American students in 1963. Local school districts modified school attendance zones to restrict African American students from attending white schools and some districts closed or privatized schools to prevent desegregation (Smith 1965). The 1960s and 1970s saw a plethora of federal district court and US Supreme Court decisions enforcing desegregation through busing (as there was considerable residential segregation that resulted in minority and majority students living in different and often distant neighborhoods). Metropolitan desegregation plans were also addressed by the Supreme Court and federal district courts to merge school districts within central cities and their suburbs. This strategy was developed because white flight to the suburbs left inner city schools racially homogeneous. The logic of the rulings was that if parents could not avoid desegregation by moving to the suburbs there might be less white flight.

When the federal government paid for school programs, as in the case of the subsidized school lunch program, or allocated support to the states for special education or bilingual education, there was less local resistance. However, in many school districts both special education and bilingual education is often underfunded and many students are not served.

By contrast, there has been substantial state and school district resistance to the implementation of NCLB and Race to the Top. State education agencies and state legislatures were particular concerned about NCLB's requirement that by the 2013–2014 academic year all students in tested grades would pass the standardized test. The law specified that only 5 percent of the students in the tested grades could be exempt from testing, generally for special education reasons. Dworkin (2008b) reported that states (and local districts) often "gamed the system", or engaged in practices that would subvert the goals of the federal legislation. States claimed that by not providing funds to develop and implement testing the federal government had forced the states to adopt an unfunded mandate. Several states sued the federal government in court. Others redefined state standards to enable most schools to meet the specified annual achievement goals (known as Adequate Yearly Progress, or AYP).

NCLB specified that schools and districts that repeatedly fail to meet their AYP goals can be subjected to the loss of some of their federal funds, lose some of their students (usually the highest achievers) to a public school choice option, be forced to close, dismiss their staff and be reopened as a charter school with new faculties and administrators, states, districts and schools engaged in an array of practices that hid academic failures. Schools encouraged low performing students not to take the test; encouraged them to drop out, but recorded them as having left to be home schooled; or had teachers give test answers to their students or changed answers after the tests were collected. In many instances these practices were implemented by the schools or districts without the cooperation of the states. States, however, sought to establish minimal standards for the tests and sometimes easy tests in order to reduce the likelihood that schools would fail to meet AYP goals (Dworkin 2005, 2008b; Booher-Jennings 2005; Booher-Jennings and Beveridge 2007).

Dworkin (2008b) interpreted the state and local action against NCLB as a form of "innovation" within the context of Merton's "Social Structure and Anomie" (1968). Innovation involves accepting the societal goals, but rejecting the means to those goals. States and local school districts and schools accepted the goal of decreasing the test score gaps between minority and majority students, middle class and economically disadvantaged students, but they rejected the means to attaining that goal—very hard work to make up for years of second-class schooling for minorities and the poor and impoverished home environments for many such students. Teachers also objected to being held responsible for the achievement of students who come to school unprepared to learn and whose parents they feel are unsupportive of their own children's education. Further, most of a child's waking hours are not in school, but subjected to many non-academic experiences. However, NCLB, Race to the Top and related school reforms that have been developed since the Standards-Based School Accountability Movement hold teachers, schools, districts and states responsible for the learning outcomes of their students. Feeling powerless to improve test scores some teachers and schools cheat (innovate). Likewise, states are often in a position of powerlessness to improve substantially student achievement. Recently, the Texas Education Agency has adopted a new formula for calculating student success called the Texas Projection Measure (Texas Education Agency 2009). Student test scores on the state-mandated standardized test created for NCLB that are below the passing threshold can be counted as currently passing if they fall within a certain range and the equation predicts that the students will pass a future standardized test. The state therefore raises the current passing rate of the school, thereby permitting it to meet AYP and not face Draconian measures specified under NCLB. It should be noted that the proposed plan was submitted to the US Department of Education and accepted.

It is neither politically correct, nor within the professional ethics of teaching to reject the goal of student academic success. When faced with a desirable goal and a barrier to its attainment, teachers, schools, districts and even states play games. The result can be that schools are seen as successful and their students are thought of as well educated, but instead the students and ultimately the society lose out to those nations that implement real standards and achieve real success within the boundaries of those standards.

CONCLUSION

Prior to the emergence of the Standards-Based School Accountability Movement in the 1980s, federal involvement in public education was generally limited to expanding educational opportunities for disadvantaged groups through various civil rights laws and court decisions and in funding school lunches for economically disadvantaged students or supporting state and local programs for language minority and special education students. However, following the release of a federal report entitled *A Nation at Risk* (1983) the federal government assumed a greater role in setting academic standards to be met by schools. The increasing role of the federal government in education can be traced to concerns regarding the competitiveness of American students and the future labor force they will form. These concerns can be linked to changes in the size of the non-European immigrant population and pressures to increase educational opportunities for ethnic minorities and children from low-income families.

The result of three decades of federal involvement has been the implementation of high-stakes achievement testing of public school students and an array of consequences for teachers, school administrators, schools and school districts if the standards are not met. The tests are high stakes for schools and school personnel because low student performance can result in the closing of schools and the termination of employment for teachers and school administrators. In a majority of states the tests are also high stakes for students, as low student achievement can result in the denial of academic promotion to the next grade or the denial of graduation and a diploma.

Federal involvement in public schools that is not accompanied by federal funding is often not welcome in many states and raises "States' Rights" issues. The result has been that states often use their States' Rights prerogative to reduce the effectiveness of federal standards intended to raise achievement and narrow the test score gaps between different categories of students. It is often not because states and districts do not want to narrow achievement gaps, although many middle-class parents object to resources being allocated to children other than their own, as they see affirmative advantages offered to previously disadvantaged students as a threat to their own children's educational privileges. Rather, for states the concern is with the cost of implementing unfunded federal mandates and the challenge to their own right to determine the nature of the schooling for their students.

The expansion of educational opportunity afforded by civil rights legislation, court decisions regarding the equality of educational opportunity, changes in the demographic characteristics of the student population and rights afforded to children of immigrants have altered the nature of competition for college access and good jobs. These changes have threatened the monopoly of the middle class over educational privilege. The threats to the middle class are exacerbated by globalization. Not only must their children compete with minority groups who previously were excluded from access to the best jobs, but they need to compete with students from many developed nations in the world. The middle and working class increasingly find that their jobs are being exported overseas, because of growing availability of skilled workers and professionals in developing nations, especially in China, India and Brazil, who are frequently paid less by the multinational corporations.

Globalization also impacts local industries as they find it increasingly difficult to compete with similar industries in the developing world. Heavy manufacturing, electronics and many high tech fields have been migrating out of the United States since the late 1960s. Not only do jobs become exported, but corporate offices also are relocated abroad. Thus, it was local industry that first sought to have the federal government impose academic standards in order to guarantee a supply of skilled labor from the US. Now, however, the multinational corporations see the value in a skilled US labor force so that workers will be able to afford the products that are now manufactured outside the United States. Heightened unemployment in the US because of the loss of jobs to developing countries presents a problem for multinationals so long as the US is the major consumer of products. Thus, federal pressure on schools to produce more talented students results not just in higher employment, but more spending money for Americans whose purchases help to support the economies of the nations to which many jobs have gone.

The response to the challenges of globalization and immigration have been increased educational accountability, which runs counter to the conceptualization of American schools as loosely-coupled systems (Weick 1976). Decentralized decision making creates a conflict between policy and practice. That is, state education agency policies are often not implemented as intended by school districts; there is a notable slippage in the implementation of district policies by schools; and finally, once teachers close their classroom doors the curricula that are offered to students may be poorly articulated with district policies.

Darling-Hammond and Berry (1988) predicted that the nexus between policy and practice across organizational levels would change with more rigorous accountability. However, when accountability systems hold teachers and school administrators responsible for student learning outcomes, and when such outcomes are measured by standardized tests, considerable conflict can arise over gaps between policies and their implementation in classrooms.

Under NCLB, federal guidelines imposed mandated standards for student passage rates with Draconian sanctions for failures to meet such standards. States, in turn, closely monitored school districts and schools, and school districts scrutinized the performances of schools. The gaps between policies and practices across levels were generally narrowed. However, because accountability assessments ultimately depend on the performances of students, student abilities and commitments to learning, parent support and involvement and myriad other social factors and social pathologies can intervene between curricula and test results, school districts, schools and teachers sometimes chafed against these regulations.

The National Commission on Excellence in Education, authors of *A Nation at Risk* (1983) and many others called for more accountability and more well-defined standards. Such calls led to the current Standards-Based

School Accountability Movement and the reforms that followed the re-authorizations of the Elementary and Secondary Education Act of 1965. In light of NCLB and other reforms that led to teacher, school and district accountability, with prescribed standards based on standardized achievement test results and prescribed sanctions for schools and personnel if standards are not met, it seems that the loosely-coupled systems portrait is no longer accurate. The disconnect between federal policy and the continued existence of loose-coupling has resulted in resistance by teachers, schools, districts and even states in the implementation of school reform. The loose-coupling could well be due to the fact that the state, district and campus actors under the aegis of states' rights innovate in their implementation of standards. The result of such innovations, in coping with accountability, may have the effect of further loosening the coupling, as it promotes actual gaps between policies and practices across levels, while creating the appearance of tighter coupling. In turn, the expansion of educational opportunity to immigrant and minority groups may be further limited by the actual gaps between policy and practice.

NOTES

1. (www2.ed.gov/about/overview/fed/ role/html): including the Second Morrill Act of 1890.
2. Smith-Hughes Act of 1917 and the George-Barden Act of 1946.

REFERENCES

Alexander, Karl L., Dorris R. Entwisle, and Susan L. Dauber. 1996. "Children in Motion: School Transfers and Elementary School Performance". *Journal of Education Research* 90(1): 3–12.

Balfantz, Robert, and Netie Legters. 2004. "Locating the Dropout Crisis: Which High Schools Produce the Nation's Dropouts?" In *Dropouts in America: Confronting the Graduation Rate Crisis*, edited by Gary Orfield, 57–84. Cambridge, MA: Harvard Education Press.

Ball, Stephen J. 1990. *Politics and Policymaking in Education*. London: Routledge.

Ball, Stephen J. 2003. *Class Strategies and the Education Market: The Middle Classes and Social Advantage*. London: Routledge Falmer.

Booher-Jennings, Jennifer. 2005. "Below the Bubble: Educational Triage and the Texas Accountability System". *American Educational Research Journal* 42(2): 231–268.

Booher-Jennings, Jennifer, and Andy Beveridge. 2007. "Gains, Strains, Gaming, and Results: the Prevalence and Impact of Elective and Defacto Test Exemption in the Houston Independent School District". In *No Child Left Behind and the Reduction of the Achievement Gap: Sociological Perspectives on Federal Education Policy*, edited by Sadovnik, O'Day, Bohrnstedt, and Borman, 77–95. New York: Routledge.

Census Bureau News—Geographical Mobility. 2009. http://www.prnewswire.com/news-releases/census-bureau-news—-geographical-mobility-2009–93287259.html

Chalmers, David M. 1968. *Hooded Americanism: The History of the Ku Klux Klan*. New York: Quadrangle Books.

Chalmers, David M. 1981. *Hooded Americanism: The History of the Ku Klux Klan* (2nd edition). New York: New Viewpoints, Franklin Watts.

Clapp, John M., Anupam Nanda, and Stephen L Ross. 2007. "Which School Attributes Matter? The Influence of School District Performance and Demographic Composition on Property Values". *Journal of Urban Economics* 63(2): 451–466.

Cohn, D'vera, and Rich Morin. 2008. Who Moves? Who Stays Put? Where's Home? Washington, DC: Pew Research Center. http://pewsocialtrends.org/2008/12/17/who-moves-who-stays-put-wheres-home

The College Board. 1996. 1996 Profile of College-Bound Seniors: National Report. New York: The College Board.

The College Board. 2009. 2009 College-Bound Seniors: Total Group Profile Report.

Darling-Hammond, Linda, and Barnet Berry. 1988. *The Evolution of Teacher Policy*. Santa Monica, CA: RAND Corp.

Dworkin, Anthony G. 2005. "The No Child Left Behind Act: Accountability, High-Stakes Testing, and Roles for Sociologists". *Sociology Education* 78(April): 170–174.

Dworkin, Anothony G. 2008a. "Dropping Out of High School: Another American Dilemma". The Latino Black Education Initiative. Atlanta, GA: Southern Education Foundation.

Dworkin, Anthony G. 2008b. "School Accountability and the Standards-Based Reform Movement: Some Unintended Consequences of Education Policies". *International Journal of Contemporary Sociology* 45(October): 11–31.

Dworkin, Anthony G., and Rosalin J. Dworkin. 1999. *The Minority Report: An Introduction to Race, Ethnic, Gender Relations*. New York: Harcourt, Brace.

Dworkin, Anthony G., and Jon Lorence. 2007. "Gaming No Child Left Behind: The Effects Of Tokenism on the Achievement of Students in Texas Schools". *In No Child Left Behind and the Reduction of the Achievement Gap: Sociological Perspectives on Federal Education Policy*, edited by Sadovnik, O'Day, Bohrnstedt, and Borman. New York: Routledge.

Fiske, Edward B. 1991. "The Practice and Pitfalls of School Reform". In *Partners in School Reform*, edited by Robert W. Houston, 7–18. Houston, TX: Texas Center for University School Partnerships.

Fujiwara, Lynn, and Dana Takagi. 1999. "Japanese Americans: Stories about race in America". In *The Minority Report: An Introduction to Race, Ethnic, Gender Relations*, edited by Anthony G. Dworkin and Rosalin J. Dworkin, 297–320. New York: Harcourt, Brace.

Gibson, Campbell J., and Emily Lennon. 1999. "Historical Census Statistics on the Foreign-Born Population of the United States: 1850–1990". Population Division Working Paper No. 29. Washington, DC: Population Division, US Bureau of the Census.

Heckman, James J., and Paul A. LaFontaine. 2007. "The American High School Graduation Rate: Trends and Levels". Discussion Paper No. 3216, Institute for the Study of Labor (IZA), Bonn, Germany.

Kobrin, Jennifer L., Viji Sathy, and Emily J. Shaw. 2007. "A Historical View of Subgroup Performances Differences on the SAT Reasoning Test". New York: The College Board.

Lewis, Sharon, Candace Simon, Renatta Uzzell, Amanda Horwitz, and Michael Casserly. 2010. "A Call for Change: The Social and Educational Factors Contributing to the Outcomes of Black Males in Urban Schools". New York: Council of Great City Schools.

Merton, Robert. 1968. *Social Theory and Social Structure: 1968* (Enlarged Edition). New York: The Free Press.

National Center for Education Statistics. 2009. NAEP 2008 Trends in Academic Progress. (NCES 2009–479). Washington, DC: Institute of Education Sciences, US Department of Education.

National Commission on Excellence in Education. 1983. A Nation at Risk: The Imperative for Educational Reform. Washington, DC: US Government Printing Office.

Passel, Jeffrey, and D'Vera Cohn. 2008. Immigration to Play Lead Role in Future U.S. Growth. U.S. Population Projections: 2005–2050. Washington, DC: Pew Research Center.

Payne, Ruby, K. 2003. No Child Left Behind (NCLB) Series. Printed in Instructional Leader. http://ccweb.colquitt.k12.ga.us/depts/AltEd/NCLBSeriesPartI.pdf

Roderick, Melissa, and Eric Camburn. 1996. "Academic Difficulties During the High School Transition". In *Charting Reform in Chicago: The Students Speak*, The Consortium on Chicago School Research, 47–65.

Rumberger, Russell W. 2003. "The Causes and Consequences of Student Mobility". *Journal of Negro Education* 72: 6–21.

Rumberger, Russell W., and K. A. Larson. 1998. "Student Mobility and the Increased Risk of High School Dropout". *American Journal of Education* 107(1): 1–35.

Rumberger, Russell W., R. K. Ream, and Gregory J. Palardy. 1999. "The Educational Consequences of Mobility for California Students and Schools". Berkeley, CA: Policy Analysis for California Education, ED 441040.

Sedgley, Norman H., Williams, Nancy A., and Frederick W. Derrick. 2008. "The Effect of Educational Test Scores on House Prices in a Model with Spatial Dependence". *Journal of Housing Economics* 17(2): 191–200.

Smith, Robert C. 1965. *They Closed Their Schools: Prince Edward County, Virginia, 1951–1964*. Chapel Hill: University of North Carolina Press.

Smylie, Mark A., and Jack W. Denny. 1990. "Teacher Leadership: Tensions and Ambiguities in Organizational Practice". *Educational Administration Quarterly* 26: 235–259.

Stasiulis, Daiva, and Nira Yuval-Davis. 1995. *Unsettling Settler Societies*. Thousand Oaks, CA: Sage Publications.

Texas Education Agency. January 12, 2009. Texas Education Agency Growth Model Pilot Application for Adequate Yearly Progress Under the No Child Left Behind Act. Austin, Texas. http://rittr.tea.state.us/student.assessment/resources/growth_proposal/011209_USDE_Growth_Proposal_Texas.pdf

U.S. Department of Education, National Center for Education Statistics. 2007. *The Condition of Education 2007* (NCESNCES 2007-064). Washington, DC: U.S. Government Printing Office.

Viadero, Debra. 2006. "Test Scores Linked to Home Prices". *Education Week* July 26, 25(43): 20.

Weick, Karl. 1976. "Educational Organizations as Loosely Coupled Systems". *Administrative Science Quarterly* 21: 1–19.

Wells, Amy Stuart. 2001. "Reaction to the Supreme Court Ruling on Vouchers: Introduction to an On-Line Special Issue". Teachers College Record. http//www.tcrecord.org ID Number: 10940

6 Building the Nation at School
Spain's Tables Turned

Mariano Fernández Enguita

The modern history of Spain is one of a failed nation-building (partially failed, although partially successful). In fact, the Spain of the Catholic Kings, with his dynastic and territorial religious and ethnic unification, is an example of protonational State before the France of the Bourbons, but its subsequent history was quite different. In the debatable but expressive dichotomy of Anthony Smith, France is the perfect example of nation-state, but Spain is the opposite, a state-nation. The why and how of two such processes, so different in themselves and in their results, is due to a multiplicity of factors, but one key factor and product has been in both cases the school system. Spain, increasingly weakened by its colonial adventure was not able to put in place a system of public education, entering a helpless way running from the denominational nature of the Constitution of Cadiz (1812), through proclaiming a fictional education system without funding or infrastructure by the Moyano Act (1857), to the exorbitant privileges granted to the Catholic Church by the concordat with the Vatican (1953); France, by contrast, would advance to a school effectively serving the nation-building from the failed laws of the Republican Convention, through the nationalization of *l'enseignement secondaire* and the University by Napoleon, to the creation of *l'école unique* by the Third Republic.

Sequelae of this are today peripheral nationalisms, including Catalan and Basque, and its most radical face, secessionism. Moreover, the twentieth century Spanish history, with a languishing monarchy, two dictatorships, civil war, a noisy but brief and tumultuous Republican intermediate and a transition to full and ultimate democracy, but settled on delicate balances, has led to its revival and reinforcement. In fact, the collapse of the legitimacy of Spanish nationalism simply resulted in collapse of the Spanish, not of nationalism, creating the best conditions for the explosion of peripheral nationalisms. From the standpoint of the analysis of the use of school systems by nationalism, the Spanish one is a case in point because it just led to *turning the tables*. That is, a situation in which centrifugal nationalisms seek, and often succeed, to use the school with the same intensity and cheek as in his day did centralist nationalism.

NATIONS ARE BUILT BY STATES, ALTHOUGH WITH VARYING DEGREES OF SUCCESS

In nationalist rhetoric, the nation always precedes the state, which sometimes translates into a happy ending, when the nation raises its own state or achieves independence from one which was not his, and other times in a long ordeal, the one of stateless nations, so oppressed, etc. This story has the virtue of putting the nation's soft side (culture, language, tradition, folklore . . .) and the state hard side, even tough (repression, taxes, laws, violence . . .), which then allows you to easily guess who is good and who is wrong when they do not match. But history and logic refute this romantic tale. In the absence of some form of power, culture extends only to be fragmented; abandoned to its fate it would step no further than a man on foot, as shown by the persistence of almost a thousand different cultures (considered as such by UNESCO) on an island the size not too big of Papua New Guinea or the entrenchment of the Aran Valley in Catalonia: one valley, one culture, approximately. On the contrary, power is able to break any unitary culture, as evidenced by the division of Spanish America in twenty countries despite the shared language, heritage and oppression of the Indian (indigenous cultures were really different between themselves, but they did not count towards the establishment of present-day nations, they are just beginning to do so now.) Conversely, once the state begins its performance, it is not without effect: neither linguistic unity, nor cultural tradition, nor interest in the economies of scale, nor the perception of a common enemy have promoted a millimeter of advancement to pan-Hispanoamericanism (barely present in musical folklore, and only on the lyrics), or pan-Arabism (despite the shared sense of grievance against the Christian West); by contrast, the artificial states born of decolonization, even if in some cases they were not able to consolidate what they had inside (and have sometimes subdivided, as is doing Sudan now), they have been able to separate from what lies outside.

In this perspective, the nation is no longer a reality that precedes the state (although certain nations may precede certain states) but, on the contrary, its result, complete or incomplete. Or, more accurately, since the term *state* corresponds to a modern form of political, cultural community (which we often call a nation when it has a territorial base and claims for an independent existence) is the product of political community (which we call state when it meets certain features of modernity such as territorial unity, the monopoly of violence, sovereignty and some kind of constitutionality). The nation-state is a state that has succeeded in building a nation, which not all succeed. It is not a nation preexistent to any state, but which has finally reached such status, as it is often claimed by nationalist theories (while other nations would be expecting to achieve it, or fighting for it), but a state that built a nation. What Smith (1971) called state-nation would be, in this view, a state that has failed that objective. And so-called stateless nations would be but the debris on the road by failed states, perhaps by themselves or more likely because of some external factor, which would make of their reconstruction a latent possibility for long (Fernández Enguita 2007). The amazing thing in the history of nations is not the European gibberish, let alone the national failure or limitations of states like the former Yugoslavia, present-day Spain and perhaps soon the UK, but the persistence and consolidation of more than fifty nations, almost all entirely artificial, in Africa. Except for the secession of Eritrea, and now the independence of South Sudan, where the lines will respond, if anything, more to the Huntington's clash of civilizations (1996) than to any national definition, we have more than fifty countries still attached to borders drawn with pen point by colonialism and the impossibility of any merger of their states, as shown by the superficiality and the failure of successive United Arab Republics, or the evidence that that neither Swahili language will suffice to unite Kenya and Tanzania nor the combined English-Afrikaans will do so with South Africa and Namibia, to take just two cases.

How can a state create a nation? With all the instruments at its disposal, which are not few: the language of administration, laws, courts and the church, the influence or manipulation of culture and cultural media, military conscription, the management of symbols, linking the provision of public services to the collective identity . . . but first and foremost, education, and more specifically universal schooling. There will be no redefinition of the community, either in terms of scope (as do the processes of unification or division, occupation or secession) or in its internal structure (reforms and political revolutions, or simply the reproduction of the existing before trends of change), which is not served at the school. In contrast, any cultural heritage that is outside of the school is now condemned, before the power of the latter, to gradually losing force and effect, even if the media can offer alternative spaces increasingly broad and family and community of life can last for a long time as a space of resistance.

THE TRADITIONAL, PRE-DEMOCRATIC SPAIN AND THE LACK OF A SCHOOL SYSTEM WORTHY OF THE NAME

In the school domain, the construction of the Spanish nation has not exactly had a brilliant career. The nineteenth-century liberal proclamations of public schools fell one after another in little more than that. The Spanish Constitution of 1812 dedicated a full title, the XI, to education, and proclaimed the intention to create "primary schools" in every town, under a "general scheme for teaching [. . .], uniform throughout the kingdom". But liberalism lasted for as long as it took King Fernando VII to return from his captivity in France, since municipalities never had sufficient means to create those schools nationwide and the Catholic Church went gaining ground through seminars and urban schools.

Nearly half a century later, the Public Education Act of 1857, also known as *Moyano Act*, established the existence of a primary school in every town and a high school in each provincial capital, but did not have the financial means for the first goal (a way to legislate for the gallery that would be used over and over again, until the Education Act of 1970). In fact, universal schooling in basic education was not effective until the mid-'80s of the twentieth century. The weakness of the Spanish state until well into the century and the counterrevolution brought by the 1936–1939 civil war and the military dictatorship between 1936 and 1976 were decisive in the shaping of the education system. In 1900, 63.8 percent of the total population were illiterate, and in 1930 so were still 44.3 percent. In September–October 1937, 52 public institutes were closed. In 1939 there were 113 public high schools, and in 1960 they had increased just to 120; by contrast, in 1946 there were 802 private schools (primary and secondary), which in 1969 reached 1,248, the vast majority of which belonged to different Catholic church organizations (Puelles 2002, 12–13). With the advent of democracy, the school enjoyed a quantum leap forward, first as a result of the so-called Moncloa Pacts of 1976 and then of the socialist government policy since 1982, but based on the acceptance of the existence of a dual network, since then on fairly stable in its distribution: two-thirds of public schools and one-third of private schools, most of them chartered.

During the Franco years, the school was crudely orchestrated in the service of an image of Spain marked by uniformity, archaism and megalomania, the one sustained by the person of the dictator as well as by ultramontane Catholic, monarchical restorationist, fascist Falange and traditionalist Carlist movements that supported and were supported by him, becoming a scene for the military-fascist paraphernalia of the period, with its iconography of the cult of the regime's leaders, military and patriotic hymns, paramilitary activities, etc. History turned onto halcyonic periods of the Spanish Empire, literature onto the epic texts, geography onto lost imperial domains. . . . There is no point in detailing this here, but it can be found in the magnificent collections digitized by the Spanish Textbook Project (MANES), which contain many textbooks from those times. On the other hand the languages of the historical nationalities (Catalan, Galician and Basque) were expelled from school, banned in public life and even demonized in the private realm. All this was preceded by the purge of primary and secondary school teachers, mostly aligned with the Republic and its ideals of progress and culture, or simply because it promoted a major expansion of the institution and the profession.

The result was a weak educational system, not universal, with little social legitimacy and largely in the hands of the Catholic Church which not only did not contribute to the consolidation of the Spanish nation, i.e., to the creation of a sense of moral community, but caused adverse reactions, of opposition among those who had another communitarian identity to fall back on and of disaffection among those who had only that one.

THE NEW PERIPHERAL NATIONALISMS: FROM THE RESISTANCE OF THE OPPRESSED TO THE OFFENSIVE OF THE PRIVILEGED

The nationalist movement repressed by the military dictatorship knew a spectacular burst since the transition to democracy. This was due to several factors, among which we must take into account not only its own dynamics, i.e., the strength of collective identities previously asphyxiated, the vigor of their languages or the dynamism of their cultures, but also the discredited collective identity of Spain as a whole as a reaction to the abuses and folklore of the dictatorial regime, the naive support of the left educated in the idea of saluting the nationalism of the oppressed against that of the oppressors and comfortable in the idea that the enemy of my enemy is my friend, and the self-reinforcing logic of the meso-governments arising from the configuration of the new federal state (*Estado de las Autonomías*). The first was simply the result of the centuries-old weakness of the Spanish state, which was able in its beginnings to adopt strength measures quite common in the early shaping of nations (territorial unification, expulsion of minorities of difficult or doubtful assimilation, subjection of intermediate power structures and recognition in the international system), but then it was hopelessly incapable of creating the mechanisms of persuasion required to build consensus around a national community, including and foremost a school system. The second was the logical or at least understandable reaction, after four decades of crude and oppressive Spanish nationalism, that of Spain *one, great and free* (*one* in front of nationalities and ethnic groups that formed, *big* on nostalgia of the empire gone and *free* from communism, liberalism, atheism and other demons of the dictatorship), which reversed the coordinates of legitimacy turning the terms Spain, Spanish nation, etc. damned, to be replaced by *state, Spanish state* or, at most, *the country*. The third is connected with the rhetorical (just rhetorical) tradition of Leninism and Stalinism, very influential on the left in the period of transition to democracy, about the liberation of oppressed nationalities, and fit to the leftist language of the new emerging nationalisms, due to their need to win popular support. Fourth, in short, it is part of the dynamics of any power superstructure, leaning from birth to persist and grow, following Parkinson's Law, especially favored in the Spanish case by a semi-proportional and territorial electoral system that often gives peripheral nationalist parties the key to parliamentary majorities in Spain, offering them a disproportionate bargaining power that is always used to claim new devolutions.

Peripheral nationalisms in today's Spain have very different character-istics from those provided in the rhetoric on oppressed nationalities, sub-jugated peoples, cultural genocide or stateless nations. Undoubtedly there was and there is yet much to do for the recovery of the right to their own language and culture, political autonomy and administrative decentraliza-tion, after two centuries and a half since the Bourbonic decrees (*Decretos de Nueva Planta*) that put an end to the separate institutions of the ancient Hispanic kingdoms and after forty years of dictatorship, a route that is particularly relevant because we deal with nationalities with important cul-tural specificities and political singularities. Moreover, it appears that the process of globalization provokes particularistic and communitarian reac-tions, a return journey to the alleged roots and the cultivation of differential identities (Castells 1997). But present peripheral nationalisms, especially those now playing with the separatist alternatives, are plain secessionist movements of the economically richest regions. In 2009, on an index of 100 for the whole of Spain, the per capita GDP of the Basque Country was at the highest place among the seventeen autonomous communities, 134.2, and Catalonia in the fourth place (after Navarre and Madrid), 117.2, both significantly above the national average.[1] The advantage of both is due to greater economic development and, in the case of the Basque Country, to a preferential tax regime. The claims for independence do not exist, however, in the case of Galicia, where the index on the same basis is 87.4, which makes the region a beneficiary of the overall interregional redistributive mechanisms and, therefore, advised to wait and save even for the most radical nationalism. Similarly, the Canary islands with a per capita GDP of 86.48 and a small but active secessionist movement did not pursue their claims for independence due also to their geographic proximity to Morocco, which claims all Spanish territories in continental Africa and could some day extend its claims on these islands. Other regions located above the mean do not show a marked cultural difference with the whole and have more reasons to fear the expansionism of the emerging nationalisms than to complain about their position in Spain, as is the case of Navarra and La Rioja (about which the radical wing of Basque nationalism maintains some claims), Aragon and the Balearic Islands (the latter, of Catalan language, are part of the pan-nationalist project of *Països Catalans*, and Catalonia was a part, indeed, of the Crown of Aragon).

The independence movements that now agitate some regions or nation-alities in Spain, in short, are not different from those that move Scotland in the UK, the imaginative Padania in Italy, Flanders in Belgium, Slovenia in the former Yugoslavia, Cabinda in Angola or Santa Cruz in Bolivia (we could also include, if we look back further, the secession of Panama from Colombia or the separate independence for Kuwait out of Iraq, if only these cases were born of a strong foreign sponsorship). All of them combine the demand of cultural liberation with the more prosaic goal of maintaining or achieving economic privilege. To a great extent they are collective fiscal revolts, but not by those who are or believe to be rich for their individual properties, but by those who are or think they are so by their collective property. Redistributive function of the welfare state can generate this type of *fiscal* or (anti)*welfare* revolts, which bring together those who believe that, being rich, they would pay less taxes if they were part of a community with less poor to benefit, with those who think that, being poor, they would receive more benefits if they had to share them with fewer people.

Some of these nationalisms, particularly the Basque and the Catalan, have an irredentist dimension. In the case of the Basque Country it is the demand for annexation of Navarre (which includes a Basque-speaking area and a Castilian-speaking one, and, by the way, had a long independent existence, as the Kingdom of Navarre, which the Basque Country never had), the *French territories* and the enclave of Treviño in an independent united Euskal Herria. In the case of Catalonia, the proposed unification of the Catalan-speaking territories, including the region of Valencia (not necessarily complete), the Balearic Islands, the Catalan-speaking strip of Aragon, the region of Carche in Murcia, the principality of Andorra, the French Roussillon and the Corsican area of Alghero.

THE LANGUAGE ISSUE: FROM THE DEFENSE OF MOTHER TONGUE TO THE IMPOSITION OF A SINGLE NATIONAL LANGUAGE

The main objection to language standardization in a multilingual context has always been the importance of learning, or at least early learning, in the mother tongue. When, under the dictatorship, Spanish was the single, uniform language at school, the demand for mother-tongue education was widespread in the territories of nationalities with their own languages, of course among nationalist forces, and usually supported from other geographical and political fields. UNESCO, for example, has been and is particularly belligerent in defending the use of mother tongue in school (UNESCO 2003). Today the teaching language, i.e., that which is taught as principal and serves as a vehicle for other non-language subjects, except maybe (just maybe) other languages learned as secondary, is the subject of conflict in each of the historical nationalities: Catalonia, the Basque Country and Galicia.

Catalonia has chosen a *linguistic immersion* model in which all students and subjects are taught in Catalan language, except the teaching of other languages.[2] In purely linguistic terms, the policy of Catalan nationalism is the most ambitious since linguistic uniformity is imposed from the top without any option, while other territories with two languages allow families to choose, with greater or lesser constraints, at least in principle. The justification for this policy is twofold: on the one side, the idea that, under equal conditions, i.e., in a situation of paritary bilingualism, Catalan would be displaced by Spanish, thus putting an end to the essence of Catalonia, etc.; on the other side, the argument that by forcing the learning of Catalan, the social disadvantage that could affect those who are not fluent in that language is avoided. That is, a convenient and timely combination of nationalist victimization and class egalitarianism. It should be noted, in any case, that the Romance languages, Catalan and Galician in particular, have a proximity to the Spanish one which makes the choice between either of them into something quite different from what would be the choice between Basque and Spanish languages, without a common structure (though with a plethora of terms imported from Spanish to Basque). Catalan nationalism, in short, had always and has now, in any case, a more modern and *decisionist* (civic) content than any other.

Apart from the more general question of what can or should be the language of citizenship in a community with a unique language that is, at the same time, part of a wider community with a shared language, this has led to four types of conflict. First, with families that even though wish to educate their children with Spanish as the teaching language, and theoretically may choose to do so, in practice they meet all sorts of obstacles to the extent that it is often impossible, at least in public school. Second, in relation to the number of hours dedicated to the teaching of Spanish as a second language, something that the Catalan government tries to restrict arguing that Catalan and Spanish being Romance languages share common linguistic structures, therefore learning the former also means learning the latter (but not vice versa). Third, with the use of Spanish in informal spaces and times such as during breaks between classes, playgrounds, etc., often suppressed or punished to the point that pupils come to see and feel it as a language of resistance against the institution's official language, Catalan. Fourth, with immigrants that often reside temporarily in the region and consider it more useful to learn Spanish, which allows them to communicate in the whole country, or who simply have it as their mother tongue as the majority of them are of Latin American origin, and who only reluctantly accept an additional obstacle to an already problematic schooling of their children.

In the Basque Country there are three models of schooling: A, which means Spanish as the teaching language, except for the hours of Basque language and literature; B, which is bilingual education, with both languages, Spanish and Basque as vehicular languages; and D, which means teaching in Basque language, except for Spanish language and literature and foreign languages (option C does not exist, or the letter C means no choice at all, because there is no such letter in the Basque alphabet).[3] In the 2009–2010 academic year, 57.3 percent of students in the basic education (considering as such preschool, primary and compulsory secondary and adult education) were schooled in model D (Basque as vehicle) versus 24.7 percent in group B (both as vehicle) and 17.4 in the A (Spanish as vehicular). But there are big differences between stages and branches inside the system:

in the initial stages (not including secondary or adults, but only preschool and primary), Model A drops to 6.6 percent and model D rises to 66 percent, while model B remains almost stable, 26.8 percent. In academic high school, model D reached 52.6 percent, but in vocational branches it fell to 23.7 percent and in adult continuing education it does not exist. When we distinguish within the basic stages, between the networks of public schools and private schools, model D amounted to 68.4 percent in the first but dropped to 45.2 percent in the second, while B model option fell to 10.3 percent and rose to 41.8 percent respectively. It can be seen, therefore, that the implementation of Basque language as vehicular is more akin to public schooling than to the private, to compulsory education than to post-compulsory, to the academic branch than to the vocational one.

In Galicia the law lays that school education is bilingual, but this general direction is rendered differently at the different stages of schooling. In preschool education, teachers will determine the language used in the circumstances of the environment, starting with a question addressed to parents about their children's language. In compulsory education (primary and secondary) it is now required by law to provide some specific subject areas in Spanish and others in Galician, and it is up to the school to decide autonomously the vehicular language for the other subjects, but requiring equality between the two. In academic high school full autonomy is left to the center to provide any subject in either language, but once again with the requirement of equality. For vocational training it is simply required *a balanced provision* and to achieve mastery in both languages.[4] In short, the law seeks parity between the unique and the common languages, Galician and Spanish. It was not always so, as a former bill forced to teach in Galician a majority of subjects both in primary and secondary schools, at least 50 percent of them in academic secondary education (so that this percentage could be overcome in Galician, but not in Spanish language), while the requirement was limited to a small number of general subjects in vocational secondary.[5] The explanation is simple: the former law was passed by a coalition government of socialists and nationalists, while the present one has been passed by a conservative government with absolute majority in the regional parliament.

(Spain has other linguistic peculiarities. Catalan is the vernacular language of two other regions or autonomous communities, the Balearic Islands and the Community of Valencia, although in the latter, where there are large areas of Spanish speakers, Catalan is officially called Valencian language and has a quite distinct pronunciation; it is also spoken in a strip of Aragon, in a small area of Murcia and in the Principality of Andorra; in the Val d'Aran in Catalonia, however, the vernacular language is Occitan, and in some others it is Spanish. Galician is spoken in the region of El Bierzo in León and in some areas of Asturias; due to its similarity with Portuguese there is ample discussion about whether they are two different languages, and if they should both converge, or should Galician approach the more widespread Portuguese. Basque language is spoken in a part of Navarre, which is another autonomous region, and less in the French Basque provinces, but not, however, in most of Álava, a Basque province. There are also other minority languages as Bable in Asturias, the *fala* [akin to Galician and Portuguese] in parts of Extremadura bordering Portugal, Aragonese in small regions of Aragon. But we can dispense with all this, because the object of this paper is not language in itself but its instrumentalization by nationalist projects.)

This institutional belligerence is not in correspondence with the preferences of families. Although in theory, families can apply for enrollment in Spanish language in public schools or go to private schools that provide it, the use of native languages as vehicular goes far beyond the expressed preferences, at least if we look at the surveys. Table 6.1 comes from a survey conducted in 2001 and compares the practices and the declared preferences of pupils' parents with what they actually get at school (Pérez Díaz et al. 2001). The first thing that can be seen in the results is that, except in Galicia (precisely where the implementation of the language via the school is more limited and mild), in all cases there is a majority of families who are usually Spanish speakers. Second, the percentage of respondents who supported the idea that education should be only or mainly in the local language was always significantly higher than those who consider it the mother tongue at home in the case of Catalonia (61 vs. 45 percent) and the Basque Country (43 vs. 17 percent) but significantly lower in those of Galicia (24 vs. 43 percent) and Valencia (22 vs. 29 percent). Third, however, the implementation of the language at school was well ahead of the preferences of parents in Catalonia (85 vs. 61 percent) and Galicia (36 vs. 24 percent), but at the same level in the Community of Valencia (22 vs. 22 percent) and the Basque Country (46 vs. 43 percent).

Table 6.2 shows the results of six surveys conducted by the *Centro de Investigaciones Sociológicas* (Sociological Research Center) in 1998, in regions with a unique language (CIS 1998a–f). For each of them we can see in which language a child (the older of schooled sieblings) is enrolled and to what extent people (with or without children at school) agree with the idea that all public schooling (the question is about neither private nor both types of schooling altogether) should take place in the unique language.[6] Although we have included the data, we should clarify the case of Navarra, which is not really one of a unique language (Basque) and a common one (Spanish), but one of two native languages in two areas and among two groups of people more or less clearly differentiated, one of which happens to be also the common language throughout Spain. In any case, in four of the six communities the proportion of pupils educated in the language only far exceeded the proportion of citizens in favor of that model.

Table 6.1 Mother Tongue, Actual and Preferred Teaching Languages

	Autonomous Communities with a unique language					Provinces overrepresented in the sample		
	Catalonia	Galicia	Valencian C.	Basque A.C.	Total	Vizcaya	Barcelona	Valencia
Child mother-tongue								
Spanish	52	43	70	76	59	83	55	66
Unique language	45	43	29	17	36	14	43	32
Both	2	12	1	5	4	2	2	1
Other	2	2			1	0	1	
No answer		2	2	2	1	0		1
In which language do your child teachers teach								
Only in Spanish	2	3	29	13	12	11	0	21
Mainly in Spanish	2	27	34	21	18	21	3	35
In Spanish and unique language, equally	11	29	13	18	16	14	14	19
Mainly in unique language	43	23	11	18	27	20	38	10
Only in unique language	42	13	11	28	25	34	43	10
In which language would you like your child to be taught								
Only in Spanish	2	11	27	13	13	11	2	23
Mainly in Spanish	4	18	30	28	17	18	4	27
In Spanish and unique language, equally	27	40	15	15	24	18	24	18
Mainly in unique language	29	11	12	15	18	18	30	13
Only in unique language	32	13	10	28	21	32	34	11
No answer	5	3	4	3	5	0	4	4
N	136	62	95	40	361	400	400	400

Source: Survey ASP 00.030 (Pérez Díaz et al. 2001, 185).

Table 6.2 The Language of Schooling; Preferences and Realities

	Catalonia	Basque C.	Galicia	Navarre	Valencian C.	Balearic I.
Could you tell me which is the general language of teaching at the school or educational establishment attended by your first child?						
Spanish only	1.7	19.2	24.0	69.8	19.8	8.2
Spanish, but unique language is also learned	2.7	23.4	29.2	10.3	50.8	09/09/11
Unique language only	39.2	35.9	3.6	14.7	9.3	29.7
Unique language, but Spanish is also learned	35.5	10.8	10.4	3.4	6.0	20.3
Some subjects are taught in Spanish and others in the unique language	17.9	8.4	27.1	0.9	12.1	25.8
Another language	0.3	1.8	0.5	0.9	0.8	3.8
No answer	2.7	0.6	5.2	-	1.2	2.2
Now I will read to you some opinions that are sometimes listened around: At the public schools of my Autonomous Community, teaching should be only in the unique language						
Rather agree	27.5	31.7	27.3	7.8	12.5	17.8
Rather disagree	69.9	53.5	59.9	86.2	84.6	75.9
Difference between agreement around schooling only in the unique language and real schooling in it						
Over-schooling in unique language	11.7	4.2	-23.7	6.9	3.2	11.9

Source: CIS, surveys on *Uso de lenguas en comunidades bilingües* [The use of languages in bilingual communities], núms. 2295–2300, 1998, and elaboration by the author.

THE CONTENT OF EDUCATION: FROM AN INVENTED
TRADITION TO ANOTHER ONE NOT LESS SO

It would be really surprising if regional meso-governments, which are not simply mechanisms for decentralization, but have been equipped with its own source of legitimacy (the parliamentary elections and autonomic systems, added to the languages, cultures and collective identities and alleged own historical legacies and trajectories), did not use the school to legitimize their present and consolidate their future, as any other political structure with a territorial basis and authority over education. Still undone, however, is a systematic investigation of the differential content of education in the different regions, particularly in the social sciences and humanities and for the historic nationalities, probably because it is politically inconvenient, one of those that neither the political authorities are eager to sponsor nor the researchers are eager to perform. But there is a substantial body of partial evidence, scattered through small documentary studies, institutional dossiers and media reports. Many of them come from sources that can be considered partisan (i.e., as opposed to decentralization or to the dismemberment of the Spanish educational system, at least beyond a certain point), and so they are, but they have never been declared false.

The most obvious area of conflict is the very definition of endogroup and exogroup, who are to be considered us and them. It has been marked, for example, the irredentism of numerous textbooks approved by the Basque and Catalan autonomous powers. In the Basque case, the priority is often given to the idea of *Euskal Herria* (the "land of the Basque language speakers"), which would consist of the current three Basque provinces, plus the community of Navarra, plus three Pays Basque provinces of France (part of the Department of Pyrenees Atlantiques) and other smaller territories (the enclave of Treviño and Villaverde valley in Santander). In the case of Catalonia, but with less emphasis, the same happens with the so-called *Països Catalans*, which would be constituted, besides actual Catalonia, by most or all of the Valencian Community, the Balearic Islands, the West Strip in Aragon, Northern Catalonia (Roussillon, which is most of the French department of Pyrénées-Orientales), the micro-state of Andorra, Carche area in Murcia and the Italian city of Alghero, Sicily. By contrast, these same texts are reluctant to use the word Spain, which is often replaced by words such as the Spanish state, Iberian Peninsula and other elusive forms. In general, there is a tendency in the educational books of many communities, and much more in these, to give prime attention to its own territory, to the detriment of the wider Spanish and the other communities that integrate with added nationalist elements such as pan-nationalist and irredentist definitions of territory or the juxtaposition of the community with Spain as separate, parallel and of similar level.

No less striking is the distortion of history in favor of an alleged independent sovereign past of the nationality in question and to the detriment of the unit or the existence of the Spanish nation. What in the old regime was a common form of relationship, marriage and inheritance agreements between royal houses, recognition of particular rights and privileges to territorial lords, cities, etc., is presented as an outstanding feature of Catalonia and the Basque Country, timeless rather than historical. Historical periods in which the communities and territories for which independence is claimed today were not but part and parcel of wider unities that would be fully integrated under the Spanish crown (the Basque country was but a part of the kingdom of Navarre, and Catalonia was but several counties integrated in the kingdom of Aragón), are presented as periods of full independence. We can read about a *Neolithic Catalonia* in the same book that avoids the name of *Hispania* in the Roman era. According to a text, the Romans occupied Catalonia, a name that would take a thousand years to see the light, and the Iberian peninsula, instead of the *Hispania(e)*. Events of recent history are reinterpreted to suit the national interest, e.g., civil war of 1936–1939, which was almost a canonical case of class warfare with little or no territorial issues, as a war of Spain against Catalonia and/or the Basque Country. Or events that are obvious to adults, but unknown by the students, are plainly manipulated, as when one speaks of the birth of ETA as an expression of Basque resistance against Franco, but without mentioning the existence of a single victim (and they are over a thousand) or states that achieving the 1992 Olympics in Barcelona was a high point of the Catalan national reconstruction. The present institutional framework is also the subject of an ongoing bargaining. The Spanish constitution of 1978, which gave rise to the federal state (*Estado de las Autonomías*), is systematically avoided in favor of the Statute of Autonomy or their presumed historical foundations. The textual or graphical indications of the central state institutions are replaced by others for autonomous institutions. Quebec and the Balkans, settings of independence movements and processes, receive exorbitant attention.

The same textbooks by large publishers can change from one region to another to bow to the demands of local authorities. The protest by an ETA assassination may appear in all other regions, but be replaced by a demonstration against racism in the Basque Country. ETA attacks in Catalonia and the separatist terrorism of Terra Lliure may not merit a line, but an interview is included with a teenager who sent anonymous threatening messages to a shopkeeper for not labeling the commodities in Catalan, as to make of him a national(ist) hero. In the textbook of the largest Spanish publisher for the fourth grade of junior high school, for example, Juan Sebastian Elcano's ship *La Vizcaína* (The Biscayne), illustrating the discovery of America in versions for other regions, is replaced in the Basque country by the centenary of the chocolate factory *La Guipuzcoana* hiding the uncomfortable evidence of integration of the Basques in the Spanish crown for half a millennium. Ferdinand *the Catholic*, first co-monarch of a unified Spain, who before and after his marriage to Elisabeth I of Castile was known as Ferdinand II of Aragon (then V of Castile), is transformed into *Ferran de Catalunya i Aragó*, never heard of before. Along with the big publishers in the state level, which simply adapt to regional requirements to keep those markets, flourish some small publishers, usually directly focused and limited to their regional territories, whose nationalist vocation is much more intense (e.g., Erein or Elkarlanean in the Basque Country or Castellnou in Catalonia). But not only national publishers have to adapt to the demands of communities governed by nationalists, on the contrary, authorities or associations of Valencia or the Balearic Islands have complained at times about the pan-Catalanist approach of textbooks arriving from Catalonia, Navarre has withdrawn books of Basque origin that included it in Euskal Herria, and Extremadura has protested the Galician Nationalist complaints about the lack of protection for the *fala* of a small border zone with Portugal that they associate without much ground to Galician language.

In the present federal state, i.e., in a Spain that was transformed from a centralized dictatorship into one of the most decentralized states in the world, but which also moved from centripetal to centrifugal jingoism, the issue is so politically uncomfortable that it is simply avoided by academics but engulfed by conflicts of interest. Accordingly, the facts have been brought originally from the arch in the political spectrum most contrary to the idea of a plural Spain (PPPV Secretariat of Education 2006), the press hostile to centrifugal nationalisms and their allies in the political left (Romero 2007), citizens' committees opposed to the nationalist excesses (*Galicia Bilingüe* [Bilingual Galicia] 2010; *Basta Ya* [Enough!] 2001) and a few researchers placed at the margins of academia (Heras 2009; Beas 1999). At some point calls for attention reached the governmental institutions as the Delegation of (Spanish) Government in the Basque Country, non-governmental institutions such as the Royal Academy of History (RAH 2000) or private ones such as the Association of Spanish Geographers (AGE 2000). Historians then entered the debate, but only to show that the vast majority had been out of step (Ortiz de Ortuño 1998; Segura 2001). Some had entered or would enter the background historical debate (Fusi 1998; Alvarez Junco et al. 2005), but most went off on a tangent or chose to stay aside. For what concerns us here, there was much discussion on the eventual interests behind every position, on the comparative evil of central and peripheral nationalisms, on the hidden agendas of institutions and authorities, but nobody questioned the data revealed by the various reports and the press. The non-university teachers and experts had not been less absent, except for very superficial hints on cases of localist or biased usage of History (Conference of Education 1998; AEPHG 1998), because what they were generally employed in was to claim more teaching hours for their subjects, i.e., more jobs for the guild, if not simply aligned with the idea that more local history is always better, without necessarily asking why (for example, Valls 2002, or Hijano c2002).

NATIONALISM AND TEACHERS: THE FOUNDATIONS
OF A MARRIAGE OF CONVENIENCE

Obviously, different communities have followed varied routes and have been governed by various forces. For reasons that cannot be explained here, the Spanish regions have accessed to self-government at different times (since 1977, when the *Generalitat* [government] of Catalonia was restored, to 2000) and under different constitutional assumptions. Table 6.3 shows the year of the grant of autonomy, the path to it and the year of transfer of competences in education. The first communities that joined the autonomous status were those which had already done or begun to do so under the II Republic, Catalonia and the Basque Country, soon followed by another nationality recognized as such by the Constitution of 1978, Galicia. The three of them followed the special or fast-track under Article 151 of the Constitution, which also involved a wider range of competences devolution. The *exceptional way* of Article 144, feasible for Navarre as it was a one-province region which did not require neither a revision of boundaries nor any territorial agreement between different institutions, and the slow way, Article 143, for pluri-provincial regions not recognized as nationalities, represented a more limited functional and power degrees of self-government, but the subsequent dynamics led to unleash a dynamic of emulation among different regions, always jealous of obtaining any concession previously obtained by any other, while Catalonia and the Basque Country clamored for recognition of their uniqueness, or *differential fact*, always wanting to be ahead, triggering a self-powered dynamic in which there is no limit to the general demands for autonomy.

Table 6.4 shows the composition of the regional governments of each of the regions concerned, since the transition to democracy up to now. Obviously, there is a correspondence between the presence of nationalist parties,

Table 6.3 Date and Way of Access to Regional Autonomy and Date of Devolution of Authority on Education

	Statute of Autonomy date	*Art. of Const./Way*	*Educational devolution*
Catalonia	1979	151/*Special*	1980
Basque Country	1979	151/*Special*	1980
Galicia	1981	151/*Special*	1982
Navarre	1982	144/*Exceptional*	1990
Valencian C.	1982	143/ *Slow*	1983
Balearic Islands	1983	143/*Slow*	1997

Table 6.4 Composition of Regional Governments in the Six Regions with Unique Language, 1977–2010*

Year	77 78	80	82	84	86	88	90	92	94	96	98	00	02	04	06	08	10
Catalonia	N+S+C		N											S+C+I			
Basque C.	S+I	N+I			N+S			N+S+I			N+I			N+I+C			S
Galicia		P			S+I			P						S+I			P
Navarre					S			P		S+R +I		P+R					
Valencian C.					S			P									
Balearic Isl.					P			S+R				S+R		P		S+R	

* N: nationalists (CiU, PNV); I: separatists (EA, ERC, BNG); S: socialists (PSOE, including PSC, PSE, PSG); C: United Left –of Communist origins (IU-EB, ICV); R: center regionalists (CG, CDN); P: conservatives (PP, UPN).

alone or in coalition, and the advancement of unique languages in education, but these simple data do not permit to tell if this is a consequence of
that or both are of some third variable, for example, a more deeply rooted
national sentiment. It seems clear, however, that a weaker push of unique
language or a greater strength of Spanish language in school are related
to the presence and duration of non-nationalist conservative governments,
whereas the opposite is associated with the presence and duration of nationalist governments (which have also been mostly conservative) and left (even
if not nationalist), or of coalition between these two.

More remarkable perhaps is the usual attribution of the education portfolio to nationalists when they have been part of coalition governments
in which, however, socialists were the major partner, which shows the
great interest of nationalism in school and the resignation of the left in
this respect. In the case of *tripartite* cabinet that has governed Catalonia
between 2003 and 2010, consisting of the PSC (socialist), IC (former com-
munists and environmentalists) and ERC (*left* separatists), the Department
of Education and Universities was for the first three years in the hands of
ERC (Josep Bargalló and Marta Cid) and, after many conflicts inside the
government, a change of president and an interim period of six months in
the hands of a socialist with no other affiliation, in came to be occupied
by a member of the nationalist wing of the PSC (Ernest Maragall) over the
next four years. In Galicia, the PSG (socialist), which has been majoritary
in coalition governments in 1987–1989 and 2005–2009, left the responsibility of education put in the hands of a moderate nationalist (Aniceto
Núñez) in his first term and of a radical one (Laura Sánchez Piñón) in the
second. Unlike the case of the Basque Country, where, during the period of
coalition between moderate nationalism (PNV) and socialism (PSE-PSOE)
the portfolio was in the hands of the socialists, when later the government
came to be formed only by nationalists the portfolio was entrusted to the
separatist member of the new coalition (EA, with counselors I. Oliveri, A.
Iztueto and J.A. Campos Granados). The assignment of Education by the
PNV to the PSE between 1987 and 1994 (José Ramón Recalde and Fernando Buesa) can be interpreted, contrary to the other cases, as a concilia-
tory stance on the side the nationalists, or exceptionally belligerent on the
one of socialists, but that was also a period of public school basquification
(*euskaldunización*). In any case, not all nationalism thought was alike, as
became clear when the terrorist group ETA killed Buesa and tried to do so
with Recalde in 2000 (the latter survived a gunshot to the head).

The inclination of nationalism to lay hands on education seems logical,
intuitive and empirically obvious; one cannot say so of the fact that this
love is reciprocated by teachers, but it appears to be. In the most general
terms, it is not a hypothesis or a new finding, the role of intellectuals in
the broadest sense, in the nationalist movements (Gellner 1983). But the
reasons for teachers' approach to nationalism can also be more prosaic.
First, the unique language, if any, becomes, in the context of bilingualism,

a source of benefits for the locals, who dominate the common language and can compete on equal terms everywhere throughout the state but, as holders of a natural monopoly of the unique language, enjoy certain advantages in the regional territory once it becomes a selection criterion. It should be noted that if mobility throughout the state territory could be in the early education system an incentive to embrace the teaching profession, especially for those who aspired to leave the rural and provincial life, to date, with the dramatic development of communications and equipment (which equalizes the territory), the strong feminization of the profession (which is less willing to geographical mobility) and improved teacher working conditions (in particular a comparatively low workload, which attract applicants with other priorities and possibly other local ties), now it can be said to have ceased to be. For example, according to statistics of teacher mobility in 2008–2009, 5.35 percent of the teachers who moved to another place in that year came from one region different from that of his new job, but in Catalonia, the only region in which monolingualism reigns alone, was limited to 0.32 percent (although those could have come from two other regions with wide dissemination of the Catalan language, Balearic and Valencia, but the same phenomenon occurred in these: 2.06 and 2.31). Among secondary school teachers rates were higher, but with the same imbalance: 10.08 percent for the whole of Spain and 0.82 percent in Catalonia.[7]

Another incentive could be wages, reaching a significant disparity between communities. Equalizing to 100 the average wage of Spanish teachers in each stage, Basque teachers lead the rankings with 112.4 for primary school teachers, 114.3 for academic secondary and 123.5 for vocational secondary. Above the national average are also, however, other regions, ruled by nationalists or not, and so are below, where it falls by little Catalonia (98.1, 98.5 and 98.9),[8] so the salience of the Basque Country can be also attributable to their income level, and above all, to the aforementioned fiscal surplus versus the central government in public budget, which is where the salaries of public school teachers comes from. Simply, each meso-government offers what it can: Catalonia can offer geographic stability, given the fact that mastery of the language is easy for Catalan teachers, but it would be difficult to offer higher salaries; the Basque Country, on the other hand, can do the latter but has to be more moderate in the first, since a good part of the teachers have a very limited domain of Basque language (in fact, this has led to a conflict between labor rights and national education policy whose effects are lasting for three decades).

In any case, teachers correspond up to some degree. In the Basque Country, the whole of the unions of nationalist influence (ELA and LAB) get 57.6 percent of the vote in union elections among workers and 63.6 percent among public teachers with (STEA); the most radical of them, (LAB) rises from 16.7 to 20.2 percent.[9] In Galicia, the nationalist union (CIG) gets 28.1 percent of the general vote but reaches 42.5 percent in public education (to which one could add a 9.6 percent for STEG, a left-corporatist teachers only union also of nationalist orientation).[10] According to a CIS post-election survey of 2004, the percentage of voters of nationalism in the whole of Catalonia, Basque Country and Galicia in general elections that year was 23.2 percent, but among teachers amounted to 28.9 percent.[11] In another post-election survey of 2009 in the Basque Country, referring to the regional elections, the percentage of intention of vote for nationalist parties was 57.9 percent in the whole population, but 65.9 percent among teachers.[12] Consider, moreover, that the very socialist parties in the nationalities, integrated into the PSOE but with a significant degree of autonomy, also heel towards nationalism. The push for public school basquification began with a Socialist counselor, but today the Socialist Party of Basque Country follows a path more clearly distanced from nationalism; in Catalonia, by contrast, there has been a progressive abduction of the Socialist Party of Catalonia by nationalism, from their government coalition with the radical nationalist sector to their current inclination to believe that they have lost the last elections because they were not nationalistic enough. Ultimately, this is just an indication. What nationalism wants from teachers is not particularly his vote, which is as good as any other citizen's, but his work on behalf of its national project, whether by conviction, interest or prudence.

The problem could lie in the very conception of the nation. The new peripheral nationalisms learned to be such in the same school as the old Spanish nationalism, even from this itself. They conceive the nation as an excluding community that is built necessarily in opposition to another, with defined and sealed borders. To deny the 500 year history of Spain, in particular the history of a civic nation that starts from the Cadiz Constitution of 1812, moving through the I and II Republics and up to the present democratic monarchy, is so arbitrary as to deny the cultural legacy, the unique language or the differential identity of Catalans, Basques and Galicians. Bridging the gap time, current methods of peripheral nationalisms are no different from those of earlier periods of Bourbon centralization, but far light years from the most recent dictatorship. But the school is in any case reduced to the category of an instrument and citizenship education and human and personal development of students are subject to their socialization in the service of a political project. A sad turn in the global era.

NOTES

1. INE, *Contabilidad Regional de España—Base 2000.* http://www.ine.es
2. Ley 1/1998, de 7 de enero, de Política Lingüística en Cataluña (BOGC 9-1-1998) [Act of Linguistic Policy of Catalonia].
3. Ley 1/1993, de 19 de febrero, de la Escuela Pública vasca (BOPV 25–2-1993) [Act of Basque Public Education].
4. Decreto 124/2007, do 28 de xuño, polo que se regula o uso e a promoción do galego no sistema educativo (DOG 28–6-2007) [Decree regulating the use and the promotion of Galician in the educational system].

5. Decreto 79/2010, do 20 de maio, para o plurilingüismo no ensino non universitario de Galicia (DOG 25–5-2010) [Decree for plurilinguism in non University education of Galicia].

6. The real question in the first part of the table is not meant in the abstract to the community or to their unique language, but to their precise denominations: Catalonia, Catalan, Basque Country and Basque (in fact, *Euskadi* and *Euskara*), etc., as appropriate. Respondents were asked about up to three children in school, but here we limit ourselves to the older one for the sake of simplicity. The question of the second part was embedded in a battery with others on the language of administration officials, the advantages when seeking a job, the duty to study the unique language or its use in public administration, but these are tangential to our topic.

7. MEC, *Estadística de la Movilidad del profesorado de centros públicos. Curso 2008–2009.* http://www.educacion.es

8. Data have been taken from *MagisNet*, who attribute them to USTA, an Andalusian teachers' union. http://www.magisnet.com/noticia.asp?ref=3479. They refer to the wage of teachers with less than 3 years of service in 2008.

9. General data from EUSTAT (http://www.eustat.es/elem/ele0004100/tbl0004129_c.html#) and teachers data from FECCOO (http://*www3.feccoo.net/bdigital/informes/Euskadi.doc*), valid in 2009.

10. General data from Palomeque Álvarez 2010; public education data from Cuadernalia. http://www.cuadernalia.net/spip.php?article28459

11. Percentages are obtained on the basis of the microdata of the CIS study 2559–0-0, *Postelectoral elecciones generales y autonómicas de Andalucía*, 2004. http://www.cis.es. The subsample of teachers in the three regions is too small to use it for any accurate measure, but it is worth to indicate a tendency.

12. Percentages are obtained on the basis of the micro-data of the CIS study 2795–0-0, *Postelectoral del País Vasco, Elecciones Autonómicas 2009.* http://www.cis.es

REFERENCES

AEPHG (Asociación Española de Profesores de Historia y Geografía). 1998. Observaciones de la A.E.P.H.G. acerca de la enseñanza de la Historia (y, complementariamente, de la Geografía y el Arte), a propósito del debate sobre la reforma de la enseñanza de las Humanidades (y en particular de la Historia) en la Educación Secundaria. http://mimosa.pntic.mec.es/~mgarciaa/debates/deb_2.htm

AGE (Asociación de Geógrafos Españoles). 2000. *La geografía en los libros de texto de enseñanza secundaria.* Madrid: AGE, unpublished manuscript. http://age.ieg.csic.es/docs/00–12-libros-text.PDF

Álvarez Junco, J. et al. 2005. *El nombre de la cosa: debate sobre el término nación y otros conceptos relacionados.* Madrid: Centro de Estudios Políticos y Constitucionales.

Basta Ya 2001. "¿Libros de texto o catecismos nacionalistas?, *Revista Hasta Aquí* 1.

Beas Miranda, M. 1999. "Los libros de texto y las Comunidades Autónomas: una pesada Torre de Babel", *Revista Complutense de Educación* X, 2.

Castells, Miguel. 1997. *The Power of Identity.* Malden, MA: Blackwell.

CIS. 1998a. 2298/0–0 *Uso* de lenguas en comunidades bilingües (ii). Cataluña. http://www.cis.es/cis/opencms/ES/1_encuestas/catalogo.html

CIS. 1998b. 2299/0–0 *Uso* de lenguas en comunidades bilingües (ii). Comunidad Valenciana. http://www.cis.es/cis/opencms/ES/1_encuestas/catalogo.html

CIS. 1998c. 2295/0–0 Uso de lenguas en comunidades bilingües (ii). Galicia. http://www.cis.es/cis/opencms/ES/1_encuestas/catalogo.html
CIS. 1998d. 2300/0–0 Uso de lenguas en comunidades bilingües (ii). Islas Baleares. http://www.cis.es/cis/opencms/ES/1_encuestas/catalogo.html
CIS. 1998e. 2297/0–0 *Uso* de lenguas en comunidades bilingües (ii). Navarra. http://www.cis.es/cis/opencms/ES/1_encuestas/catalogo.htmla
CIS. 1998f. 2296/0–0 Uso de lenguas en comunidades bilingües (ii). País Vasco. http://www.cis.es/cis/opencms/ES/1_encuestas/catalogo.html
Conferencia de Educación.1998. *Dictamen sobre la enseñanza de las humanidades en la educación secundaria.* Task Force of the Conference of Education (Grupo de Trabajo de la Conferencia de Educación). Madrid: MEC.
Fernández Enguita, Mariano. 2007. "No hay naciones sin estado, ni estados sin nación". In *Escritos sociológicos: En homenaje a Salvador Giner*, edited by T. Pérez Yruela, T. González de la Fe y T. Montagut, 379–390. Madrid: Centro de Investigaciones Sociológicas.
Fusi, Juan Pablo. 1998. "Bajo el signo de la historia", lecture delivered at the seminar La *educación que queremos*. Madrid: Fundación Santillana, mimeo.
Galicia Bilingüe. 2010. "Adoctrinamiento en la enseñanza en Galicia". http://issuu.com/galiciabilingue/docs/adoctrinamiento?viewMode=presentation
Gellner, Ernest. 1983. *Nations and Nationalism.* Ithaca: Cornell University Press.
Heras Caballero, Pedro. 2009. *La España raptada: La formación del espíritu nacionalista.* Barcelona: Áltera.
Hijano, Manuel. c2002. "La historia de Andalucia en los libros de texto". http://servidormanes.uned.es/
Huntington, Samuel. 1996. *The Clash of Civilizations and the Remaking of World Order.* New York: Simon & Schuster.
Ortiz de Orruño, Jose Maria. 1998. *Historia y sistema educativo.* Madrid: M. Pons.
Palomeque, Manuel, and Jose Manuel Alvarez. 2010. *Derecho del trabajo.* Madrid: Editorial Universitaria Ramón Areces, 18th edition, actualized.
Pérez Díaz, V. et al. 2001. *La família espanyola davant l'educació dels seus fills.* Barcelona: Fundació "La Caixa".
PPPV (Partido Popular del País Vasco, Secretaría de Educación). 2006. "Libros de texto de Educación Primaria en el País Vasco. Resumen del informe. El adoctrinamiento nacionalista entre los 8 y los 12 años". Madrid: FAES.
Puelles Benitez, Manuel. 2002. "La educacion en la Espana del Siglo XX: Politicas, instituciones, logras y dracasus". In *Cien anos de educacion en Espana. En torno a la creacion del Ministerio de Instruccion Publica y Bellas Artes*, edited by Pedro Alvarex Lazaro, 3–25. Madrid: Ministerio de Education/Funacion BBVA.
RAH (Real Academia de la Historia). 2000. *Informe sobre los textos y cursos de Historia en los centros de enseñanza media*, Madrid, MEC.
Romero, Manuel. 2007. "Sembrando la diferencia: Radiografía del escándalo silencioso que va minando España". *El Mundo*, 20–26/11/2007
Segura, Antoni. 2001. *Els llibres d'història, l'ensenyament de la història i altres històries.* Barcelona: Fundació Jaume Bofill.
Smith, Anthony. 1971. *Theories of Nationalism.* New York: Harper & Row.
UNESCO. 2003. *Education in a Multilingual World.* Education position paper. Paris: Unesco.
Valls, Rafael. 2002. "Informe sobre los manuales escolares de Historia en la Educación Secundaria Obligatoria y Bachillerato valencianos". http://www.ahistcon.org/docs/ayer/ayer30_13.pdf

7 The Politics of Education in Post-War Germany

From Europeanized Nationhood to Multicultural Citizenship?

Daniel Faas

This chapter looks at citizenship education, European education and intercultural education from a historical perspective to critically analyze the politics behind German educational approaches. It argues that, at various points in time, government ideologies were implemented through education including the promotion of a 'Europeanized national identity' (Faas 2007; Goetz 1996) especially in geography, and the development of citizenship education from promoting de-Nazification in the West and state socialism in the East to emphasizing common citizenship in a multicultural society.

The German school system has included elements of citizenship education since the Weimar Republic introduced *Staatsbürgerkunde* (civics studies) in 1919. The aim was to strengthen the civic dispositions (*staatsbürgerliche Gesinnung*) of students, in addition to their morals and work ethic. German schools have since taken a wide range of approaches to the task of instilling desired political skills and values. Authoritarian governments under the Nazis and the Communist rulers of East Germany centralized the school system and aimed for blind loyalty. After World War II and up to the 1960s, citizenship education was carried out rather apolitically as formal knowledge of democratic institutions and procedures. The Allied powers occupying Germany saw citizenship education as part of a broader policy of de-Nazification. In the West the general emphasis was on teaching people to resist the use of state authority for immoral ends, while in the East the aim was to instill support for state socialism. In the 1960s and 1970s, traditional learning about democratic institutions was replaced with a more realistic picture of the political praxis. Students should thus not simply accept sociopolitical processes but develop critical and reflective thinking and question state attempts to breach 'inviolable' human rights (see Dahrendorf 1965; Händle 2002)[1].

Recent years have also seen fresh interest in citizenship education. Many commentators believe that this reflects the belated recognition that the country has become the destination of large-scale immigration. In this context, many politicians now argue that German civic consciousness must be actively inculcated, rather than simply being passed down the generations (see Engel and Ortloff 2009). Larger numbers of immigrants began claiming German citizenship only from the mid-1990s. After years of impasse in citizenship for migrants, many described the 2000 citizenship reform as having 'historical' importance (e.g., Koopmans, Statham, Giugni and Passy 2005; Green 2000). In addition to reducing the standard waiting period from fifteen to eight years of residence, the reform introduced provisional dual citizenship for children born to foreign parents in Germany (children would have dual citizenship until the age of 23, then have to choose a single citizenship). Researchers see the change as a shift away from an exclusively 'ethnic' conception of German identity, whereby citizenship was accessible only by descent, to a more territorial definition of citizenship (see Brubaker 1992). Alongside the principle of *ius sanguinis* (citizenship by birth), the reform introduced the concept of *ius soli* (citizenship by territoriality). But in recent years, a number of commentators have argued that the practical implications of the citizenship reform are limited (e.g., Green 2005; Howard 2008; Thränhardt 2008), mostly because fewer people have taken advantage of easier access to citizenship due to the restriction on dual citizenship (Skrobanek 2009). Since this change, school curricula have placed greater emphasis on common citizenship in a context of cultural and religious diversity. I return to this point later.

Unlike Germany's century-long tradition of citizenship education, European and intercultural education have been the result of post-World War II political orientations towards the West and sociocultural changes due to migration. In the first three decades following the War, successive German governments employed the concept of Europe as an identity and quickly developed an idealistic relationship with Europe. As a founding member of both the European Coal and Steel Community in 1951 and the European Economic Community in 1958, the government redefined German's concept of nationhood shattered by the War, in European terms. In recent decades, politicians have remained ardent proponents of a politically integrated Europe. Europe has thus become a focal point for national political identities in German schools. As early as 1978, attempts were made to include a European dimension in schools. Building on such initiatives, in 1990 and again in 2008, the Standing Conference of the Ministers of Education published the revised document 'Europe at School' (*Europabildung in der Schule*). It stated that the goal of education must be 'to awaken in young people the consciousness of a European identity; to prepare them to be aware of their responsibilities as citizens of the European Community' (Kultusministerkonferenz 2008, 6f.). This exemplifies the role of education in shifting German identity towards a more European agenda. In some respects this makes for an unusually broad conception of the political community, but risks that the European focus could serve to portray non-European cultures and people as inferior.

The theme of multiculturalism and intercultural education is an even more recent one and has led some (see Kiesel 1996) to focus on the ideological dimension of this concept while others (e.g., right-wing political parties) have regarded multiculturalism as a threat; some (see Bukow, Nikodem, Schulze and Yildiz 2001) have defined this concept as an everyday life normality in the age of globalization; and others (see Schulte 1999) have emphasized the potential of multiculturalism for the democratization of society. In the 1990s, many German curricula moved from emphasizing *Ausländerpädagogik* ('foreigner' education) to *interkulturelle Erziehung* (intercultural education). This reflects in part the belated recognition that many of the labor migrants of the 1960s and 1970s, and hence their German-born children, had in fact settled in Germany for good. The children of immigrants were no longer obliged to learn the languages of their parents—originally introduced to ensure they would be able to 'return' to the homelands of their parents—and instead were told to integrate into German society. In response to anti-immigrant violence in the early 1990s, there was also a change in emphasis for native German children, who were instructed to practice tolerance. The two trends were encapsulated in an agreement between the education ministers of the 16 federal states on 'Intercultural Education in Schools' (*Interkulturelle Bildung und Erziehung in der Schule*) stating that federal states should 'overhaul and further develop their curricula and guidelines of all subjects with regard to an intercultural dimension [and] develop teaching materials which address intercultural aspects as an integral part of school and education' (Kultusministerkonferenz 1996, 6). Previously, separate goals were pursued for migrants and natives; this was one of the first statements of civic values for all students.

The 1949 Constitution (*Grundgesetz*) put education under the control of the federal states, but it is beyond the scope of this chapter to focus on variations across federal states. Instead, this chapter continues to prioritize generic features and hones in on the southwestern state of Baden-Württemberg to illustrate how national politics affect regional educational legislators. In Germany, compulsory education generally starts at the age of 6. Children spend four to six years in primary school (*Grundschule*). The focus is on providing children with key skills in German and mathematics. Pupils are also introduced to the natural and social sciences, art, music and sport. The constitution requires that all public schools offer religious education (those who opt out attend ethics classes). The 1949 constitutional requirement of state neutrality over religious matters resulted in the creation of separate Protestant and Catholic classes in most of the country; at the time these were the only two religions in question. German schools have been slow to introduce a Muslim version of religious education (for more on Islamic religious education in Germany see Faas 2010) in part because it is very difficult for the Islamic associations that could certify teachers to achieve the required status. The educational system in many federal states sends children either to vocational (*Hauptschule, Realschule*) or to academic schools (*Gymnasium*), typically at the age of 11 or 12. Immigrants and their descendents are underrepresented in the academic track with one in three native Germans graduating from the *Gymnasium* compared with only one in ten migrants (Paritätischer Gesamtverbund 2010).

A NOTE ON METHODOLOGY

The study is designed to shed light on how macro-level European and intercultural issues have infiltrated geography, history and citizenship education curricula in Germany. This leads on from the work of Schissler and Soysal (2005) who, among others, argued that history and citizenship textbooks and curricula tend to recast the nation in European terms because of a broadening of human rights discourses, decolonization, social movements of the 1970s and the end of the Cold War and subsequent European integration processes. They also refer to the difficulties textbook authors and curriculum planners face when dealing with migrants. Historically, geography, history and especially citizenship education have represented the state's most formal and direct means of creating citizens and shaping young people's values and identities (see Osler 1994).

It is beyond the scope of this chapter to capture the full diversity of approaches across the sixteen federal states. The education ministers are represented in the *Kultusministerkonferenz* (the Standing Conference of the Ministers of Education and Cultural Affairs), and together they agree common guidelines but these are not binding. Hence one might expect considerable variation depending on the political constellation of the states, especially in a subject like citizenship education. To check this, I selected two states with very different political backgrounds in order to set bounds on the likely range of approaches, Baden-Württemberg and Berlin. Other curricula, such as geography and history, show less variation across the federal states. This is in part due to an emphasis on Europe, a much less politically contested field compared with migration.

Baden-Württemberg has been ruled by the Christian Democratic Union for the entire post-war period. The region's conservative reputation was recently reinforced by the refusal of the education ministry to employ a teacher who wished to wear a headscarf in the classroom. The case was taken to the constitutional court, which refused to make a clear decision, allowing Baden-Württemberg and other regions to pass their own legislation on the issue. The law adopted in Baden-Württemberg prohibited teachers wearing headscarves but explicitly allowed for Christian symbols in the classroom, and for nuns to teach wearing the habit. This was justified on the grounds that German educational and cultural values are fundamentally Christian. Most of the other German states that have introduced legislation banning headscarves include a similar provision to make clear that Christian (and Jewish) symbols are *not* affected (see Joppke 2007). In contrast, Berlin was ruled by the Social Democratic party for 42 of the past 60 years, and in recent years by a 'red-red' coalition of the SPD and the Left Party. Berlin, like Baden-Württemberg, recently passed legislation to prevent teachers from bringing religious symbols into the classroom, but the law applies to *all* religions.

Part of this chapter compares the citizenship curricula for children in the later stages of compulsory education, between ages 10 and 16. Berlin is somewhat unusual in that secondary education begins later and lasts just four years (from 12 to 16). To ensure comparability with Baden-Württemberg (and most other parts of the country) I therefore also included the final two years of primary school in my analysis of the Berlin curricula. In Berlin, the curricula apply to all schools, but Baden-Württemberg issues separate instructions for vocational and academic schools. At this stage it is important to mention one methodological caveat. This chapter does not provide information on the actual implementation of subject-specific curricula. Existing research suggests that this varies from school to school, depending, for example, on the socioeconomic background of students and teachers (see Faas 2010). Schiffauer, Baumann, et al. (2004) even argue that schools and some regions have commonly-agreed but rarely articulated hidden curricula.

The cross-state analysis of citizenship curricula is triangulated with European and multicultural ideologies promoted especially in geography and history. This approach is unique because curriculum analyses have hitherto largely focused on national and European values (see Hinderliter Ortloff 2005; Keating 2009; Michaels and Stevick 2009) or multicultural and global values (see Wilhelm 1998; Graves 2002; Marshall 2009), thus neglecting the ways in which these dimensions and ideologies intersect. However, there is more general literature that deals with issues of intra-European diversity and citizenship. For example, Sultana (1995) fears a potential Eurocentrism and Tulasiewicz (1993) argues that confining the European dimension to the EU, 'may help to present a more compact whole, but is also open to the accusation that it ignores the rest of the world'. There is a need for dissociation from a Eurocentric or 'fortress Europe' approach and the notion of Europe should thus also include 'all those recent Europeans who live in Europe whose roots are in Morocco, Bangladesh or Turkey' (ibid., 241). Various studies have emphasized the ethnocentrism of educational materials and textbooks in particular (see Nieto 1996; Coulby 2000) and, similarly, the Eurocentrism (Hansen 1998). Europe has been 'invented' over the centuries in Eurocentric ways to exclude various 'others' (Delanty 1995). Yet another body of literature has developed around global citizenship education, notably in England (see Osler and Vincent 2002). However, there is a scarcity of literature on the ways in which national, European *and* multicultural ideologies have been promoted through curricula.

To sum up, my content analysis of curriculum documents included the latest citizenship, geography and history curricula from the federal state of Baden-Württemberg and, additionally, citizenship curricula from the final phase of primary schooling and first phase of secondary schooling in Berlin. The quantitative part of the analysis referred to the presence of European, multicultural and citizenship topics in the curriculum. To this end, I counted which units and subunits across the age groups (10–16) in the subject areas referred to Europe, multiculturalism and the nation-state. The qualitative analysis focused on the discourses employed in the curriculum including the emergence and space given to concepts like tolerance and interculturalism. Most documents consisted of an introductory part or explanatory notes, which covertly or overtly addressed my research agenda, and a part where teaching units and activities were listed in bullet points.

EDUCATING FOR MULTICULTURAL EUROPEAN CITIZENSHIP IN GERMANY

The impact of European and national policies on education has been investigated for quite some time by social scientists. Research has described how Europe and European integration became part of the German secondary school curricula and textbooks in the 1990s. Hauler (1994) found that, out of seventy Year 10 (ages 15 to 16) annual lesson plans, twenty included eight or more hours of teaching the European dimension; thirteen did not cover this teaching unit at all; and in almost half the classes a mere three lessons were spent on 'European Integration and Unification'. Kesidou's (1999) analysis of geography, citizenship and history curricula of grammar schools (*Gymnasien*) in Baden-Württemberg found that teaching units in both geography and citizenship education specifically dealt with European unification. However, at the time, the term Europe referred to central and western Europe without mentioning Eastern Europe.

The notion of Europe has been particularly integrated into geography and history (Kultusministerium Baden-Württemberg 2004). In the geography curriculum of Baden-Württemberg, the entire Year 7 (ages 12 to 13) in the vocational-track Hauptschule is spent on Europe; in the university-track Gymnasium, three out of four teaching units in Year 6 (ages 11 to 12) also deal with Europe. The Baden-Württemberg geography curriculum is a good example of what I would call an inclusive European curricular approach. About one-third of geography teaching units deal with national (e.g., cities and industrial areas in Baden-Württemberg, mountains in southwestern Germany, areas of Germany), European (e.g., European integration, the continent of Europe, socioeconomic processes in Europe) as well as intercultural and global topics respectively (e.g., culture zones including the

Muslim world, living in one world, India and China)². Arguably, this may be the result of *Kultusministerkonferenz* (KMK) guidelines around both European (2008) and intercultural education (1996), mentioned earlier. The introductory notes of the current geography curriculum refer to the importance of a local, national, European and global perspective thereby promoting the creation not just of European citizens but self-reflective, ethically responsible world citizens (Kultusministerium Baden-Württemberg 2004). At the same time, one of the stated goals of this subject is to awaken the value of, and understanding for, other peoples and cultures.

The country's 'Europeanized national identity' can perhaps best be seen in history, where one would expect an ethnocentric view as is the case in many other European countries (see Faas, forthcoming). However, a simple count of the teaching modules revealed a relatively equal balance between national (45.5 percent) and European (36.4 percent) history topics. Such topics include Europe and Charles the Great, European unification, the Enlightenment in Europe and Germany after World War II. Up to half an academic year (Year 6 in the case of *Hauptschulen* and Year 7 in the case of *Gymnasien*) is spent on Europe whilst issues of cultural and ethnic diversity are somewhat marginalized in the history curriculum framework (13.6 percent), especially compared with geography. This is suggestive of the general struggle Germany, including regional education policymakers, face of redefining the country's 'Europeanized national identity in intercultural terms'. Notably, the introductory note to the history curriculum refers to the importance of developing a European identity when dealing with the different historical epochs (Kultusministerium Baden-Württemberg 2004) as well as the need to promote tolerance and values of a pluralistic democratic society. Students are required to learn about the importance of antiquity for the development of European civilization and culture and, in doing so, are taught that the notion of European identity has a long history. They are also taught about the processes of European integration from the 1957 Treaties of Rome to the 2002 launch of the Euro as a single currency. Despite the national-European emphasis, there are topics that address interculturalism including past and present migration from the 'folk wandering' between the third and sixth centuries and the emigration from central Europe through World War II expulsions to present-day integration problems and refugee movements.

A combination of intercultural and anti-racist education has been Germany's prevailing educational response to migration. Some federal states (e.g., Saarland, Thuringia) have developed intercultural teaching units and others (e.g., Berlin, Hamburg, Schleswig Holstein) introduced intercultural education as a cross-curricular theme. Still others (e.g., Bremen, Hesse, Rhineland-Palatinate) have carried out intercultural projects during special project days in school and some (e.g., Baden-Württemberg, Bavaria, Brandenburg) have taken a combined approach of the above. North-Rhine Westphalia and Hamburg were amongst the states that took a leading role in implementing intercultural education. Hamburg's revised school law today states that 'schools have the task to educate for a peaceful living together of all cultures and the equality of all human beings' (Behörde für Bildung und Sport 2003, 9). Baden-Württemberg delivers intercultural education in a range of subjects, including geography, history and citizenship education. Moreover, as a result of the poor performance in international student assessment tests, and the particular underachievement of Turkish and other migrant youth (see OECD 2006, 2010), the Standing Conference of the Ministers of Education agreed on national educational standards and also revised the standards for teacher training to enhance knowledge of the social and cultural backgrounds of students and the role of schools in responding to increasingly diverse populations.

Another controversial issue raised by migration to Germany is the provision of mother-tongue education, and the perceived value of the linguistic and cultural capital that migrants bring into schools. Until the 1980s, children of migrants were sent to separate schools for 'foreigners' so that they could retain linguistic and cultural ties to their countries of origin, and be prepared for their eventual return. This educational strategy has shifted however, and policymakers now emphasize integration and German language acquisition, typically to the exclusion of mother-tongue education. The swing from one policy extreme to the other largely ignores the findings of many academics, who argue that mother-tongue language ability complements, rather than competes with, the process of learning German (see Gogolin and Neumann 2009). In addition, proficiency in the mother tongue has also been found to provide a source of stable 'identity', which is important for success in school (Krumm 2009).

The recent quest for common citizenship and cohesiveness is also expressed through numerous government initiatives. For example, the two coalition governments under Angela Merkel (since 2005) have hosted three so-called integration summits (*Integrationsgipfel*) with political and societal representatives to discuss issues of German language learning, education and job opportunities. Several additional Islam conferences (*Islamkonferenz*) have sought to focus on the interaction between the national majority and Muslim minorities, addressing religious topics, German law and values and employment policies. This appears to reflect recognition that 'people with a migration background' will play a large role in shaping the country's future, an important change since around one-third of the children now entering German schools have a migrant background (Schäfer and Brückner 2008). Academics and politicians agree that current policies must make up for the 'mistake' of ignoring integration in the past. Bade (2007) for instance speaks of 'catch-up integration' (*nachholende Integration*). However, this recognition is not leading to straightforward acceptance of migrants. Rather, these people are increasingly called upon to demonstrate that they are 'willing' to integrate and, until now, there has been a deadlock between the two main political parties over the meaning of 'integration'—the Social

Democratic Party views naturalization as a precondition of successful integration whereas the Christian Democratic Union mostly views integration as a precondition for naturalization.

The reorientations of Germany's approach to managing migration at the national level have also included youth integration summits (*Jugendintegrationsgipfel*), bringing together young people from diverse backgrounds to discuss their ideas about language and education, local integration and cultural diversity. A National Integration Plan was launched at the second integration summit in 2007, consisting of ten thematic priority areas such as improving integration courses, promoting early German language learning, integration through sports, using the diversity of the media and strengthening integration through civic commitment and equal participation (Bundesregierung Deutschland 2007). In this respect the German Government, like its counterparts in North America and elsewhere, appears to be taking a new interest in civil society organizations. In Germany, this interest appears largely instrumental however, since the government is arguing that civil society organizations should be encouraged not so much because membership is of intrinsic value, but because they facilitate government influence over processes that are hard to steer from above. Jann (2003) describes this as a new style of governance in Germany. The National Integration Plan, for example, states that it is not possible to legislate for integration, but goes on to list over 100 commitments on the part of various levels of government and non-governmental organizations.

At the same time, policymakers and politicians at the regional level, particularly in conservative-controlled states, have continued to perceive national and multicultural values and ideologies as largely incompatible. In 2003, Germany's highest constitutional court found that the federal state of Baden-Württemberg was wrong to ban Fereshta Ludin, a German teacher of Afghan descent, from wearing a headscarf in school, but declared that states could in principle legislate on such issues (Bundesverfassungsgericht 2003). Unlike in France, there was no serious question that students have the legal right to wear headscarves in Germany (see Wallach Scott 2007, Weil 2004). School authorities in Baden-Württemberg argued that the headscarf could be seen as a political symbol, and is thus inappropriate in a public classroom. The teacher in question argued that she should be allowed to wear the headscarf on the basis of her constitutional right to freedom of religious expression, and further that public schools should mirror the pluralism of German society rather than imposing secularism (Joppke 2007, 329).

The states of Baden-Württemberg, Bavaria, Bremen, Thuringia, Lower Saxony, North-Rhine Westphalia, Saarland and Hesse subsequently introduced legislation banning teachers from wearing headscarves. This is important because it privileges the Christian cross over other religious symbols in schools and society at large and is therefore counterproductive to integration efforts. For example, in April 2004, the Baden-Württemberg parliament added the following paragraph to the law on education:

Teachers in schools [. . .] may not make statements on politics, religion or ideology that could endanger the neutrality of the State with respect to children and parents, or which may disturb the peaceful operation of the school. In particular, it is forbidden to behave in such a way as to give children or teachers the impression that the teacher is opposed to the constitutional guarantees of human dignity, equal rights according to Article 3 of the Constitution, the rights to personal and religious freedom or the liberal-democratic basis of the State. The transmission of Christian and western educational and cultural values is not affected by [these stipulations]. The requirement of religious neutrality does not apply to religious education, following Section 1 Article 18 of the Constitution of Baden-Württemberg. (Regierung des Landes Baden-Württemberg 2006)

This paragraph is remarkable in several ways. The first sentence evokes the image of female teachers in headscarves posing a 'danger' to pupils and school order. The second sentence encompasses many of the arguments commonly used against wearing a headscarf, including the idea that it is an insult to human dignity and that it is likely to have been imposed upon the woman in question by a patriarchal religion. The third and fourth sentences ensure it will still be acceptable for a crucifix to hang in classrooms in Baden-Württemberg and for nuns to teach wearing the habit. This was justified on the grounds that German educational and cultural values are fundamentally Christian. Most of the other German states that have introduced legislation banning headscarves include a similar provision to make clear that Christian (and Jewish) symbols are *not* affected (see Joppke 2007). Only in Berlin does the reform in question explicitly apply to all religions. In Berlin the ban applies not only to teachers but also to other higher-level state officials; this is also true of the headscarf ban in the state of Hesse. In no part of Germany were there substantial numbers of teachers actually wearing headscarves when the legislation was passed. During the past decade, Muslims have been quite successful in claiming rights and, at the same time, Germans have been more willing to concede these rights which are further signs of the ideological shifts that have occurred. However, as evidenced by the legislation in Baden-Württemberg, policymakers and parts of the general population are finding it hard to accept this accommodation of Muslim rights and the development towards a more multicultural concept of citizenship.

Between Tolerance and Interculturalism: Citizenship in Baden-Württemberg and Berlin

The main purpose of citizenship education in Germany is to continue to remind young Germans that their country is a federally-organized parliamentary democracy. Students get to know and discuss democratic elections,

democratic forms of government, political parties, Germany's constitution
and the meaning of the freedom of press. For decades, a 'gap' has existed
between the constitutional ideal of one German national identity and the
reality of two German states. The 1990 reunification was a crisis for West
Germany as it regained full political sovereignty and thus had to reinter-
pret its role in European and world politics; for East Germany, it was a
different crisis as it had to come to terms with economic, social and ideological changes created by a new political union of two national identities whose historical paths had been diverging for two generations (Piper
1998). Despite an emphasis on the fragility of democracy, current citizenship curricula address the living together of different cultures. Students are
familiarized with the ways in which increasing mobility results in cultural
meetings and exchanges and how to develop respect and understanding
for other cultures. Yet, there are subtle differences between federal states
around migration-related challenges, as exemplified when comparing citizenship curricula in Baden-Württemberg and Berlin.

Schools in Berlin are instructed to orient their teaching to students 'of
various backgrounds' rather than trying to impose a unitary model (Senatsverwaltung für Bildung, Jugend und Sport Berlin 2007b, 7). Themes
of 'intercultural competence' and 'cooperation with people of different
backgrounds' run throughout the curricula of all courses (ibid., 21; Senatsverwaltung für Bildung, Jugend und Sport Berlin 2007a, 5). This applies
not just to content but also to skills. Besides analytic and methodological
competence, the ability to negotiate daily life in a context of diversity is a
key skill. The curricula also emphasize the importance of being open to
new sources of information 'in the context of accelerated globalization'.
Berlin aspires to make the best of its high proportion of migrant children,
given that 'international employers now expect their workers to be able to
understand and give presentations in foreign languages' (Senatsverwaltung
für Bildung, Jugend und Sport Berlin 2007a, 7).

Students in citizenship classes in Berlin are to be reminded that democracy can be fragile and that its stability depends on the engagement of
citizens. The special emphasis on democracy derives in part from the
city's tumultuous twentieth-century experience. Besides democracy, key
themes are children's' rights and peace. Although there are few explicit
references to the German constitution, it seems to be the source for various topics and phrases (e.g., 'human dignity', the topic of the first line of
the constitution). In the Berlin curricula, references to 'culture' are either
to the 'open and democratic learning culture' of the school, or to 'other
cultures'. There are no references to German culture. The Berlin curricula
do not always specify the geographic level at which relevant organizations
and institutions are to be studied, but make frequent references to the
local political context, especially to democracy within the school and in
the local municipality. Examples of topics to be covered in years five and
six refer to German institutions and to international organizations such
as UNICEF. There is only a single reference to Europe (Senatsverwaltung

für Bildung, Jugend und Sport Berlin 2007b, 28–29). But in the curriculum for students in years 7 through 10 there are about as many references to European topics and the EU as there are to Germany and the German political system. In the later years students are also introduced to international topics and organizations.

Citizenship curricula in Baden-Württemberg are sufficiently different, depending on whether students are in the vocational or academic tracks, to merit separate analysis. Students in the *Hauptschule* (the less prestigious of the two kinds of vocational schools) study 'World–Time–Society'. This covers the subjects of history, citizenship, geography and economics (Kultusministerium Baden-Wurttemberg 2004). The focus is on 'people living together in the past, present and future'. Students are taught about the importance of sustainable development, to understand the historical background of German society, to respect the views of others and to address conflict through democratic procedures. This curriculum promotes 'intercultural learning', and valuing other people and cultures. Topics include 'orientation in space and time', 'power and authority' and 'democratic society', in which the content is primarily German and European, with a major focus on the Nazi past. Another topic is 'living together with different groups', in which the focus is on 'other cultures' (ibid., 4). The final two broad topics are 'conflicts over resources' and 'Earth and environment'; here the focus is on environmental problems, often in other parts of the world or at a global level.

Students in the *Realschule* (the more prestigious of the vocational schools, which aim to prepare students for skilled blue-collar employment) are encouraged to develop 'social engagement' through classes that promote membership in civil society organizations such as the Church or sports clubs (Kultusministerium Baden-Württemberg 2004). In addition to building confidence in their ability to participate, the aim is to instill 'sensibility and tolerance'. Students in the *Realschule* are also taught to behave responsibly with regard to 'People and Environment' (Kultusministerium Baden-Württemberg 2004). Instruction should prepare students to deal with current political and social issues, and should be able to appreciate their 'historical-cultural context'. A paternalistic tone predominates. The aim is that students should be responsible and self-sufficient in matters of clothing and feeding themselves, and should understand the importance (and some of the practicalities) of caring for others in need. There is much less attention to intercultural differences than in the previously described curricula for the *Hauptschule*; the concept of intercultural education receives no mention.

Students in the academic *Gymnasium* are to be taught about the history and mechanics of existing political institutions in greater detail. Understanding democracy and its social foundations is the single most important theme (Kultusministerium Baden-Württemberg 2004). The Gymnasium curriculum in Baden-Württemberg makes no reference to intercultural perspectives and few to the importance of working together with people from diverse backgrounds. Students should internalize tolerance of other ways of life, religions, ideologies and people (Kultusministerium Baden-Württemberg 2004). The curriculum makes only two references to culture: to European culture and to the thesis of the 'clash of civilizations' (Huntington 1996). There are frequent references to the principles and values espoused in the German constitution. The geographic and institutional focus is predominantly on Germany. Local political participation is a topic in lower years, and the great majority of topics in Year 10 focus on German politics. The curricula for the *Gymnasium* specifies a total of ten topic areas, of which two focus on youth politics, two on international issues such as globalization and human rights, one covers the European Union, and the remaining five are on German history and the German political system (Kultusministerium Baden-Württemberg 2004). One of the German history topics is 'Migration to Germany', including a focus on the 'opportunities and problems of integration in a pluralistic migrant society'. Overall, citizenship classes for the most academically successful students in Baden-Württemberg are oriented less towards everyday social competence than towards existing political institutions.

Citizenship curricula in Baden-Württemberg overlap with those in Berlin in certain respects, but there are also important differences. They share an emphasis on the fragility of democracy and the need for citizens to be vigilant and active in protecting it. They pay considerable attention to the ideals of the German constitution. And all of the curricula studied make at least some reference to diversity within the citizenry, and the challenges that this brings. The differences appear not only between the states but also between different kinds of schools in Baden-Württemberg. In general, the citizenship curricula in Baden-Württemberg pay less attention than those in Berlin to 'intercultural' perspectives and questions of collective welfare in diverse populations. In Baden-Württemberg the concept of 'tolerance' is preferred. Critics of this concept argue that it implies and reinforces a sense of superiority among the people who tolerate over the objects of their tolerance (e.g., Brown 2006). One need not fully accept this position to appreciate that this is a different approach to that taken in Berlin, more abstract and arguably less open to the perspectives of migrants themselves. But it is interesting to see that within Baden-Württemberg, the curriculum for the *Hauptschule* (the schools with the lowest reputation) is much more similar to the Berlin curricula. These are also the schools in which immigrants and their descendents are overrepresented—over 40 percent of children with a migration background attend the *Hauptschule*, compared to around 20 percent of native Germans. This suggests the possibility that teachers and curriculum developers have responded to this diversity by emphasizing intercultural participation, rather than more abstract ideals of citizenship and tolerance.

CONCLUSION

This chapter shed light on the ways in which educational policies and curricula were designed to reflect government ideologies in Germany. The

German educational approach in the 1960s and 1970s, also known as 'foreigner pedagogy' (*Ausländer-pädagogik*), was viewed as the key means of assimilating migrant children into a monocultural conception of Germany. Germany was reluctant to reconceptualize her national identity as multicultural, perhaps as a result of the fact that policymakers and politicians had just shifted the country's national agenda towards European integration. The result has been that Germany, a founding member of the European integration project, has used schools and the curriculum to construct a 'Europeanized national identity' since the 1980s and 1990s. Education policy documents stressed the political justification for a European dimension in education, arguing that Europe was more than just a geographical term and that the painful experiences of two World Wars as well as the developments in Western and Eastern Europe since 1945 had given Europeans every reason to reflect on their common origins. The task of the school was seen as conveying insights into geographical diversity, political and social structures, formative historical forces and the history of the European idea. Residues of these governmental ideologies enacted since World War II can still be found in schools today (see Faas 2010).

Despite paradigm shifts from 'foreigner politics' and 'foreigner pedagogy' to a 'politics of integration', Germany is still struggling to leave behind the image of the third-generation 'foreigner' (*Ausländer*) or 'foreign citizen' (*ausländische Mitbürger*). This has to do with the ideological power struggle between the two main political parties. For example, the conservative Christian Democratic Union sees citizenship as a reward for successful integration whereas the Social Democratic Party considers citizenship as an incentive or stimulus for migrants to integrate. At the same time, the struggle to change how immigrants are seen is related to the ingrained insensitivities formed over five decades of politicians and policymakers rejecting the notion of Germany as an immigration country. One of the challenges now lying ahead is how to balance the country's 'Europeanized national identity' with migrant values.

What is interesting is that the relationship between national, European and multicultural ideologies and values is put together in rather different ways depending on the school subject and, at times, also the federal state. History curricula by and large promote national and European values whereas geography curricula indicate Germany's recent attempts to add more multicultural values to the prevailing European ideology. Citizenship education has become a major tool to promote common citizenship in a multicultural Germany although there are nuances with some federal states (e.g., Berlin) emphasising aspects of tolerance and others (e.g., Baden-Württemberg) notions of interculturalism. But all converge around the importance of reminding young Germans that their country is a federalized parliamentary democracy, that democracy is fragile and that citizens must be alert to the risk that state authority is put to immoral ends.

There is evidence that the challenge of helping the children of immigrants succeed in the German school system is forcing new thinking on the means and ends of education. Indeed, this is true not just of Germany but also of many neighboring countries (see Commission of the European Communities 2008). German politicians seem in recent years to have developed a more nuanced understanding of the issues involved. The single most common refrain is still the need for better German language skills, but other changes are now discussed, including some minor reforms of German institutions. Language also features prominently among the ten thematic priority areas of the German national integration plan. But there is little discussion of deeper issues. For example, the emphasis on the need for immigrants to do well in school ignores the fact that schools play a role not just in opening the way for upward mobility, but also in perpetuating the stratification of society. Since students are ranked rather than compared to an absolute standard, it is impossible for *every* child to do better. The evidence to date is that the children of immigrants by and large remain at the bottom of the heap.

Another underlying but rarely mentioned issue is the irony of providing citizenship education to millions of children who are not actually citizens, despite being born in Germany. The reform of citizenship laws in 2000 was meant to put an end to this, but in fact around half of the children born to foreign parents since that time lack German citizenship (Statistisches Bundesamt 2009, 57). The reluctance to address this issue is hence another example of politicians playing down the need for large-scale reforms. The latest curriculum reform in the federal state of Baden-Württemberg was not necessarily triggered by macro-political events such as terrorism and calls for more social cohesion but by the introduction of national educational standards and subject clusters to monitor variations from one federal state to another. There is thus still some way to go in shifting educational policies and curricular approaches from the prevailing Europeanized concept of nationhood to a more multicultural notion of citizenship. The presence of large migrant populations as well as high-profile events including Turkey's EU accession negotiations are continuing to shape government ideologies and their educational implementation.

NOTES

1. Today, 'citizenship education' in Germany is taught in a subject that has many different names, depending on the federal state and type of school (Derricott 2000). For example, in the federal state of Baden-Württemberg, Hamburg and Saxony the subject is called *Gemeinschaftskunde*; in Bavaria, Mecklenburg Western Pomerania and Saxony Anhalt it is called *Sozialkunde* whereas in Brandenburg it is called *Politische Bildung*.
2. Given that there is little if any difference between those three types of schools (Hauptschule, Realschule, Gymnasium) in terms of addressing the interface of a European and intercultural curricular dimension, I focus on more general findings with regard to the geography and history curriculum framework in Baden-Wüttemberg.

REFERENCES

Bade, Klaus. J. 2007. "Versäumte Integrationschancen und nachholende Integrationspolitik". In *Nachholende Integrationspolitik und Gestaltungsperspektiven der Integrationspraxis*, edited by H.-G. Hiesserich, 21–95.Göttingen: V&R unipress.

Behörde für Bildung und Sport ed. 2003. Hamburgisches Schulgesetz vom 16.4.1997 geändert am 27.6.2003. Hamburg: Behörde für Bildung und Sport.

Brown, Wendy. 2006. *Regulating Aversion: Tolerance in the Age of Identity and Empire*. Princeton: Princeton University Press.

Brubaker, Rogers. 1992. *Citizenship and Nationhood in France and Germany*. Cambridge: Harvard University Press.

Bukow, Wolf-Dietrich, Claudia Nikodem, Erika Schulze, and Erol Yildiz. 2001. *Die multikulturelle Stadt: Von der Selbstverständlichkeit im städtischen Alltag*. Opladen: Leske und Budrich.

Bundesregierung Deutschland. 2007. *Nationaler Integrationsplan: Neue Wege, Neue Chancen*. Berlin: Presse- und Informationsamt der Bundesregierung.

Bundesverfassungsgericht. 2003. 2 BvR 1436/02.

Commission of the European Communities. 2008. *Green Paper Migration and Mobility: Challenges and Opportunities for EU Education Systems*. Brussels: Commission of the European Communities.

Coulby, David. 2000. *Beyond the National Curriculum: Curricular Centralism and Cultural Diversity in Europe and the USA*. London: Routledge.

Dahrendorf, Ralf. 1965. *Gesellschaft und Demokratie in Deutschland*. München: Piper.

Delanty, Gerard. 1995. *Inventing Europe: Idea, Identity, Reality*. London: McMillan.

Derricott, Ray. 2000. "National case studies of citizenship education". In *Citizenship for the 21st Century: An International Perspective on Education*, edited by John Cogan and Ray Derricott, 23–92. London: Kogan Page.

Engel, Laura, and Deborah Hinderliter Ortloff. 2009. "From the Local to the Supranational: Curriculum Reform and the Production of the Ideal Citizen in Two Federal Systems, Germany and Spain". *Journal of Curriculum Studies* 41: 179–198.

Faas, Daniel. 2007. "The Europeanisation of German Ethnic Identities: The Case of German and Turkish Students in Two Stuttgart Secondary Schools". *International Studies in Sociology of Education* 17: 45–62.

Faas, Daniel. 2010. *Negotiating Political Identities: Multiethnic Schools and Youth in Europe*. Farnham: Ashgate.

Faas, Daniel. forthcoming. "The Nation, Europe and Migration: A Comparison of Geography, History and Citizenship Education Curricula in Greece, Germany and England". *Journal of Curriculum Studies*.

Goetz, Klaus. 1996. "Integration Policy in a Europeanized State: Germany and the Intergovernmental Conference". *Journal of European Public Policy* 3: 23–44.

Gogolin, Ingrid, and Ursula Neumann. (Eds.). 2009. *Streitfall Zweisprachigkeit [The Bilingualism Controversy]*. Wiesbaden: Verlag für Sozialwissenschaften.

Graves, Jaya. 2002. "Developing a Global Dimension in the Curriculum". *The Curriculum Journal* 13: 303–311.

Green, Simon. 2000. "Beyond Ethnoculturalism? German Citizenship in the New Millennium". *German Politics* 9: 105–124.

Green, Simon. 2005. "Between Ideology and Pragmatism: The Politics of Dual Nationality in Germany". *International Migration Review* 39: 921–952.

Händle, Christa. 2002. "The Burden of History? Civic Education at German schools". http://www.jsse.org/2002/2002-2/pdf/haendle-germany-2-2002.pdf

Hansen, Peo. 1998. "Schooling a European Identity: Ethno-Cultural Exclusion and Nationalist Resonance Within the EU Policy of The European Dimension in Education". *European Journal of Intercultural Studies* 9: 5–23.

Hauler, Anton. 1994. *Die europäische Dimension in der schulischen Wirklichkeit: Eine quantitative Analyse des Europa-Unterrichts im historisch-politischen Unterricht an baden-württembergischen Realschulen.* Weingarten: Forschungsstelle für politisch-gesellschaftliche Erziehung.

Hinderliter Ortloff, Deborah. 2005. "Becoming European: A Framing Analysis of Three Countries' Civics Education Curricula". *European Education* 37: 35–49.

Howard, Marc M. 2008. "The Causes and Consequences of Germany's New Citizenship Law". *German Politics* 17: 41–62.

Huntington, Samuel P. 1996. *The Clash of Civilisations and the Remaking of World Order.* New York: Touchstone.

Jann, Werner. 2003. "State, Administration and Governance in Germany: Competing Traditions and Dominant Narratives". *Public Administration* 81: 95–118.

Joppke, Christian. 2007. "State Neutrality and Islamic Headscarf Laws in France and Germany". *Theory and Society* 36: 313–342.

Keating, Avril. 2009. "Nationalizing the Post-National: Reframing European Citizenship for the Civics Curriculum in Ireland". *Journal of Curriculum Studies* 41: 159–178.

Kesidou, Anastasia. 1999. *Die europäische Dimension der griechischen und baden-württembergischen Lehrpläne und Schulbücher der Sekundarschule: An den Beispielen Geographie, politische Bildung, Geschichte und Literatur.* Frankfurt am Main: Lang.

Kiesel, Doron. 1996. *Das Dilemma der Differenz: Zur Kritik des Kulturalismus in der interkulturellen Pädagogik.* Frankfurt am Main: Cooperative.

Koopmans, Ruud, Paul Statham, Marco Giugni, and Florence Passy. 2005. *Contested Citizenship: Immigration and Cultural Diversity in Europe.* Minneapolis: University of Minnesota Press.

Krumm, Hans-Jürgen. 2009. "Die Bedeutung der Mehrsprachigkeit in den Identitätskonzepten von Migrant(inn)en". In *Streitfall Zweisprachigkeit [The Bilingualism Controversy]*, edited by Ingrid Gogolin and Ursula Neumann, 233–248. Wiesbaden: Verlag für Sozialwissenschaften.

Kultusministerium Baden-Württemberg. 2004. "Bildungsplan 2004". http://www.bildung-staerkt-menschen.de/service/downloads/Bildungsplaene

Kultusministerkonferenz. 1996. Interkulturelle Bildung und Erziehung in der Schule Bericht der KMK vom 25.10.96. Bonn: Sekretariat der Ständigen Konferenz der Kultusminister der Länder in der Bundesrepublik Deutschland.

Kultusministerkonferenz. 2008. Europabildung in der Schule: Beschluss der KMK vom 08.06.1978 in der Fassung vom 05.05.2008. Bonn: Sekretariat der Ständigen Konferenz der Kultusminister der Länder in der Bundesrepublik Deutschland.

Marshall, Harriet. 2009. "Educating the European Citizen in the Global Age: Engaging With the Post-National and Identifying a Research Agenda". *Journal of Curriculum Studies* 41: 247–267.

Michaels, Deborah L., and Doyle E. Stevick. 2009 "Europeanization in the 'Other' Europe: Writing the Nation Into 'Europe' Education in Slovakia and Estonia". *Journal of Curriculum Studies* 41: 225–245.

Nieto, Sonia. 1996. *Affirming Diversity: The Socio-political Content of Multicultural Education.* New York: Longman.

Organisation for Economic Cooperation and Development. 2006. "Where Immigrant Students Succeed: A Comparative Review of Performance and Engagement in PISA 2003". Paris: OECD.

Organisation for Economic Cooperation and Development. 2010. *Closing the Gap for Immigrant Students: Policies, Practice and Performance.* Paris: OECD.

Osler, Audrey. 1994. "Education for Development: Redefining Citizenship in a Pluralist Society". In *Development Education: Global Perspectives in the Curriculum*, edited by Audrey Osler, 32–49. London: Cassell.

Osler, Audrey, and Kerry Vincent. 2002. *Citizenship and the Challenge of Global Education*. Stoke-on-Trent: Trentham Books.

Paritätischer Gesamtverbund. 2010. Bildungschancen von Migrantinnen und Migranten: Fakten, Interpretationen, Schlussfolgerungen. Berlin: Paritätischer Gesamtverband.

Piper, Nicola. 1998. *Racism, Nationalism and Citizenship: Ethnic Minorities in Britain and Germany*. Aldershot: Ashgate.

Regierung des Landes Baden-Württemberg. 2006. "Schulgesetz für Baden-Württemberg". http://www.smv.bw.schule.de/Gesetze/schulgesetz.pdf

Schäfer, Thomas, and Gunter Brückner. 2008. "Soziale Homogenität der Bevölkerung bei alternativen Definitionen für Migration: Eine Analyse am Beispiel von Bildungsbeteiligung, Erwerbstätigkeit und Einkommen auf der Basis von Mikrozensusdaten". Wirtschaft und Statistik 12: 1046–1066.

Schiffauer, Werner, Gerd Baumann, Riva Kastoryano, and Steven Vertovec (Eds.). 2004. *Civil Enculturation: Nation-State, School and Ethnic Difference in Four European Countries*. Oxford: Berghahn Books.

Schissler, Hannah, and Yasemin N. Soysal. (Eds.). 2005. *The Nation, Europe and the World: Textbooks and Curricula in Transition*. Oxford: Berghahn Books.

Schulte, Axel. 1999. Demokratie als Leitbild einer multikulturellen Gesellschaft". In *Medien und multikulturelle Gesellschaft*, edited by Christoph Butterwege, Gudrun Hentges and Fatma Sarigöz, 187–206. Opladen: Leske and Budrich.

Senatsverwaltung für Bildung, Jugend und Sport Berlin. 2007a. Rahmenlehrplan für die Sekundarstufe 1: Sozialkunde. Berlin: Wissenschaft und Technik Verlag.

Senatsverwaltung für Bildung, Jugend und Sport Berlin. 2007b. Rahmenlehrplan Grundschule: Politische Bildung. Berlin: Wissenschaft und Technik Verlag.

Skrobanek, Jan. 2009. "Perceived Discrimination, Ethnic Identity and the (Re-) Ethnicization of Youth With a Turkish Ethnic Background in Germany". *Journal of Ethnic and Migration Studies* 35: 535–554.

Statistisches Bundesamt. 2009. Statistisches Jahrbuch. Wiesbaden: Statistisches Bundesamt.

Sultana, Ronald G. 1995. "A Uniting Europe, a Dividing Education?" *International Studies in Sociology of Education* 5: 115–44.

Thränhardt, Dietrich. 2008. Einbürgerung: Rahmenbedingungen, Motive und Perspektiven des Erwerbs der deutschen Staatsangehörigkeit. Bonn: Friedrich Ebert Stiftung.

Tulasiewicz, Witold. 1993. "The European Dimension and the National Curriculum". In *The Multicultural Dimension of the National Curriculum*, edited by Anna S. King and Michael J. Reiss, 240–258. London: Falmer.

Wallach Scott, J. 2007. *The Politics of the Veil*. Princeton: Princeton University Press.

Weil, Patrick. 2004. "Lifting the Veil". *French Politics, Culture and Society* 22: 142–149.

Wilhelm, Ronald W. 1998. "Issues in Multicultural Education". *The Curriculum Journal* 9: 227–246.

8 Multiculturalism, Education Practices and Colonial Legacies
The Canadian Case

Neil Guppy and Katherine Lyon

Ancestry, ethnicity and race are key dimensions of identity and experience in Canadian society. The vast majority of Canadians trace their ancestral roots, from two or three generations ago, to a wide array of other regions of the world. Three key social processes have contributed to this multiplicity of cultural identities: European colonization of First Nations peoples, linguistic and cultural inequality between the British and French founding charter groups, and high rates of in-migration from diverse source countries. While many nations have encountered similar cultural developments, no other country shares all three of these processes to the same degree as Canada. It is out of these overlapping struggles that a national approach to multiculturalism has arisen, often in unexpected and contentious ways, but always in response to political pressure from interest groups, changing political parties, new conceptions of diversity and variations in ethnic migration to Canada.

Schools play an important role in shaping our identities and allegiances. They help us to construct a sense of self. How our particular heritage is portrayed, or not, in the school curriculum is important to this process because the curriculum can either reflect or ignore, valorize or demonize, the groups with whom we identify and align. Schooling processes thus can help in constructing multiculturalism by influencing our own 'ethnic' identities, while simultaneously affecting how we think of other ethnicities. Unlike other Western nations, the Canadian education system is politically decentralized because education is a provincial rather than a federal responsibility. This structure influences the political processes through which federal government initiatives, such as multiculturalism, are integrated into educational mandates across the nation.

In this paper we review the rise of multiculturalism, discussing approaches to and criticisms of multicultural education in Canada. To measure the effectiveness of current educational approaches, we employ three different forms of evidence: changes in textbook content over time, the educational achievement rates of visible and non-visible minority students and the ethnic composition and classroom practices of teachers. While multiculturalism has led to important changes since its formal inception in 1971, we contend that the current multicultural framework in education still lacks a deep appreciation of the more structural and systemic aspects of racialized forms of inequality.

HISTORY OF MULTICULTURALISM

Despite Canada's international reputation as a model of cultural pluralism, Canadian history has been marked by extensive conflict and inequality among cultural groups. From European colonization until the middle of the twentieth century, forms of blatant discrimination supported an Anglocentric, assimilationist government agenda. Beginning in the 1600s, conflict erupted between British and French immigrants as they competed to colonize land inhabited by First Nations[1] peoples. After the British defeat of the French in 1759 on the Plains of Abraham, French territory was limited to what is now the Province of Quebec. In 1774, the Quebec Act was passed by the British, protecting and entrenching the French language, culture, religion and other institutions. The legal recognition of two languages and cultures in Canada set the grounds for continuing struggles between the two founding charter groups in a bilingual and bicultural nation.

Claiming the remaining territory as their own, the British took a strong assimilationist stance by devastating Aboriginal culture, languages and land access and creating legislation to permanently entrench their dominance (Hare 2007). In an act often considered cultural genocide, many Aboriginal communities were legally required to send their children to government-run residential schools. With multiple forms of abuse, child labor, minimal academic teaching and bans on the use of Aboriginal languages, these institutions were places of humiliation and cultural shaming for First Nations peoples.

Continued resistance from both the French and the First Nations led to the British creating some accommodative legislation. Although self-serving and stratifying, this legislation laid the groundwork for the recognition of multiple cultures and rights within one nation (Joshee and Winton 2007, 22). For example, to pacify First Nations and gain their favor against the French, the same Royal Proclamation (1763) that limited French territory also established the right to Aboriginal self-government and the principle of negotiating land ownership (Joshee and Winton 2007, 22; Hare 2007, 53–54). The 1876 Indian Act gave the government the power to "protect" and control Aboriginals while also granting First Nations peoples official status and formal rights. The British inadvertently generated a framework that First Nations would later draw upon to claim their special rights and their place in Canada as neither ethnic minorities nor members of the founding charter groups. In both cases the accommodations created frameworks for competing cultural claims, a fundamental prelude to the establishment of Canadian multiculturalism.

Canada also has a legacy of massive in-migration, first dominated by flows from Europe and then from Asia. Since the turn of the twentieth century, immigration has been crucial for population growth. With 19.8 percent of its total population foreign born, Canada is second only to Australia (22.2 percent) as the country with the most foreign-born citizens (Statistics Canada 2006). This immigration, though, is riddled with discrimination. Until the 1960s the government gave preferential treatment to white Americans, British and Northern Europeans while blatantly excluding immigrants from other source nations (Derwing and Munro 2007, 93–94). The 1910 Immigration Act gave the government freedom to arbitrarily select immigrants based on factors such as their perceived compatibility with the Canadian climate and the needs of the nation. By 1923 a formal list of desirable and undesirable source countries was in place.

The treatment of immigrants of Chinese descent is a particularly telling example of biased policies. Chinese immigrants were disenfranchised in 1875, exploited as laborers on the Canadian Pacific Railway in the late 1880s, targeted with a prohibitive head tax in 1885, and subjected to an exclusionary Chinese Immigration Act in 1923 (Chan 2007, 136). Only recently has Canadian multiculturalism policy led to formal apologies and financial compensation from the government for these actions.

A significant shift towards the current policy of multiculturalism occurred after World War II when ethnic diversity came to be seen more positively. For the first half of the century, cultural variation was perceived as a threat by the Anglo-Canadian majority (Fleras and Elliot 1992, 71). As a young nation Canada struggled with identity. Canadians began articulating a progressive conception of ethnic diversity, defining themselves in opposition to the intolerant Nazi regime and even the more assimilationist British and American approaches (Joshee and Winton 2007, 18–19). Collectively supporting the war effort as a nation, regardless of ethnic origin, also promoted a more accepting approach to cultural differences. The large inflow of Europeans after World War II further forced authorities to reconsider the stratification of immigrants (Fleras and Elliot 1992, 71).

In 1947 the Canadian Citizenship Act granted native-born Canadians and immigrants similar rights and legitimacy, further solidifying a collective Canadian identity marked by diversity. As multicultural sentiments increasingly resonated with an ethnically mixed population, cultural diversity became associated with the strength of the nation and the meaning of Canadian citizenship (Joshee and Winton 2007, 18, 23).

With a new conception of citizenship and legal grounds from which ethnic minority groups could oppose the status quo, the 1960s were a time of political unrest (Fleras and Elliot 1992, 71). Liberal Prime Minister Lester B. Pearson needed to respond. Most critical was the growing Québécois separatist nationalism arising from the power imbalance between French and English Canada (Fleras and Elliot 1992, 72; Forbes 2007, 30). In response to French Canadian protest, Pearson approved the Royal Commission on Bilingualism and Biculturalism in 1963 to explore the status of bilingualism and biculturalism between the two founding charter groups.

The commission reaffirmed the importance of equality between French and English Canada through a bicultural and bilingual framework. The 1969 Official Languages Act granted the two charter groups equal linguistic status within the federal government and public service (Forbes 2007, 31). However, the Act did not address the problem of the small number of French speakers in Western Canada and neglected the contributions of other ethnic groups, including more recent immigrants and First Nations (Fleras and Elliot 1992, 72). Dissatisfied with the emphasis on French and British language and culture, many ethnic minorities protested. In 1969, the final volume of the Royal Commission on Bilingualism and Biculturalism, "The Cultural Contribution of the Other Ethnic Groups", questioned the acceptability and equality of an exclusively bicultural and bilingual framework when Canada had a large and growing non-charter immigrant population.

In the international context of the Universal Declaration of Human Rights, the Civil Rights movement in the US, and the national disputes over bilingualism and biculturalism, Aboriginal people also began pressing for greater recognition. The key issues were Aboriginal identity, self-government, land rights and special status to negotiate with the Canadian government.

Facing pressure from French-Canadians, Aboriginals and the 'Other' ethnic groups, the Liberal Prime Minister Pierre Elliott Trudeau presented a policy of multiculturalism within a bilingual framework in 1971. Trudeau's vision was to retain English and French as the two official languages while promoting the status, history and rights of non-charter ethnic minorities (Fleras and Elliot 1992, 72). Canada became a nation with two national languages, supposedly no formally dominant culture and an ongoing negotiation of special status and rights to limited self-government for Aboriginals.

Early attempts at promoting multiculturalism focused on festivals, organizations and language classes in order to encourage cross-cultural sharing and the preservation of distinct cultures. Constructed with the needs of well-established ethnic minority groups in mind, Trudeau's multiculturalism mainly provided minorities with symbolic cultural preservation, recognition and legitimacy in relation to the French and British majority (Ley 2010, 196–197).

By the late 1970s a new points-based immigration system implemented in the 1960s had resulted in a further ethnic diversification of immigrants. The removal of the biased birthplace requirements resulted in a shift in major source countries, with immigrants from Asia becoming the largest group by the end of the twentieth century. With the growth of large numbers of new visible minority immigrants, multiculturalism needed revision because newer immigrants required adequate employment, housing and education in the face of systemic discrimination (Dewing and Leman 2006,

5). No longer solely an issue of culture and linguistics, race relations policies were designed to remove systematic barriers to fuller participation in Canadian society.

A permanent anti-racist multicultural framework was written into Section 27 of the Canadian Charter of Rights and Freedoms in 1982 (Dewing and Leman 2006, 5; Ley 2010). This legislative measure meant that Canadian courts had to consider Canada's multicultural past and present in their decision making. Section 15(1) of the Charter also guaranteed equal and fair treatment under the law, regardless of any socially significant status, including race, national or ethnic origin and religion among others. The next section, 15(2), further qualified that special measures may be necessary to help disadvantaged groups.

In 1988 Prime Minister Brian Mulroney's Progressive Conservative government produced the Multiculturalism Act, the first national multiculturalism law in the world. This Act was intended to strike a careful balance, advocating cultural preservation and intercultural understanding, while ensuring institutional change, the reduction of discriminatory barriers and full participation in Canadian society for all members (Dewing and Leman 2006, 7). The Employment Equity Act, first passed in 1986 and amended in 1995, also developed one of the strongest legal systems supporting minority rights. With the passage of these acts, multiculturalism was placed within the context of human rights and social justice.

FEDERAL MULTICULTURALISM AND PROVINCIAL EDUCATION

While multiculturalism was originally implemented at the federal level, education is a provincial responsibility. Since provinces are in charge of school districts, curricula, approval of textbooks, funding grants and teacher certification, federal involvement in education is indirect. In fact, Canada is the only Western nation without a national education policy or a federal office of education (Ghosh 2004, 545). The only exception to this is First Nations reserve education, which is federally controlled, and even here First Nations peoples are pushing for more educational autonomy (Hare 2007).

The Canadian provinces, each with unique ethnic composition, immigration rates and political leanings, differ in their implementation of federal multiculturalism. Provincial multicultural policies are complicated by the fact that the Multiculturalism Act of 1988 offers no specification regarding educational mandates. As a result, multicultural frameworks vary across the nation. Saskatchewan was quick to create a multicultural policy in 1974 (Dewing and Leman 2006, 12; Fleras and Elliot 1992, 80), Newfoundland and Labrador did not take an official position until 2008 (Human Resources, Labour and Employment 2008), while most provinces developed legislation during the 1980s. Ontario and British Columbia are noticeably more advanced in their institutionalization of multiculturalism, mainly because of their large immigrant populations (Ghosh 2004, 555).

Quebec, the only officially French province, has a particularly unique multicultural policy. Drawing upon an 'intercultural' rather than 'multicultural' framework, Quebec's legislation encourages recognition of and contact between culturally diverse groups, yet French is held as the dominant language and culture of the province (Fleras and Elliot 1992, 83). For example, Bill 101, which was passed in 1977, required all children to attend French schools unless they had parents who had been educated in English (Ghosh 2004, 557). French-Canadians are generally opposed to federal multiculturalism as it is seen to dilute their status to that of an 'Other' ethnic minority rather than a founding charter group. Fear for the survival of the French language in North America abounds, particularly with the exceedingly low Québécois birth rate and high numbers of allophone immigrants settling in the province.

COMPETING APPROACHES TO MULTICULTURAL EDUCATION

Much like multiculturalism itself, multicultural education is necessarily an imperfect and ongoing process. Its meaning is constantly renegotiated within the nation's collective consciousness through legal battles, public protests and media debates. In Quebec, for example, conflict erupted when a school board denied a Sikh student the right to carry the Kirpan, a small symbolic dagger, sewn inside his clothing. By 2006, the conflict had reached the Supreme Court of Canada which unanimously ruled that Sikh students had the constitutional right to carry this meaningful religious symbol. This case highlights the unclear relations between provincial and federal multicultural policies and legislation, as well as the complex balance between individual rights (to safety in this case) and group rights to religious freedom. New tests for multiculturalism will undoubtedly continue to arise, especially as more recent immigrants to Canada come with higher levels of commitment to more diverse religions.

Clearly, multiculturalism is politically contentious and open to continuous dispute. No definition or application of the term is accepted by all, especially in the classroom. Two contrasting perspectives on multicultural education reveal the objectives of different political interests in Canada. For the government, as codified in legal policy, education is one of many institutions responsible for ensuring not only that "cultural and racial diversity" is respected, but also that people's cultural heritage is "preserved, enhanced, and shared". In particular this means that education ought to help in guaranteeing the "full and equitable participation" of all citizens and their communities, with attention paid to the "elimination of any barrier to that participation" (quoted from the Canadian Multiculturalism Act 1988). This policy envisions acculturation, tolerance and cultural harmony but it falls well short of a model for assimilation in which everyone marches to the same drummer. Consensus is the implicit watchword of the Act; issues of conflict are marginalized. Nevertheless, diversity is clearly understood as an acceptable, legitimate political outcome.

Were it merely education that did the heavy lifting of promoting cultural tolerance and equitable participation, one might dismiss the Multiculturalism Act and this version of multicultural education as more rhetoric than reality. However, as noted above, other institutions pursue similar objectives, which are laid out most fundamentally as human rights protected by the Canadian Charter. Supporting the Charter are many other institutionalized policies and practices promoting multiculturalism (see Ley 2010) including employment equity, equal treatment before the law and gradual recognition of aboriginal land claims and self-government. It is within this larger context that multicultural education must be understood.

A more radicalized version of multicultural education, promoted especially by progressive educators leaning more to the political left, understands the former perspective as too embedded in a liberal rhetoric of "equality of opportunity", and thus insufficiently attuned to issues of unequal power among groups and particularly blind to issues of racism, discrimination and exploitation. Indeed the practices and policies stemming from the Multiculturalism Act are seen from this angle as anemic panderings failing to address the root causes of inequality and exploitation. From this perspective the slippage to a language of culture, away from a language of race, has permitted an approach that stresses "cultural richness" while making invisible "racial discrimination". Furthermore, a more radicalized version of multicultural education resists the sequestering of ancestry, ethnicity and race into a special compartment, and instead insists on a variety of intersecting bases for inequality (including gender, religion, sexual orientation and disability). A broader social justice motif is envisioned. The "equality of opportunity" form of multicultural education examines "richness", promotes tolerance and encourages participation, while a multicultural education program informed by anti-racist ideals examines "discrimination" and seeks broader social justice.

In our judgment the first model of multicultural education meshes more closely with what actually occurs in most Canadian classrooms. It is not that issues of race and discrimination are ignored, but these topics are certainly not as central to the curriculum as those promoting an anti-racist agenda would like them to be. In what follows we use the term multicultural education to signify mainly the first of the two perspectives outlined above.

MULTICULTURALISM IN THE CURRICULUM AND IN TEACHING PRACTICE

To begin this section of the paper we first explore criticisms of multicultural education—how is it found wanting? After reviewing these criticisms, we turn to empirical evidence to assess the viability of multicultural education as we have defined it and as we see it practiced in most Canadian classrooms.

Multicultural education is frequently criticized as merely "additive" or "tacked on". Rather than starting from scratch and infusing multicultural issues into a newly revitalized curriculum, the claim is that multiculturalism has been added at the margins, worked into the old approach where opportunities permit. Sensoy et al. (2010, 4) maintain that "content about particular ethnic or racial groups is added to (without changing the structure of) the existing school curriculum". The implication is that issues of ancestry, diversity, ethnicity, human rights and race are excluded from the "mainstream curriculum" (ibid.).

A second and quite different criticism of multicultural education is that it celebrates rather than challenges diversity. By celebrating cultural diversity multicultural education is thus accused of fomenting the containment and marginalization of essentialized ethnic identity (Bissoondath 1994). First, by celebrating multicultural fragments, ethnic identity is made into a master status identity but not one that all members of any ethnic group necessarily share. Cultural groups (e.g., Irish-Canadians) come to be understood as internally homogeneous and static, lacking internal diversity and hybridity. Second, this celebrating of assumed homogeneous clusters eclipses issues of discrimination and marginalization that people face. Schick and St. Denis (2005, 296) argue that in schooling "the rhetoric of multiculturalism is enacted as a symbol of the 'good' nation" . . . with a "narrative of the nation as raceless, benevolent, and innocent . . .". In particular they argue that the school curriculum will always be insufficient in promoting social equality unless it challenges students and teachers to examine "how and why race matters". Third, cultural diversity places an emphasis upon difference, stressing what separates groups while making invisible the cultural practices that are shared both within and across diverse groups. In Willinsky's (1999) language this approach stresses what divides us, not what unites us.

Third, multicultural education also stands accused of two contrasting sins: either forgetting the foundational origins of Canada, in its European, and especially British and French, heritage (e.g., Granatstein 2007), or of neglecting the diversity of new Canadians and ignoring the First Nations peoples who were colonized by the French and British (e.g., Schick and St. Denis 2005). On this score the content of the school curriculum is found wanting in two opposing ways. From one angle, schooling is now too focused upon diversity, thereby valorizing group-rights, ethnic identities and cultural practices that effectively make European roots less visible and hence fragment the nation. As Granatstein (2007, 97) argues, we teach everyone's history, except Canada's. From an opposing angle schooling is seen to retain a Eurocentric bias in which the dominion of the British and the French remains privileged. Furthermore, even when ethnic diversity and cultural difference are made visible, this is done only superficially while the systemic inequality associated with these differences is eclipsed (e.g., Schick and St. Denis 2005).

A related concern is that multicultural education downplays content and focuses overdue attention on process. By using progressive, child-centered schooling, students are made to "feel good about themselves", to the detriment of content (Granatstein 2007, 35–36; Sensoy et al. 2010). Here the notion of celebration is again central. Making students feel welcome, whatever their dress, dance or dining preferences, is highlighted in ways that make the ethnocultural struggles and conflicts of history less central to schooling. At least this is the claim.

A fourth criticism of multicultural education is that only the knowledge of privileged groups is found in the curriculum. This criticism addresses not just who defines knowledge, textbook authors and government bureaucrats for example, but also who are the authorities that disseminate this knowledge in classrooms. To the extent that administrators, authors and teachers, the main definers of official school knowledge, come from dominant ethnic or racial groups, then this validates their kind of knowledge and makes it difficult for students to see the legitimacy of the authoritative understandings of others.

In reading the research literature pertinent to these criticisms, however, the observation of Mansfield and Kehoe (1994, 418) remains germane: "most of these contentions are speculative and unsubstantiated". Furthermore, the claims may have been germane to some early incarnations of multicultural education, but current practice has moved well beyond them. As Ley (2010, 196) argues, in "Canada today multicultural policy is only indirectly concerned with the maintenance of old-world cultures". Furthermore multicultural education critics often point to visible minorities being "overrepresented in the criminal system" or facing "penalties . . . in the labour market", as though the school system ought to be held solely accountable for these outcomes (Kirova 2008, 103). Misplaced criticism and specious evidence are often evident in critical assessments of multicultural education.

Given these critiques, we provide three windows through which to assess multicultural education. First, we do a close reading of textbooks used in British Columbia (and elsewhere) to ascertain how they represent issues of ancestry, diversity, ethnicity, human rights and race. Second, we present evidence on the relative school achievement of members of different ancestral, ethnic and racial groups on the basis that differential achievement would be possible grounds for believing that the school system did not accommodate everyone relatively equally. Third, we examine the viewpoints and procedures of teachers to examine whether or not they engage in practices that promote multicultural education. These different measures allow us to consider three distinct yet equally important aspects of multiculturalism.

Textbooks: The Politics of Representation

One way to evaluate multicultural education is to examine the historical record as represented by the texts that are approved for classroom use.

Texts are a powerful cultural product since they "reinforc[e] certain ways of thinking and de-legitimat[e] others" (Bickmore 2006, 360). In the 1960s, as the Biculturalism and Bilingualism commission was underway at the federal level, at the provincial level the Ontario Human Rights Commission funded a study to assess school textbooks. The Commission had received complaints from members of the public about the portrayal of specific groups. In promoting the study, William Davis, then Ontario Minister of Education, stated:

> We are about to make a thorough examination of all school textbooks, not just for the purpose of removing material which may be offensive to any of the groups which make up our multi-national family, but more important, to make sure that our textbooks do contain the type of material which does full justice to the contributions of many peoples to the development of our Province and Nation. (McDiarmid and Pratt 1971, vii)

The commission study was undertaken by two university scholars, Garnet McDiarmid and David Pratt (1971). Their aptly titled book, *Teaching Prejudice*, was based on a careful examination of 143 English- and French-language texts used in Social Studies (e.g., History, Geography, Civics). Most of the texts were published in the 1950s and 1960s. McDiarmid and Pratt (1971, 45) concluded that students were "most likely to encounter in textbooks devoted Christians, great Jews, hardworking immigrants, infidel Moslems, primitive Negroes, and savage Indians". These adjectives reflected the evaluative terms most commonly associated with the six groups they examined. Christians, Jews and immigrants were much more favorably presented than were Muslims, Blacks and Aboriginal peoples. Indians were sometimes portrayed as "friendly" but in combination, adjectives like "savage", "fierce", or "hostile" were more common. Clearly school textbooks contained material offensive to members of the negatively stereotyped groups and to others.

Using a smaller sample of textbooks, we assessed how the early findings of McDiarmid and Pratt compare to the material that students are reading in recent years. We identified 14 textbooks recommended for use in Grade 12 History, Grade 11 Civics and Grade 11 Social Studies in the province of British Columbia (the vast majority of these books are used in many other provinces as well). Using an approach similar to McDiarmid and Pratt's we then sought to identify "evaluative assertions"—that is, claims that are judgmental, invoking emotive terms.

The findings are dramatic. The kinds of evaluative assertions found in McDiarmid and Pratt are virtually absent in modern texts. In contrast to their findings of "Indians" making "savage raids" or being called "savages" or described as acting "hostile", Table 8.1 shows a representative slice of the types of statements made in contemporary texts. There is very

Table 8.1   Representative Comments About First Nations/Aboriginal Peoples in
Ministry of Education Recommended Textbooks in British Columbia

Text	Sentence	Page
Canada: A Nation Unfolding	"There treaties stripped Natives of title to most of the fertile land of the southern Prairies"	81
	" . . . severe restrictions were placed on Native people by the Indian Act"	89
	"In recent years, [Native peoples] have become increasingly militant in order to assert their rights"	412
Canadian by Conviction	"Canada's Aboriginal peoples developed a series of unique governmental systems"	18
	"Many studies have shown that Aboriginal people are more likely to be arrested than are Whites"	147
Canadian History	"North American societies were examined in the context of European values and were dismissed as primitive"	44
	" . . . some recent historians have pointed out that the criticisms and negative comments made about Aboriginal peoples could easily have been applied to Europeans living at the same time"	82

*A full listing of the textbooks reviewed is presented in an appendix.

little in modern texts that is overtly offensive, that casts negative aspersions on any particular group. Below we review some of the reasons why this change has occurred.

To reinforce their overall findings, McDiarmid and Pratt (1971, 55–86) also examined "critical incidents" that texts might have omitted because of their "sensitive" nature, particularly where this might reflect poorly on "those who colonized North America". Here they found that issues of French–English relations were reasonably well covered, including the conscription crisis of World War I, but on eight of the other nine critical issues they examined, they concluded that the historical treatment was "unsatisfactory" (and "borderline" on the ninth).

We chose to focus on three of the eleven issues they highlighted, seeking representation across issues. The first was treatment of First Nations peoples in Canada, and especially the issues of self-government and land claims. The second was the internment of Japanese Canadians in World War II, many of whom had been born in Canada, but were nonetheless removed from the Pacific coast and relocated elsewhere in Canada. The third was the use of conscription by the Government of Canada to recruit soldiers in World War I, a practice that was particularly opposed among French Canadians.

Table 8.2   Treatment of Three "Critical" Historical Incidents in Canada in Nine Different Textbooks Used in British Columbia

Book Title & Date	First Nations	Japanese Internment	Conscription WWI
1 *Canada: A Nation Unfolding,* 1994	Good	Good	Good
2 *Canada: Face of a Nation,* 2000	Good	Good	Fair
3 *Canada Today,* 1979	Poor to fair	No Mention	Fair to Good
4 *Canada Today 2nd edition,* 1988	Fair	Good	Fair to Good
5 *Civics Today,* 2000	Good	No Mention	Poor
6 *Canadian by Conviction,* 2000	Good	No Mention	No Mention
7 *Canadian Citizenship in Action,* 1992	Good	Good	No Mention
8 *Canadian History,* 2003	Good	Fair	Poor to fair
9 *Civics: Participating in a Democratic Society,* 2000	Fair to good	No Mention	Poor

*Some of the fourteen books we reviewed were organized in ways that meant these issues would not have been covered (e.g., more focus on world or comparative issues). Poor, fair and good were measured on a simple ordinal scale in relation to what McDiarmid and Pratt offered as the "gold standard."

We followed McDiarmid and Pratt in using their renditions of these critical issues as the touchstone for establishing the accepted facts (1971, 55–86). In judging how modern textbooks fared, we assessed the presentation of each critical incident along four dimensions: validity (accuracy), comprehensiveness (major points addressed), balance (nuanced, inclusive) and concreteness (specificity not platitudes). Good ratings came when texts met all four of these criteria and poor ratings when the texts failed adequately to meet any of these criteria.

In comparison to the findings of McDiarmid and Pratt, attention to both First Nations peoples and the Japanese improved noticeably, while consideration of the conscription crisis deteriorated. Based on our small selection of both books and incidents, we need to interpret these results carefully but there is evidence here that issues of Aboriginal Canadians and of Asian Canadians have risen in prominence and improved in coverage while the focus on French–English tension was made less visible (although to some extent more contemporary issues are now discussed here; e.g., the use of the War Measures Act in 1970 to deal with a political crisis in Quebec). In an important sense, however, this rebalancing also represents an important historical shift from the 1960s to 2010, involving the rising centrality of non-French and non-English ethnic and ancestral issues. Further, there is little doubt that a sampling of textbooks from British Columbia, Canada's most westerly province, presents a different picture from that found in texts from Quebec.

A second important theme that emerges in studying current textbooks is a concerted attempt to move beyond difference to include aspects of similarity, as well. In large part this is accomplished by examining multiple cases as illustrations of larger issues. For example, students might be asked to compare and contrast the Declaration of the Rights of Indigenous People (UN 2007) to the Universal Declaration of Human Rights (UN 1948; as in *Civics Today*, 2003). Or alternatively, students might be asked whether or not the freedoms of the Canadian Charter should be equally applicable to people who enter Canada illegally, to people who arrive here by boat from foreign shores and to people who are born outside of Canada but to Canadian parents. Here discussions of sense of belonging, nationhood, human rights and global citizens all can potentially converge (see also Shields, 2000). In ways that belie some of the critics of multicultural education, many of the presentations in textbooks have moved beyond portrayals of a single cultural heritage (e.g., traditional foods and fashions of the Chinese), to examining challenging debates that cross multiple lines of ancestry, ethnicity and race (e.g., debating policy initiatives aimed at reducing discrimination; as in *Canada Today*, 1988).

These changes have come about because a variety of interest groups have insisted that students should be presented with accurate and challenging information. Textbooks are now subject to close reviews at various levels, including Ministries of Education and textbook publishers. As an illustration, Gage published *Canada: Face of a Nation* in 2000 and used four consultants (including Ed Swain of the Métis National Council) and twelve reviewers (including seven students). The same is true for *Canadian History: Patterns and Transformations,* published in 2003 by Irwin Publishing, which used five consultants (including Zubeda Vahed, a race relations expert with the Peel School Board) and eight reviewers. Review processes do not guarantee unbiased representation of issues, but the checks and balances of teachers, parents, social movements (e.g., the Canada Race Relations Foundation) and students help to minimize the unbridled distortion that was clearly evident in McDiarmid and Pratt's *Teaching Prejudice.*

In Provincial Ministries of Education, guidelines for the approval of textbooks for classroom use are now pro forma and are relatively similar in all provinces. The following is from the Ontario Ministry of Education (2008, 7):

Bias
The content must be free from racial, ethnocultural, religious, regional, gender-related, or age-related bias; bias based on disability, sexual orientation, socioeconomic background, occupation, political affiliation, or membership in a specific group; and bias by omission. The material should present more than one point of view, and be free from

discriminatory, exclusionary, or inappropriately value-laden language, photographs, and illustrations.

This approach shows an awareness of the complexity of textbook content by paying attention to the problematic elements of representation and lack of representation in both text and images. A more radical mandate may also require the inclusion of texts from a diversity of authors and regions, in order to allow students access to multiple worldviews and experiences. The current framework focuses mainly on ensuring that existing mainstream publishers and authors (likely from dominant cultural groups) work to be "inclusive" in their writing.

School Achievement

A second method of examining the effectiveness of the school system, especially as it pertains to how schools deal with students of culturally different backgrounds, is to examine scholastic achievement. "Equitable participation", as outlined above, ought to mean that one's ethnocultural background would make no difference to scholastic achievement. Conversely, if achievement varied by ancestral, ethnic or racial background that would be *prima facie* evidence of barriers to learning that required elimination (i.e., contravening the Act).

We first compare educational test scores of children born to Canadian parents with the scores of children whose parents were born outside of Canada. Evidence that multicultural education was failing would be found if the children of immigrant parents were less successful at schooling. This evidence would be especially troubling if children born to parents whose ethnic origin was neither French nor English were less successful. Worswick (2004) has compared test results on three dimensions—vocabulary, reading and mathematics—for children of Canadian and foreign-born parents. Table 8.3 shows that in vocabulary tests children of Canadian-born parents do better than children born to either Francophone or Anglophone immigrant parents (100.45 vs. 98.9), and they do much better than the children of allophone immigrant parents (100.45 vs. 88.8). These scores are for children in kindergarten and Grade 1. On tests of reading and mathematics ability, where children are in Grade 2 or above, differences are not as drastic, but the children of allophone parents still fall slightly behind in reading. Worswick concluded,

> There is evidence of lower performance early in the school system by the children of immigrant parents. This is especially true for the case of parents having mother tongues other than English or French and for the case where the family has recently arrived in Canada. However, these children are found to have performance that is comparable to that of children of the Canadian-born by age fourteen. (Worswick 2004, 76)

Table 8.3   Average Test Scores of School-Aged Canadians, by Parents'
Immigration Status

Test Score Categories	Children of Canadian-born Parents	Children of Anglophone or Francophone Immigrant Parents	Children of Allophone^ Immigrant Parents
Vocabulary	100.45	98.9	88.8*
Reading	100.07	103.2	97.0
Mathematics	99.86	101.2	100.3

^ Allophone parents list neither English nor French as their mother tongue.
*The difference in vocabulary scores between children of allophone parents and both other groups is very unlikely to be due to chance (p < .01).
Source: Worswick (2004, 57).

The equalization of skills by the teenage years is an exceedingly important result in that it demonstrates the education system is doing a remarkable job in enhancing the abilities of young immigrant students. On this evidence Canadian schools are providing test results that augur well for the notion that multiculturalism ought "to promote the full and equitable participation" of all.

A second form of evidence comes from examining university degree attainment for young people from different ancestral and ethnic backgrounds. Table 8.4 shows that on average young visible minority people exceed young whites in the attainment of university degrees—29.6 percent versus 23.7 percent. Second, the experiences among visible minority groups are very different, with over 40 percent of Asians having a university degree. In sharp contrast,

Table 8.4   Percentage of Canadians Between Ages 25 and 34 with a University
Degree, by Visible Minority Status, 2001 Canadian Census

Visible Minority Status	Percentage with a University Degree
Aboriginal	6.2
Asian*	41.0
Black	18.3
Hispanic	18.8
Other Visible Minority	33.9
Subtotal (visible minorities)	29.6
White	23.7

*Asian includes East, Southeast and South Asians.
Source: Frenette (2005).

only 6.2 percent of Aboriginal people have a university degree. Among both blacks and Hispanics, about 18 percent have university degrees.

Again the politics of education intervenes because these attainment measures can be interpreted, from one perspective, as irrelevant to certain objectives of multicultural education. If by multicultural education one wants to see political reform to the societal processes of discrimination, racism and exploitation, then success in mathematics and reading is at best secondary. On the other hand, such an outcome makes it very hard to argue that systematic discrimination against visible minorities occurs in school testing. There is some evidence, however, that on fostering tolerance of, and respect for, diversity, the school system is not doing a very good job of meeting objectives (Peck, Sears and Donaldson 2008). However, other evidence suggests that at least in comparison to students in Belgium, Canadian youth show higher levels of multicultural tolerance (Harell 2010).

Conversely, if multicultural education is examined in the context of providing fair opportunity for all young people, then the attainment results shown above are markers of success that demonstrate a school system that is beneficial for students from diverse backgrounds, save for First Nations, and to a much lesser extent Blacks and Hispanics. Certainly schools ought to be expected to help with ameliorating societal ills such as discrimination and exploitation, but that is only one among many ways of measuring the success of multicultural education.

Teachers and Teaching

A final window through which to examine multicultural education is to ask about teachers and their practices. First, diversity among teachers is valuable for a variety of reasons. Teachers are role models and diversity among role models demonstrates compliance with the Multiculturalism Act and with Employment Equity legislation. Furthermore, a diversity of ethnocultural backgrounds in the teaching workforce helps to ensure a richer tapestry of cultural knowledge and experience, increases teachers' likelihood of relating to the diversity of students in their classes (Banks 2001), and often provides a point of more comfortable initial contact between parents and teachers (e.g., someone who might better understand a family's cultural concerns). Second, teaching practices are also important as instances of how multicultural education is implemented. We provide some evidence on both of these issues.

Teaching Labor Force

As Table 8.5 highlights, the proportion of teachers who are visible minorities (6.9 percent in 2006) is significantly below the proportion of the Canadian population that has visible minority ancestry (16.2 percent).[2] Furthermore although the doubling rate among visible minority teachers is greater than for the Canadian population, which is a positive outcome with respect to

Table 8.5　Visible Minority Members in Canadian Population and in Teaching Labor Force*

Canada	% Visible Minority	
	Teaching Labor Force	General Population
2001	5.4	13.4
2006	6.9	16.2
Doubling Rate	14.4	18.3

*Adapted from Ryan, Pollock and Antonelli (2009,598); teaching labor force includes elementary and secondary teachers as well as school counselors. The doubling rate shows the estimated duration, in years, for the numbers to double.

representation, the proportions will not equalize for many decades given current doubling rates. As well, we also know that teaching lags behind many other professions in accommodating visible minority members. For example, in Ontario in 2001 7.4 percent of teachers and 11.6 percent of the general population were visible minorities (Ryan, Pollock and Antonelli 2009, 598), while 9.2 percent of lawyers, 15.2 percent of university professors, 25.9 percent of physicians and 27.3 percent of engineers were members of visible minorities (Ornstein 2004, 14).

This trend means that the Canadian teaching work force will not completely represent the visible minority population for the foreseeable future, unless visible minority teachers are to be recruited from elsewhere. And here again politics intervenes, because one viable solution to rebalancing the teaching labor force would be to hire teachers who have been trained abroad. However, Canada does a poor job of employing people with teacher training credentials and experience who migrate to Canada, many of whom are visible minority members (Ryan et al. 2009, 603–605). The lack of credential recognition is the key political obstacle in implementing a more diverse workforce.

Beyond the teaching workforce is the issue of what teachers actually do in the classroom. We begin here with a brief review of recent research by Frohard-Dourlent (2010). She completed 35 interviews with teachers in Canada (N = 15) and France (N = 20), asking about how the topic of cultural diversity was addressed in the classroom. Her results show that in Canada there is a much greater awareness of cultural diversity which promotes more attention to this issue in teaching practice. Frohard-Dourlent notes that Canadian teachers were more comfortable addressing diversity, had received some professional development training in dealing with diversity, could give concrete illustrations about how they addressed diversity in the classroom and were very aware of government policy related to diversity. While aspects of 'celebration' were high on the list of 'multiculturalism in practice', which is not too surprising given that these were students in Grades 1 through 7, racism and multicultural challenges were not totally ignored. In contrast French teachers lacked the common vocabulary that Canadian teachers easily adopted, and French teachers had fewer concrete examples about addressing diversity in the classroom, reported less previous training around diversity, and were not as informed about clear policy guidelines related to cultural diversity.

However, when issues of language ability intersect with diverse student needs, as with students who are recent immigrant ELLs (English language learners), Canadian secondary teachers are often not prepared or willing to assist these students effectively (Pappamihiel 2007, 43). In particular, teachers do not feel that they are responsible for teaching necessary literacy skills or restructuring their lesson plans to account for the learning styles of students who are in the process of learning English (Gunderson 2000). While many teachers respect and celebrate abstract and symbolic diversity, accounting for and responding to practical language differences in classroom learning are not adequately addressed.

Finally we want to return to the criticism that multicultural education downplays content and focuses undue attention on process, using progressive, child-centered schooling (see previous). As Frohard-Dourlent (2010) observed, and as Sensoy et al. (2010) lament, in Canadian classrooms there is still the recognition of diverse religious holidays, the display of cultural artifacts from around the world and the singing of songs from various regions of the globe. Part of schooling is this celebration of diverse world cultures, but increasingly there is emphasis, too, on intercultural communication and conflict resolution, both of which tie in directly to multicultural education.

Bickmore (2006) recently reviewed the Grades 1–10 curriculum in Manitoba, Ontario and Nova Scotia, examining "representations of social conflict". Among the prominent themes was an emphasis on "students' development of skills and inclinations for civil interpersonal communication and co-operation" (ibid., 366) as well as on "appreciation for diversity, and conflict management/avoidance" (ibid., 365). In conclusion she argued that there was "considerable space for teachers . . . to use these curricula in relatively conservative or relatively transformative ways" (Bickmore 2006, 381).Once again, teaching practices must be considered in order to understand how this content is applied and interpreted in the classroom.

Finally there is the issue of teacher training. To what extent are Canadian teachers prepared for discussion and debate regarding multicultural education? Frohard-Dourlent noted that most of the Canadian teachers she interviewed reported some professional development regarding cultural diversity. Dunn, Kirova, Cooley and Ogilvie (2009) reported that intercultural inquiry was incorporated in various teacher education courses they examined. Nevertheless, the training could be in more depth, needs to be sensitive to pockets of resistance among some new teachers, and requires as much work in actual field experiences in culturally diverse settings as is possible. For thoroughly engrained biases, assumptions and privileges to be recognized, challenged and used to inform constructive pedagogical approaches, more than a single course or training session is required (Pappamihiel 2007, 44).

CONCLUSION

Our purpose has been to examine provincially mandated education within the context of federal multiculturalism. Importantly, historical legislation has shaped the political climate in which multiculturalism has developed and been practiced in Canada. Early political decisions framed important accommodations between the British and the French, and then the Federal Government and First Nations peoples. These accommodations mandated a more inclusive diversity than that which has occurred in many other modern nations. Although Canadians and their governments have not always been quick to promote diversity, the school system has been one institutional sphere in which gradual, if uneven, policies and practices of ancestral, ethnic and racial inclusion have taken hold.

Given this historical backdrop, we considered multicultural education policies and practices to assess how issues of cultural diversity have been dealt with in Canadian schools. Our findings show promising results but suggest that further changes to the conception and implementation of multicultural education are necessary. Today's textbooks represent ethnic groups in a much less stereotypical manner than they did decades earlier. More comparisons and contrasts of issues of diversity are featured and much less prejudice and pejorative framing now exist in the official school curriculum. Measures of academic achievement also suggest that the education system is performing well in its quest to provide visible minority students equal access to skills in core subjects and to promote post-secondary education. In this case, however, inequalities *among* visible minority groups remain significant, especially the disadvantages experienced by First Nations peoples. Finally, the ethnic composition of the teaching labor force lags behind that of the general population and many other professions. Although in cross-national perspective Canadian teachers seem better trained to manage classroom diversity than other teachers, more diversity among teachers and more thorough training programs are needed.

While a variety of approaches to multicultural education exist across the nation, most fall within the more conservative framework of cultural preservation and equitable participation. This emphasis downplays current conflicts and inequalities. There can be little doubt that the curriculum stresses issues of multiculturalism that resonate with difference and diversity more so than with issues of power and privilege. However, it would be wrong to suggest that teachers or textbooks ignore uncomfortable questions about inequality and discrimination. A more radical educational approach could recognize and deal with systemic racism and discrimination as ongoing barriers to equality of outcome.

NOTES

1. "First Nations" refers to Indigenous or Aboriginal Canadians (terms we use interchangeably). First Nations, which is used in preference to Indians almost invariably now, was coined by an Aboriginal chief. The term refers to the ancestors of the original inhabitants of what is now Canada. The widespread use of this term illustrates an important transition in cultural awareness among Canadians. The term "Indian" originated with Christopher Columbus and his mistaken belief that he had discovered the Antilles off the coast of India. Hence we have the term Indian since Europeans referred to the people of South and South East Asia as Indies.

2. Ryan et al. (2009) used the "general population" including all age groups. An age-adjusted comparison (because most teachers are over the age of 25) would reveal a closer fit between the two groups than the table shows. This is because in 2006, the visible minority population was younger (38.1 percent under 25) than the non-visible minority population (30.0 percent under 25). The comparison of the teaching labour force with the *general* population is thus distorting in this case.

REFERENCES

Banks, James A. 2001. "Citizenship Education and Diversity: Implications for Teacher Education". *Journal of Teacher Education* 52(1): 5–16.

Bickmore, Kathy. 2006. "Democratic Social Cohesion (Assimilation)? Representations of Social Conflict in Canadian Public School Curriculum". *Canadian Journal of Education* 29(2): 359–386.

Bissoondath, Neil. 1994. *Selling Illusions: The Cult of Multiculturalism in Canada*. Toronto: Penguin.

Canadian Multiculturalism Act. 1988 [date of Royal Ascent]. http://laws.justice.gc.ca/en/C-18.7/index.html

Chan, Adrienne S. 2007. "Race-Based Policies in Canada: Education and Social Context". In *Multicultural Education Policies in Canada and the United States*, edited by Reva Joshee and Lauri Johnson, 131–145. Vancouver: UBC Press.

Derwing, Tracy M., and Murray J. Monro. 2007. "Canadian Policies on Immigrant Language Education". In *Multicultural Education Policies in Canada and the United States*, edited by Reva Joshee and Lauri Johnson, 93–106. Vancouver: UBC Press.

Dewing, Michael, and Mark Leman. 2006. "Canadian Multiculturalism". Current Issue Review—Parliamentary Research Branch, Library of Parliament Research Publications. (93–6E). http://www2.parl.gc.ca/content/lop/researchpublications/936-e.htm

Dunn, William, Anna Kirova, Miriam Cooley, and Greg Ogilvie. 2009. "Fostering Intercultural Inquiry in Subject-Area Curriculum Courses". *Canadian Journal of Education* 32(3): 533–557.

Fleras, Augie, and Jean L. Elliot. 1992. *Multiculturalism in Canada*. Scarborough: Nelson Canada.

Forbes, Hugh D. 2007. "Trudeau as the First Theorist of Canadian Multiculturalism". In *Multiculturalism and the Canadian Constitution*, edited by Stephen Tierney, 27–42. Vancouver: UBC Press.

Frenette, Marc. 2005. *Is Post-Secondary Access More Equitable in Canada or the United States?* Ottawa: Statistics Canada, Analytical Studies Branch, Catalogue no. 11F0019MIE No. 244.

Frohard-Dourlent, Hélène. 2010. "Once You Win Their Hearts and Minds, What Are You Gonna Do With It?" Master's dissertation, University of British Columbia.

Ghosh, Ratna. 2004. Public Education and Multicultural Policy in Canada: The Special Case of Quebec. *International Review of Education* 50 (5–6): 543–566.

Granatstein, Jack. 2007. *Who Killed Canadian History?* Toronto: HarperCollins.

Gunderson, Lee. 2000. "Voices of the Teenage Diasporas". *Journal of Adolescent and Adult Literacy* 43: 692–706.

Hare, Jane. 2007. "First Nations Education Policy in Canada: Building Capacity for Change and Control". In *Multicultural Education Policies in Canada and the United States*, edited by Reva Joshee and Lauri Johnson, 51–68. Vancouver: UBC Press.

Harell, Allison. 2010. "The Limits of Tolerance in Diverse Societies: Hate Speech and Political Tolerance Norms Among Youth". *Canadian Journal of Political Science* 43(2): 407–432.

Human Resources, Labour and Employment. June 3, 2008. *Government Announces Provincial Policy on Multiculturalism.* http://www.releases.gov.nl.ca/releases/2008/hrle/0603n05.htm

Joshee, Reva. 2004. "Citizenship and Multicultural Education in Canada: From Assimilation to Social Cohesion". In *Diversity and Citizenship Education: Global Perspectives*, edited by James A. Banks, 127–156. San Francisco: Jossey-Bass.

Joshee, Reva, and Susan Winton. 2007. "Past Crossings: US Influences on the Development of Canadian Multicultural Education Policy". In *Multicultural Education Policies in Canada and the United States*, edited by Reva Joshee and Lauri Johnson, 17–27. Vancouver: UBC Press.

Kirova, Anna. 2008. "Critical and Emerging Discources in Multicultural Education Literature: A Review." *Canadian Ethnic Studies* 40 (1): 101–124.

Ley, David. 2010. "Multiculturalism: A Canadian Defence". In *The Multiculturalism Backlash: European Discourses, Policies and Practices*, edited by Steven Vertovec and Susanne Wessendorf, 190–206. London: Routledge.

Mansfield, Earl, and John Kehoe. 1994. "A Critical Examination of Anti-Racist Education". *Canadian Journal of Education* 19(4): 418–430.

McDevitt, Daniel, Augus Scully and Carl Smith. 1988. Canada Today (2nd edition). Scarborough: Prentice Hall (original work published in 1979).

McDiarmid, Garnet, and David Pratt. 1971. *Teaching Prejudice: A Content Analysis of Social Studies Textbooks Authorized for Use in Ontario*. Toronto: Ontario Institute for Studies in Education.

Ontario Ministry of Education. 2008. "Guidelines for Approval of Textbooks". http://www.curriculum.org/occ/trillium/Textbook_Guide_English_2008.pdf

Ornstein, Michael. 2004. *The Changing Face of the Ontario Legal Profession, 1971–2001*. A Report to the Law Society of Upper Canada.

Pappamihiel, Eleni. 2007. "Helping Preservice Content-Area Teachers Relate to English Language Learners: An Investigation of Attitudes and Beliefs". *TEFL Canada Journal/Revue TESL Du Canada* 24(2): 42–59.

Peck, Carla L., Alan Sears, and Shanell Donaldson. 2008. "Unreached and Unreasonable: Curriculum Standards and Children's Understanding of Ethnic Diversity in Canada". *Curriculum Inquiry* 38(1): 63–92.

Ryan, James, Katina Pollock, and Fab Antonelli. 2009. "Teacher Diversity in Canada: Leaky Pipelines, Bottlenecks, and Glass Ceilings". *Canadian Journal of Education* 32(3): 591–617.

Schick, Carol, and Verna St. Denis. 2005. "Troubling National Discourses in Anti-Racist Curricular Planning". *Canadian Journal of Education* 28(3): 295–317.

Sensoy, Ozlem, Raj Sanghera, Geetu Parmar, Nisha Parhar, Lianne Nosyk, and Monica Anderson. 2010. "Moving Beyond Dance, Dress, and Dining in Multicultural Canada". *International Journal of Multicultural Education* 12(1): 1–15.

Shields, Carolyn M. 2000. "Learning from Difference: Considerations for Schools as Communities". *Curriculum Inquiry* 30: 275–294.

Statistics Canada. 2006. "2006 Census of Canada Census Analysis Findings: Immigration in Canada: A Portrait of the Foreign-Born Population, 2006 Census: Driver of Population Growth". Last modified November 20, 2009. http://www12.statcan.ca/census-recensement/2006/as-sa/97-557/p3-eng.cfm
Watt, Jennifer, Ivor Sinfield, and Charles Hawkes. 2000. *Civics Today*. Toronto: Irwin Publishing.
Willinsky, John. 1999. "Curriculum, After Culture, Race, Nation". *Discourse: Studies in the Cultural Politics of Education* 20(1): 89–112.
Worswick, Christopher. 2004. "Adaptation and Inequality: Children of Immigrants in Canadian Schools". *Canadian Journal of Economics* 37(1): 53–77.

APPENDIX

List of Recommended Texts Reviewed (British Columbia)

History 12

DeMarco, Neil. 1987. *The World This Century*. London: Unwin Hyman.
Quinlan, Dan. 2003. *Twentieth Century Viewpoints* (2nd edition). Don Mills: Oxford University Press.

Civic Studies 11

Brune, Nick, and Mark Bulgutch. 2000. *Canadian By Conviction: Asserting our Citizenship*. Toronto: Gage Publishing.
Fretts, Derald, Pamela Perry-Globa, Martin Spiegelman, and Reginald Stuart. 1992. *Canadian Citizenship in Action*. Edmonton/Regina: Weigl Publishers.
Ruypers, John, Marion Austin, Patrick Carter, and Terry Murphy. 2005. *Canadian and World Politics*. Toronto: Emond Montgomery Publications.
Skeoch, Alan, Peter Flaherty, and Lynn Moore. 2000. *Civics: Participating in a Democratic Society*. Toronto: McGraw-Hill Ryerson.
Watt, Jennifer, Ivor Sinfield, and Charles Hawkes. 2000. *Civics Today*. Toronto: Irwin Publishing.

Social Studies 11

Bolotta, Angelo, Charles Hawkes, Fred Jarman, Marc Keirstead, and Jennifer Watt. 2000. *Canada Face of a Nation*. Scarborough: Gage Publishing.
Cranny, Michael, and Garvin Moles. 2001. *Counterpoints: Exploring Canadian Issues*. Toronto: Prentice Hall.
Fielding, John, and Rosemary Evans. 2001. *Canada: Our Century, Our Story*. Scarborough: Nelson Thomson Learning.
Francis, Daniel. 1998. *Canadian Issues: A Contemporary Perspective*. Toronto: Oxford University Press.
Hundley, Ian, Michael Magarrey, Rosemary Evans, and Brian O'Sullivan. 2003. *Canadian History: Patterns and Transformations*. Toronto: Irwin Publishing.
McDevitt, Daniel, Angus Scully, and Carl Smith. 1988 *Canada Today* (2nd edition). Scarborough: Prentice Hall. (Original work published 1979)
Newman, Garfield, and Diane Eaton. 2000. *Canada: A Nation Unfolding*. Toronto: McGraw-Hill Ryerson.

9 Educational Politics and Cultural Diversity in Greece

Gitsa Kontogiannopoulou-Polydorides

This chapter is concerned with educational policy and practice with a commitment to a view of education which promotes respect of difference and social justice. The emphasis on multiculturalism as a perspective of viewing Greek education is relevant and timely because:

(a) the education system serves mainly a monocultural school practice (see, for example, May 1999b, 1);
(b) the country and the nation have for a long time been considered homogeneous;
(c) there is an influx of immigrants and refugees in the last forty years, intensified since the beginning of the 1990s;
(d) intercultural education has been introduced as an institutional framework for curriculum policy making;
(e) education practice regarding differences adheres to an oversimplified view of how social power relations affect the lives of minority students (May 1999b, 2); and
(f) recent educational policies are in the midst of contested politics and economic crisis bearing immediate effects on combating discrimination against minority students.

Multiculturalism, in line with what Young terms as voice discourses (see next), answers the knowledge-socializing divide by privileging (a) the socialization of youngsters in their own community culture, and (b) the educational provision which privileges local knowledge and experience.

In the Greek context, education has been geared to the transmission of knowledge aligned to the traditional divisions among disciplines. The socialization function until the '70s has been centering on discipline and national identity building based on the continuity of the nation and Orthodox Christianity. The prevailing notion about which knowledge is worth teaching the young followed the encyclopedic tradition of Germany and France of the late nineteenth and early twentieth centuries. This is of no surprise since the education system has been intentionally designed having the respective education systems as models.

The importance of knowledge geared to specific, well established traditional subjects has been intensified by a multiplicity of structural patterns coupled by discourses which support and are intensified by such patterns (established in a number of cases, e.g., Kontogiannopoulou-Polydorides et al. 2009). To name a few: (a) unemployment of scientists (including humanities) and their channeling to secondary teaching posts; (b) expansion of cramming schools (*frontistiria*) on the basic-important school subjects, catering for the majority of students at the upper secondary level; (c) further channeling of unemployed scientists to serve as teachers in *frontistiria* across the country.

In this context, there are a number of practices missing in Greece, a fact rendering multiculturalism in education as difficult at the moment. For it is realistic to assert that a multicultural turn would require: (a) a fundamental change in the ethnocentric discourse; (b) most certainly, a change in the prevailing discourse on what education is about; and (c) a change in the structures and interests related to an extensive segment of the labor market. So, the quest for a multicultural dimension as required by the fundamental rights and real life experiences of youngsters living in the country is constrained by the above structures, interests and discourses.

The approach taken in this paper addresses multicultural issues drawing from perspectives which (a) respect difference and the rights of multicultural groups and individuals, and at the same time accept the universality of the republic (Matustik 1993, 21); (b) do not align with what Young terms as "voice discourses" (Young 2008, 4–5) in the sense that the "implication of 'voice discourses' approaches is a relativism". Furthermore, Young argues: "The voice discourse position . . . does not distinguish between knowledge and experience and gives equal validity to the perspectives of all groups, whether expert or not . . ." (Young 2008, 8–9).

Finally, Young suggests that a way of overcoming current difficulties is by providing "grounds for: avoiding both the a-historical givenness of neoconservative traditionalism and a reliance on such notions such as relevance . . . ; maintaining an autonomy for the curriculum from the instrumentalism of economic or political demands; . . ." (Young 2008, 34).

For the purposes of this paper, I accept the concerns set forth by multiculturalism, while at the same time I support that there is a need for an extensive examination—grounded on scientific work and dialogue—of the question 'which knowledge is worth' in a way involving the above guidelines set forth by Young. In what follows I present three cases of conflict and educational politics in Greece which indicate the lack and the urgent need for the type of analysis pointed out by Young as important for school knowledge. The choice of a variety of theoretical works as the backdrop is based on the analytic tools they offer in the examination of the issues at hand. So, my analysis makes use of the theoretical work of Matustik (1993 on Habermas), May (1999a, 1999b), Coulby (2006), Bradley (1996), Arnove (2008) and Cascardi (1992).

The three issues that will be presented in this chapter have emerged fairly recently in the Greek political arena:

1. Curriculum politics and the education of migrant children in mainstream schools;
2. International politics and segregation in Thrace; and
3. The debate on the subject of history.

It has been well established that Greece was never a completely homogeneous society as ethnocentric discourse has argued for a long time (Frangoudaki and Dragonas 1997). Furthermore, in recent years, there has been an influx of people coming from other countries of the world (Embirikos at al. 2001; Tsitselinis and Christopoulos 1997). In summary, there has been a movement of population since the 1970s including repatriation of Greeks from Germany, Eastern Europe, the US, Canada, Australia and South Africa. In the 1980s this has been intensified and reached a peak after the changes in the former USSR and Eastern Europe. Many Greeks from Albania entered the country and kept coming in until about 2005. At the same time there has been an influx of immigrants and refugees from Asia and Africa. As a result, since 1991 immigrants in Greece have undergone a sharp increase from about 300,000 to 1.2 million people (Pavlou 2007, 2).

The Greek State has introduced policies to deal with the education of both repatriate children as well as migrant children in a specific law introduced in 1996 under the pressure of EU guidelines and local situations (see Liddicoat and Diaz 2008, examining the quite similar Italian case).

CURRICULUM POLITICS AND THE EDUCATION OF MIGRANT CHILDREN IN MAINSTREAM SCHOOLS: THE CASE OF THE 132ND ELEMENTARY SCHOOL

The case of the 132nd elementary school is an example of the influence of politics in education, especially concerning issues such as the concept of the "other" that is often perceived as a threat to national identity and social homogeneity.

The 132nd elementary school is located in the centre of Athens and constitutes one example of a school with multicultural characteristics. According to the school principal (1999–2007), Stella Protonotariou, 72 percent of the students that attended the school were immigrants, originating from 11 different countries. According to the principal, when she was appointed to the school, the situation was quite difficult, meaning that the school had students coming from various ethnic origins, while the majority of the students—of indigenous as well as immigrant origin—came from vulnerable social groups and had minimum familial support. The parents of the immigrant students had almost no participation in the school, mainly due to their difficulty in speaking the Greek language. The parents of the Greek students were particularly skeptical towards the school, as their children were proportionally a minority, a fact that was constantly evaluated in a negative way. As a result, according to the principal, serious problems emerged in the school, including tension among the parents as well as the students. The school's teachers, within this context, were unable to come up with solutions that could promote communication among students and ensure a working learning environment for everyone (*Eleftherotipia* 2010).

The school principal attempted to "implement" an educational program supported by the Ministry of Education in the context of the Olympic Games of Athens (2004) and allowed teaching immigrant students their native language in the school premises. The school's classrooms were used for this purpose, and teachers were assigned to teach immigrant students their native languages, mainly Albanian. At the same time, programs for learning Greek were organized for the parents, aiming at overcoming the language barriers and to facilitate communication between parents and teachers. This was envisaged so that immigrant parents, too, could take part in school life; their inability to speak Greek was perceived to be a major hindrance in participating, making existing difficulties more acute.

In the context of promoting intercultural communication, the school's council of teachers decided to replace the morning prayer with a poem, so that the majority of the students, who were not Orthodox Christians, would be able to participate in a way not compromising their religious identity. The results of the initiatives undertaken were very positive within the school, and highlighted the importance of actions that promoted an honest dialogue/interaction among cultures without political expediency. According to the school principal, the results were positive not only for the students, but their parents and the teachers, too, at many levels. More specifically, the students' self-esteem and self-respect seemed to have strengthened, the relationships with each other improved and phenomena of exclusion and marginalization were limited. That resulted to the reduction of student drop-out rate, and the reduction of violence and racist incidents among the children and among their parents. Immigrant students were integrated into school life in an easier way, while the achievement of those who took classes in their native language was improved (*I Avgi* 2010).

Furthermore, a 'parents association' was formed, and parents of both Greek and immigrant students were participating and cooperating on an equal basis. The parents developed relationships with each other, as well as with the teachers, they communicated with the school for advice and they supported the school's activities by participating. Moreover, according to the principal, the teachers gained knowledge and methodological tools to manage the diversity of the student population in a creative way, and to communicate effectively with the parents (*I Avgi* 2010). Those positive results were welcomed by the majority of the educational community (including universities), and the school was considered a model of intercultural education.

The important role that politics play in education cannot be disputed; especially regarding issues that are considered sensitive and are related to the imaginary construction of the nation-state, where the presence of the "other" is perceived as a threat to national identity and social homogeneity. The subsequent decision to remove the principal and her prosecution as well as the teacher's who taught the Albanian language, constitute one grave example of the influence that xenophobic groups can exert on politics, and the resulting political action that can follow from such pressure.

The debate between the deputy minister of education at the time and the opposition spokesperson, right after the school principal had been removed and transferred to another school, is very revealing. The government (of the conservative party), through the Minister of Education, pointed out that the important issue was not that the principal's initiatives were effective, and promoted intercultural interaction and the integration of immigrant students. On the contrary, what was of greater importance was the implementation of the law, strictly to the letter. Thus, under pressure from right wing xenophobic groups, a decision was taken to discontinue all related activities and intercultural practices. As the opposition spokesperson in charge of education, pointed out later on, the state has functioned as an inspector in charge of the control of the educational process by enforcing discipline rather than encourage the teachers' initiatives and deal with the problems in an institutional way. The opposition spokesperson went on to strongly suggest that the role of politics was to create contexts, not to inspect the rules (according to the discussion held in the Parliament on June 16, 2008 regarding the 132nd elementary school)

The previously-mentioned initiatives in the 132nd elementary school were interrupted in 2007 with the appointment of a new principal. The new principal denounced the former principal, because, as he stated, the initiatives undertaken constituted dereliction of duty. He also filed a report against the former principal, pointing out that the material used for teaching the Albanian students their native language and civilization were anti-Greek and part of propaganda for the creation of problems in the relations between the two countries (*Vima* 2009). In a report drawn up by the Office of the Ombudsman regarding this issue, it is mentioned that after talking to the new principal, *"it was made obvious that his appointment to this school was accompanied by oral instructions by his superiors regarding managing the specific school unit, with the aim to suspend all previous additional activities considered 'illegitimate/improper'"*.

The official position of the Minister of Education appeared neutral, arguing for the state's responsibility to enforce the law and prevent teacher "arbitrary" actions. Eventually, the former principal and the teacher of the Albanian language stood trial on January 22, 2010. After a period of fierce reactions by the educational (and university) community and part of the political world for this prosecution, the two teachers were acquitted. This case ended by reinstating the school principal to her previous position. It is obvious though that of great importance for the vindication of the teachers was the massive publicity that the issue received rather than the realization that such practices did not pose a threat to national identity and social homogeneity. It is also necessary to point that while these events were unfolding there were elections in the fall of 2009 which resulted in a new government led by the socialist party which may have contributed in shaping the course of events.

It is important to stress that the political conflict and arguments were plenty. What was not very clear in the process is the development on the part of the scientific community of educators and teachers of arguments and an explicit dialogue on curriculum content and educational practices within a multicultural society. So, the principal and the teachers involved were glorified and/or punished more as politically correct citizens or as dissidents or even as rebels, rather than knowledgeable and active professionals dealing with what is their everyday professional circumstances and duties. This is in line with the findings of the analysis by Lerner (2008) of how new global habitus and educational approaches and practices exist in parallel with major old approaches and practices in current educational circumstances. Furthermore, it is in line with what Arnove (2008, 112) terms the revival of conservatism manifested through "patriotic-nationalist commitment" and traditional values identified in recent education changes in Eastern Europe.

INTERNATIONAL POLITICS AND SEGREGATION IN THRACE

Education for the minority in Thrace constitutes the most unique example of the influence of politics on education in the Greek social and educational context, as it is mainly determined by the changes or fluctuations of Greek–Turkish relations. In short, the Thrace Muslim minority constitutes the only officially recognized minority in Greece and its education is ruled by specific laws that derive from international conventions (Treaty of Lausanne 1923). The Muslim minority children have the option of enrolling in either minority schools (that apply to minority children only) or mainstream Greek schools, teaching Greek and Christian issues. The large percentage of the Muslim minority attend the minority schools through elementary school (Cummins 2000, 9). Minority schools have a bilingual curriculum: some subjects are taught in the Greek and some in the Turkish language (Cummins 2000, 9). However, there exist many problems that surface quite often, for example: "textbooks prepared by the Turkish government have been rejected by the Greek government . . . while textbooks prepared by the Greek government in the early 1990's were burnt" by the (Turkish origin community of the) Muslim minority (Cummins 2000, 9). Furthermore, the divided curriculum, the insufficient preparation of teachers and the lack of knowledge on how to teach Greek as a second language, usually leads to poor educational results. Apart from that, as it is pointed out, the deeper reasons for the problems regarding education for the minority are connected with its political dimension (Askouni 2006, 13–14).

More specifically, education for the minority depends mainly on the progress of Greek–Turkish relations. The Turkish ethnic identity of most of the people in the minority, and the Turkish governments' policies, have contributed to the conception of the minority as a "national threat" (for the Greek state) and led to the decision to marginalize the minority as a control policy. Thus, education constituted an ideological mechanism for exercising influence from the Turkish part towards the minority, while at the same time, the Greek side tried to limit the Turkish influence and the threat they thought it represented. In any case, it is clear that the political dimension was the main issue that drove the educational agenda, and not the actual educational needs of the minority (Askouni 2006, 14).

A characteristic of the minority is its diversity with regards to language and ethnic background. Thus, the minority is constituted by Turks speaking the Turkish language, which is the majority group, Pomaks who speak a Slavonic language and Roma, part of which speak Romani (Askouni 2006, 34).

The religious or ethnic definition of the minority constitutes a major field of political controversy between the Greek and the Turkish states. The Turkish side tries to emphasize the characteristics of the minority which, according to them, constitute a unified and solid group ascribing to them ethnic attributes. Apart from, for example, the common religion of the minority, it is stressed that the biggest part of the population speaks Turkish. On the other hand, the different ethnic interests of the Greek side, as they are perceived, lead to different arguments that aim at highlighting the ethnic and linguistic diversity of the minority and therefore the deconstruction of common identity. The Pomaks are an interesting example, as they are "claimed" by three states: Greece, Turkey and Bulgaria. So, Bulgarians consider Pomaks as Muslim Bulgarians, the Turks consider them descendants of Turkish tribes established in the Balkans, and in Greek bibliography they appear to be mainly descendants of Thracian tribes. All three cases have in common the effort to impose on the Pomaks an ethnic identity to serve their "national" interests (Askouni 2006, 35–36).

Until the beginning of the 1990s, the Thrace minority, identified as Turkish, was treated with a policy of isolation, discrimination and violation of civic and political rights that had completely opposite results to the ones pursued by the Greek side, meaning the formulation from the part of the minority of a collective conscience. The change in the Greek policy led to significant interventions in the field of education, through an extensive educational program for educating Muslim children. In the context of this program and as a result of the change in policy, a comprehensive intervention in minority education was attempted that aimed at removing discrimination towards the minority and promoted equal rights in practice. Thus, among other things, new school textbooks were written that corresponded to the specific educational needs of a population with limited knowledge of the Greek language. Multilevel initiatives for the limitation of school drop-outs were also developed aiming at enhancing minority children's actual ability to continue school beyond primary education (Askouni 2006).

A very important axis of this intervention concerned teacher education in order to make them capable to cope with the particular social and educational context of the minority. As it is mentioned in the bibliography, the work that the teachers have to do in school environments, where the students come from lower socioeconomic groups and the language of the minority is not their native language, is very demanding. Teachers need, through intensive training, to obtain the skills necessary to help them deconstruct concepts of the "other" in the context of nation-state, so that these concepts do not develop in discrimination practices at school level (Bartolome 2010). The case of the Greek teachers of the minority was the exact opposite until recently, as the people in charge did not care for the difficulties the teachers faced, difficulties that mainly derived from the fact that the majority of the students spoke another language. And that was not accidental, as the main aim was not to educate minority children or teach the Greek language but political control (Askouni 2006, 97). The opportunity to educate teachers in the context of the program education for Muslim children derives from the change of policy from the Greek side at the central state level.

In this case, the discussion on the education of Muslim children in Thrace, with the noticeable exception of the work in the Programme for the Education of the Muslim Minority at the University of Athens, is highly political, involving the international as well as the local political arena. The issue has not so much generated a public dialogue regarding the education provided as it has generated a debate about the national identity of the communities involved. The minority's position and its relation to the majority group can be understood only in the context highlighted earlier regarding the special political dimension of the issue. The developments in this case indicate that the way social subjects define themselves is not one-way and stable on the basis of certain characteristics such as language, but is connected to the actual and symbolic value that these characteristics acquire in the sociopolitical context (Askouni 2006, 38). On the one hand, ethnicity is not just a natural category: instead, it is socially constructed, while boundaries and membership are negotiated (Shimahara 2001, 2). On the other hand, ethnicity, more often than not, is coupled by material disadvantage and social class positioning which magnifies inequality (Bradley 1996, 143–144). As it is argued, the structural conditions of national society viewed in terms of institutional arrangements constitute one of the most important conditions influencing the formation, development, decline and assimilation of ethnic groups and communities (Shimahara 2001, 2).

Thus, these groups' social success or failure is not entirely determined by their cultural orientations, but we have to illuminate their positions in the structural conditions of society at the local and national level. The developments in Thrace indicate that although sensitivity to cultural orientations is very important, it is the economic and political conditions of society to which attention must be given if one is to gain insight into the dynamics of ethnicity (Shimahara 2001, 2). According to the critical theory of the concept of race (and ethnicity), it is argued that the importance of historical context and contingency has to be recognized in the framing of racial categories and the social construction of racially defined experiences. Thus, such a theory must apply to contemporary politics, across historical time and in an increasingly global context in order to examine the interrelation of race and or ethnicity with social developments (see, for example, Omi and Winant 2005, 7).

THE DEBATE ON THE SUBJECT OF HISTORY

The History Book in 2006

History teaching at school and the prescribed textbooks constitute an extreme example of the way politics and education interweave in some social contexts. The case of compiling a new history textbook for elementary school Grade 6, which was assigned to a team led by an Associate Professor at the Aristotelian University of Thessaloniki, merits attention in this context. The textbook was supposed to follow modern conventions about compiling a history textbook, the primary concern being to produce a history textbook that did not promote and reproduce ethnocentric and racist concepts; rather, it aimed to ease national passions and promote respect among people.

The criticism against the textbook, (when it was published in September 2006) was fierce and came from a variety of sources: the educational community, political forces in the conservative extreme of the political system, as well as the Greek Orthodox Church. At the same time, there was fierce criticism posted on many Internet sites. In these cases the team of authors—and mainly the head of the team—was practically accused of national treason. On the other hand, 500 university professors signed a text in which they expressed their support for the textbook and the team of authors (*Vima* 2008).

The authors of the textbook argued that the main aspects of the conflict were neither pedagogical nor historical. On the contrary, this issue was used by people who aimed at maintaining or acquiring electoral clientele, converting thus the educational field into a political party arena (*Kathimerini* 2007). In the majority of cases, the criticism was not based on principles of scientific research, but rather on a nationalistic fury. Moreover, the authors were accused, even by members of the university community, of "an attempt to deconstruct the nation, the national state and national identity" (*Eleftherotypia* 2009, cutting and mending history) and to mitigate the Ottoman yoke, undermining the events of the Greek revolution and the actions of the Greek leaders (*Kathimerini* 2007).

The author of the textbook, responding to these accusations later, pointed out that her aim was not to question national identity, but to point out that there was not one unchangeable, closed and phobic national identity. National identity changes over time. The call (for writing the textbook) was addressing an open identity, which did not exclude the citizen identity, and did not see the right of immigrants to acquire citizenship as a danger towards national identity (Repousi 2010). A sentence in the textbook about "crowding" of the Greeks at the port of Smyrna, part of the description of the Asia Minor Catastrophe, a historical event deeply imprinted into national collective memory, constituted one of the references which caused a nationalistic outbreak which quickly spread to public opinion at the end of 2006. Thus, a peculiar debate started, among experts and non-experts regarding the role of history, as well as the "truths" and the "lies" of Greek historiography (*Eleftherotypia* 2010, replacement of the sinful textbook).

The leader of the team of authors, referring to the description of the events of Asia Minor Catastrophe, pointed out later that whoever tries to interpret these events discovers a different truth from the truth projected by the nationally correct rhetoric. Therefore, in the first case, truths about the Greek–Turkish war of the period 1919–1922, and interpret, without justification, massacres occurred by both sides emerge. On the other hand, in the context of the nationally correct version, interpretation of the phenomenon is not of interest; what is of interest are the misfortunes of the Greeks and the images of slaughtering, as a construction element of their national character. As the head of the team (Repousi 2009) mentions, all the truths that question this representation and reduce the victimization of the Greek world, are dismissed as nationally harmful and historically inaccurate.

The case of the sixth-grade history textbook constitutes perhaps the most extreme example of the mutual influence of politics and education, as this issue gained such impact that led to political decisions and developments. Thus, the Minister of Education (at the time) in order to soothe reactions decided (a) to amend the parts of the textbook that caused the rage of certain people and groups; and (b) to distribute a literary book to accompany the textbook; this literary book refers to the Asia Minor Catastrophe and has the characteristic title "land soaked in blood". Developments were not possible to slow down at that point, as this issue had received massive publicity. The Minister of Education was outvoted at the national elections that followed, and the new Minister of Education reinstated the previous history textbook, assigning the compilation of a new textbook to a new team of authors. The impact of these events to the political life was very intense. When the former Minister of Education was put in lead of the ballot of her political party for the European Parliament elections she was accused by extreme conservative forces and people were asked to vote her down (*Eleftherotypia* 2009, comment by G. Karatzaferis). The assertion was that the person in charge of defining government educational policy was considered the puppet of the group that was supposed to be in charge of applying that policy, a kind of reversed responsibility and authority. Even important personalities, who were considered to belong to the political and ideological Left, considered this textbook as an insult to national identity. Therefore, political and ideological views contrary to each other found a convergence point on the criticism.

The educational community at first had a positive attitude towards the textbook; however, the head of the team herself admitted that the gradual intensive reactions and all the rhetoric focusing on the danger for the deconstruction of national identity, as well as the fact that positioning in favor or against the textbook gained political characteristics, resulted in a climate gradually shifting against the textbook (Repousi 2010). Finally, it is important to note that criticism regarding the intervention of politics—as it was considered to be expressing the conservative views of the government at the time—was expressed for the new team of authors who were appointed to compile a new sixth-grade textbook (*Vima* 2008).

THE SUBJECT OF HISTORY IN 2010

A recent proposal focusing on the structure of the upper secondary school last fall (2009) has also caused fierce political reactions. The proposal was part of the so-called modernist reform of education put forward by the Socialist government (elected in office in 2009). The nature of the proposal seemed to shift towards a more European view on the subject of history; a major aspect of the change was that it converted the subject into an optional subject for Grades B and C at the upper secondary education level. It should be noted though, that the bill of this reform (as of November 2010) was not yet officially public, neither did it constitute an official proposal by the Ministry. The leaks alone, however, were enough to initiate a new cycle of conflict. The opposition member responsible for education rushed to characterize the alleged change as a sad phenomenon which aims at the abolition of Modern Greek history in upper secondary school, its transformation into an optional subject, as well as the so-called European orientation that is attempted. An extreme conservative political party spoke of a "total detachment from our roots as a people and as a nation" (*Kathimerini* 2010).

The discussion was passionate, the Ministry of Education presented that there is no such plan, and one professor at a high post resigned for personal reasons. The discussion centered on the same topics as in the previous conflict regarding the history textbook of the sixth grade. The extent of the debate in the daily press, at a time when local government elections were at the centre of the political debate, brought to the fore the issue with almost the same fierce arguments as the Memorandum of Understanding between Greece, the IMF and the EU regarding the current economic crisis in the country.

In this case, too, the issue was important to too many people. These people did not have an expert knowledge on the subject (as required in the scheme by Young). Matustik argues that nationalism "wins over those anomic, fragmented individuals who, having emerged from the processes of societal modernization without resisting the oppositional politics of identity and difference via radical self-choice, become susceptible to manipulative misuse by political elites" (Matustik 1993, 21). There were two university professors, nevertheless, who presented in the daily press arguments about the need for a concrete scientific and sober exchange of arguments by the experts concerning what history at school should entail. But to no avail. In this case, too, the politics concerning educational matters are strong in a way leading to oversimplified rhetoric which does not allow for a debate and a dialogue regarding major issues about the scope of knowledge at school in a way even faintly approaching the argument by Young presented in the beginning of this chapter.

CONCLUSION

The three issues presented previously and the related events can be reviewed in a number of ways. The following choice presents two alternatives, not necessarily mutually exclusive, focusing on current as well as past arguments regarding characteristics of modernity and Greece's positioning. In his excellent analysis Axelos wrote back in the 1950s that contemporary Greece is thought of as promoting ethnocentrism in the sense that Greece is considered as a centre with many but unclear assertions—answers to the question: the center of what? (Axelos 2010, 21–22).

He then moved on to juxtapose the argument that perhaps Greece is not modern in the sense that it adopts and tries to absorb (western modern) processes and achievements while the people do not themselves create their own world (Axelos 2010, 19–20). Greece, nevertheless, functions in the centre of the modern world (Axelos 2010, 27–28), adopting what is created elsewhere.

If ethnocentrism is the issue, then right-wing politics are to this date taking advantage of an ideology, which they take good care to reproduce through educational (and other) conflicts, in a way which safeguards the constituency they need in order to perpetuate a stronghold in the political arena. In the course of doing that and in order to achieve the expected political gains the conservative right does not hesitate to destroy any process that stands in the way, including the much needed dialogue for educational content and, indeed, the education process itself.

If the positioning of Greece in modernity is the case, then we need to examine in such a context why the much needed dialogue in education is rendered inconsumerate. Axelos presents that modernity is established on active subjectivities, on self-consciousness which explains both the self and the world; the subject of modernity has a will of power to understand and change the world, to create its own world having instruments of thought and action those derived from philosophy (Kant, Hegel, Marx), science, politics and techniques (Axelos 2010, 16, 29–30).

In an excellent analysis of his own context (India) Chatterjee argues that the nation does not accept or reject in a wholesale way the (western modern) ideas, processes and techniques promoted in the modern era. Rather, the nation maintains, as much as possible, the cherished indigenous core practices regarding language, family, religion and culture and adopts the (western modern) techniques that have to do with everything else in life (Chatterjee 1993).

So, it is possible that there is a different way of dealing with the pending dialogue on education in Greece, something that needs to be investigated. Such an investigation might include a perspective of treating education as part of the (maintained indigenous) core practices and at the same time as part of the adopted (modern western) techniques. Let us acknowledge, nevertheless, that the missing dialogue (on education in the western modern world in the last thirty to forty years) as established by Young in the beginning of this chapter, and the one emerging as inconsumerate in Greece— cases presented here—do not have the same origins.

If, in addition, we observe the analysis of Axelos, we might find as a worthwhile option to conceptualize the potential and/or necessary dialogue in Greece as one having its roots in the core (essence in Axelos's wording) of Greek "creative (poetic meaning piitiki) thinking towards its realization" (Axelos 2010, 35). For it is reasonable to consider that such a dialogue needs to have characteristics of modernity: the actors need to be modern in the sense that "the becoming emerges from the being" (Axelos 2010, 29–30). Furthermore, in order for Greece to move in that direction, Greece needs to adopt "a movement not towards 'modernization' but towards 'modernity'" (Axelos 2010, 31).

In theory, what is at stake here is the choice between a postcolonial view (Chatterjee) and a modernity view geared to the Greek context (Axelos) as a *modus operandi* in an attempt to create and maintain a dialogue on education, a rather complicated issue, well beyond the scope of this chapter. The fact that a dialogue on education is missing in the western world relaxes the agony about the pending dialogue in Greece, without rendering any excuses acceptable.

REFERENCES

Arnove, Robert F. 2008. "Educational Reform Around the World: To What Ends?" In *The Production of Educational Knowledge in the Global Era*, edited by Judith Resnik, 109–120. Rotterdam: Sense Publishers.
Askouni, Nelly. 2006. *Education for the Minority in Thrace* (in Greek). Athens: Alexandria.
Axelos, Kostas. 2010. *The Fate of Contemporary Greece* (in Greek). Translated by Katerina

Chatterjee, Partha. 1993. *The Nation and its Fragments: Colonial and Postcolonial Histories.* Princeton: Princeton University Press.

Daskalaki. Athens: Nefeli. Originally published in French. 1954. "Le destin de la Grece moderne". In *Esprit*, July.

Bartolome, I. Lilia. 2010. "Daring to Infuse Ideology into Language-Teacher Education". In *Critical Multiculturalism: Theory and Praxis*, edited by Stephen May and Cristine E. Sleeter, 47–59. London and New York: Routledge.

Bradley, Harriet. 1996. *Fractured Identities: Changing Patterns of Inequality.* Malden, MA: Polity.

Cascardi, J. Anthony. 1992. *The Subject of Modernity.* Cambridge: Cambridge University Press.

"Comment by G. Karatzaferis" (in Greek). 2009. *Eleftherotypia*, May 18.

Coulby, David. 2006. "Intercultural Education: Theory and Practice". *Intercultural Education*, 17(3): 245–257.

Cummins, Jim. 2000. *Language, Power, and Pedagogy: Bilingual Children in the Crossfire.* Clevedon UK: Cambrian.

"Cutting and Mending History" (in Greek). 2009. *Eleftherotypia*, January 19.

Empirikos, Leonidas, Alexandra Ioannidou, Eleni Karantzola, Lambros Mpaltsiotis, Stamatis Beis, Tsitselikis Konstantinos, and Demetrious Christopoulos. 2001. *The Linguistic Diversity in Greece* (in Greek). Athens: Alexandria.

"Everybody is Dusting the History Textbook" (in Greek). 2007. *Kathimerini*, March 6.

"Fierce Reactions About History" (in Greek). 2010. *Kathimerini*, October 12.

"The Former Principal of the 132nd Elementary School in Grava Stella Protonotariou Stands Trial" (in Greek). 2009. *Vima*, June 12.

Frangoudaki, Anna, and Thalia Dragonas. 1997. *What is our Country: Ethnocentrism and Education* (in Greek). Athens: Alexandria.

"Intercultural Work gives our Children Values" (in Greek). 2010. *Eleftheortypia*, January 24.

Kontogiannopoulou-Polydorides, Gitsa, Maria Ntelikou and Christina Polydorides. 2009. "Country Case Study—Greece". In *Secondary School External Examination Systems—Reliability, Robustness and Resilience*, edited by Barend Vlaardingerbroek and Neil Taylor, 197–212. Amherst, New York: Cambria Press.

Lerner, Julia. 2008. "We Teach our Students to do Science Like in the West". In *The Production of Educational Knowledge in the Global Era*, edited by Julia Resnik, 187–213. Rotterdam: Sense Publishers.

Liddicoat, J. Anthony and Adriana Diaz. 2008. "Engaging With Diversity: The Construction of Policy for Intercultural Education in Italy". *Intercultural Education*, 19(2): 137–150.

Matustik, J. Martin. J. 1993. *Postnational Identity: Critical Theory and Existential Philosophy in Habermas, Kierkegaard, and Havel.* New York: The Guilford Press.

May, Stephen. 1999a. "Critical Multiculturalism and Cultural Difference". In *Critical Multiculturalism: Rethinking Multicultural and Antiracist Education*, edited by Stephen May, 11–41. London: Falmer.

May, Stephen. 1999b. "Introduction: Towards Critical Multiculturalism". In *Critical Multiculturalism: Rethinking Multicultural and Antiracist Education*, edited by Stephen May, 1–10. London: Falmer.

Omi, Michael, and Howard Winant. 2005. "The Theoretical Status of the Concept of Race". In *Race, Identity and Representation in Education*, edited by Cameron Mc Carthy, Warren Crichlow, Greg Dimitriadis and Nadine Dolby, 3–10. New York and London: Routledge.

Pavlou, Miltos. 2007. "Racism and Discrimination Against Immigrants and Minorities in Greece: The State of Play" Annual Report. HLHR-KEMO. http://www.hlhr.gr/hlhr-kemo/docs/hlhr-kemo_ar_2007.pdf

"The Phenomena of Violence and Racism Between Children and Parents Have Stopped" (in Greek). 2010. *I Avgi*, March 11.

"Replacement of the Sinful Textbook" (in Greek). 2010. *Eleftherotypia*, September 5.

Repousi, Maria. 2010. "Interview with Maria Repousi" (in Greek). From: http://www.nooz.gr/page.ashx?pid=9&cid=1&aid=1086620

Repousi, Maria. 2009. "The Version That is Considered 'Nationally Correct' Could Not Care Less for Interpreting the Phenomenon" (in Greek). *Kathimerini*, August 1.

Shimahara, N. Ken. 2001. "Introduction: Contemporary Constructions of Ethnicity and Race". In *Ethnicity, Race and Nationality in Education*, edited by Ken N. Shimahara, Ivan Z. Holowinsky and Saundra Tomlinson-Clarke, 1–14. New York: Routledge.

"They are Re-Writing History Towards a More 'National' View" (in Greek). 2008. *Vima*, June 1.

Tsitselikis, Konstantinos, and Demetrious Christopoulos. 1997. *The Minority Phenomenon in Greece* (in Greek). Athens: Kritiki.

Young, F. D. Michael. 2008. *Bringing Knowledge Back In: From Social Constructivism to Social Realism in the Sociology of Education*. London: Routledge.

10 An Ecological Approach to Understanding the Development of Racism in Schools
A Case-Study of a Belgian Secondary School

Peter Stevens

Since the late 1970s, educational researchers, in particular in the UK and the US, have given considerable attention to ethnic stereotyping and discrimination in schools. Most of these studies apply a social-constructivist approach and focus mainly on students' experiences of ethnic stereotyping and discrimination, teachers' stereotypes of ethnic minority students and the processes and effects of selection, the distribution of classroom resources and the nature of the knowledge and values taught and sanctioned in schools.

While educational research on ethnic stereotyping and discrimination focuses primarily on establishing if and how teachers and school processes are racist and discriminate against ethnic minority students, theories explaining the development of stereotypes are mainly derived from social psychology, with a strong focus on micro-sociological interactions between actors (for example, drawing on the contact hypothesis: Allport 1954). Despite the continued relevance of such theories, research in this area has been criticized for focusing almost exclusively on interactions between participants and for not measuring adequately or not investigating the importance of and interactions between larger institutions, social-processes and structures of inequality.

This chapter builds on these rich traditions of educational and sociopsychological research by exploring the usefulness of an ecological or embedded context approach in studying the development of racism in educational settings. Hence, instead of investigating the prevalence and nature of teachers' ethnic stereotypes and discriminating practices, this chapter explores the importance of and interactions between social characteristics and processes situated at different levels of analysis in developing teacher racism in schools. Furthermore, it focuses on teacher racism directed to

Turkish minority students in Flanders (Belgium), a group which has been relatively neglected in this field of enquiry.[1] First, this chapter integrates existing research on racism in schools by adopting an ecological or embedded context approach in studying the development ethnic stereotypes and discriminatory behavior by teachers. Secondly, the methods section briefly discusses the case-study research on which the analysis is based. Thirdly, the analysis section explores how interactions between students and teachers, characteristics of the school and the national education system interact with each other and influence teachers' stereotypes of Turkish minority students. A final section brings the findings together and discusses the implications of this study for future research on ethnic stereotyping in schools.

AN ECOLOGICAL APPROACH TO UNDERSTANDING THE DEVELOPMENT OF RACISM

A developing body of international research explores the importance of *face-to-face interactions* between young people, their teachers and parents to account for differences in expressions or perceptions of racism and discrimination. For example, Connolly shows that peer-group interactions in primary schools reinforce each other in developing specific stereotypes of Asian and African Caribbean pupils. Other studies point to interactions between parents and their children, teachers and students or interactions between teachers in developing ethnic stereotypes or experiences of racism and discrimination.

Some studies indicate the importance of *school and classroom characteristics* in researching racism and discrimination in schools. A large scale quantitative study in the Netherlands suggests that ethnic minority students experience less racism when classrooms are more mixed in terms of ethnicity and when teachers punish expressions of racism. Similarly, in his ethnographic study of an English secondary school Foster concluded that while the allocation of students to different schools might well operate in a discriminatory fashion, there was no evidence of teacher racism in this school, something that might in part be explained by the explicitly multicultural and anti-racist agenda of the school. Research in Flanders shows that students in lower status streams (vocational and technical education) have more negative views of ethnic minority students than their peers in higher status streams (general education).

Finally, a few studies emphasize characteristics of the *larger social and institutional environment* in which schools are embedded and interact with schools in developing ethnic stereotypes and discrimination in schools. Recent research in England suggests that students develop more negative attitudes to ethnic out-groups when their neighborhoods are characterized by competitive relationships between different ethnic groups over space and control in their area. Furthermore, other studies illustrate the importance of students' social and economic background, the influence of the educational market and international political relationships in understanding in-out group attitudes between students.

In highlighting the importance of particular institutional characteristics that are situated on different levels of analysis, these bodies of literature suggest the usefulness of employing an 'integrated' or 'ecological' approach in studying the expression and perception of ethnic stereotyping and discrimination in schools. This approach has its origins in developmental psychology and classifies environmental context measures according to the level in which they are situated. In line with such an approach, the different

Political/socioeconomic context
- International political relationships;
- National curriculum and evaluation mechanisms;
- Ethnic/racial mix and segregation neighborhood;
- (...)

School, family and peer-group characteristics
- School, family and peer-group cultures;
- Tracking system;
- Social composition school and peer-groups;
- Anti-racist and multicultural schoo;
- classroom policies;
- Socio-economic status family;
- (...)

Proximal school, family and peer-group processes
- Teacher-student interactions
- Student-student interactions
- Parent/caregiver-student interactions
- (...)

Teachers' mental frames of reference
- Preconceptions
- Motivations
- Attitudes
- Values
- Norms
- Knowledge
- (...)

Figure 10.1 Conceptual model of embedded institutional contexts.

institutional characteristics considered in the literature can be classified as 'political/socioeconomic institutional contexts' (national or local government school policies, ethnic/racial mix and segregation neighborhood), 'characteristics of institutions' (school mix and adoption of multicultural and anti-racist policies) and 'proximal school processes' (face-to-face interactions between students, their parents/caretakers and staff). These various institutional characteristics interact and inform *teachers' mental frames of reference*, which includes (racist) beliefs, perceptions, evaluative judgments, knowledge and attitudes. Based on the research literature, we can develop the following conceptual scheme in studying the expression and perception of ethnic stereotypes in schools:

This chapter builds on existing research in this area by exploring, through case-study research, the importance of and interactions between various social characteristics and processes situated at different levels of analysis in developing teacher racism in schools. More specifically, this study will investigate the relevance of (1) students' interactions with teachers, particularly students' strategies in response to perceived teacher racism and teachers' strategies in response to accusations of teacher racism; (2) school characteristics in terms of multicultural policies and ethnic composition of student and staff population; and (3) characteristics of the national educational system in Flanders, related to the way in which students are evaluated and policies towards multiculturalism. This study focuses on the development of teachers 'ethnic stereotypes' of Turkish minority students, which is a particular form of prejudice and defined as "an antipathy based upon a faulty and inflexible generalization".

METHODS

This chapter reports on ethnographic research carried out in one small Flemish (Belgian) secondary, multicultural school called *Riverside*[2]. *Riverside* is situated in a highly urbanized region and welcomes a substantial number of Turkish speaking minority students (15 percent of the students were of Turkish descent and 28 percent of non-native Flemish descent). The school offers technical and vocational programs (or tracks), which prepare students to find employment after finishing secondary education at the age of 18 or (in case of technical education) prepare students for specific, more applied forms of higher education. *Riverside* counts very few female students because the kinds of programs offered (mechanics, electricity, ICT) appeal more to boys than to girls.

We focus on one particular group of students (5VC) in *Riverside* and their deputy form-tutor, Mr. Gerrard. 5VC counted 18 students, all of whom were in their 5th year (out of six) of secondary education enrolled in a program 'Vocational Car Mechanics'. This group of students allowed for an 'extreme case analysis', as the average exam outcomes in this group were the lowest of the whole school. Furthermore, teachers considered this particular group as a very difficult group to teach and argued that there was overt racial hostility between Flemish and Turkish or Moroccan students. 5VC comprised nine Turkish students, six Flemish students, three Moroccan students and one Albanian student. Most of the students in 5VC shared a lower socioeconomic background and the average age of these students was well above what should be expected (17 years old) from their year-group.

Although the analysis focuses on data collected from students in 5VC and some of their teachers, this study investigates data collected from a larger sample of students and teachers in *Riverside*. Face-to-face, semi-structured (tape-recorded) interviews were analyzed from 11 teachers individually (9 male and 2 female) and 31 male students (16 Flemish and 15 non-EU) divided over 7 interview groups. Furthermore, over the course of one school year I observed, mainly as an 'observer as participant', 9 different tutor groups for three to four weeks each. Considering the sensitive nature of racism, I never mentioned to respondents in the field that I focused on issues related to teacher racism. Racism and discrimination were only discussed explicitly during student interviews.

The data analysis adopts a Grounded Theory approach, in which a substantive theory, related to a particular setting, is developed through mainly inductive analysis of qualitative data. The initial findings emerged from the analysis very much in line with Glaser's 'open coding' approach, in which the researcher did not rely on a specific set of questions in analyzing the data but rather relied on general 'coding families' or groups of concepts derived from reading relevant literature and following training as a social scientists.

RESULTS

The analysis will first investigate how teachers in *Riverside* perceived Turkish minority students. The second part of the analysis explores the potential role of various embedded contexts on the development of teachers' negative views of Turkish students.

Exploring Teachers' Attitudes to Turkish Students

In *Riverside*, structured interviews and informal conversations with teachers and administrative staff revealed strong, negative attitudes towards Turkish and Moroccan (both mainly Muslim) students. Turkish students in particular were often criticized for having low educational aspirations and not communicating in Dutch and for being lazy and arrogant or disrespectful towards teachers, particularly to female members of staff:

One of the secretaries claimed that both Turkish and Moroccan people don't respect women, "we are nothing to them!" She advised the newly appointed secretary to let her hair grow if she wanted to receive some more respect from them. (Field notes *Riverside*—staff room)

"On my way to the workshop of metal-working, I pass by a teacher who is sitting outside (. . .). He seems to be a senior teacher in electricity. When I ask if there are differences between native and Turkish and Moroccan students, he explains that "immigrant students" have a different, more negative attitude toward studying, they also cause more behavioral, discipline problems, apart from the language problems. Nevertheless, there are differences between the different immigrant groups, Moroccan people are *even more* lazy and hypocritical than Turkish people" (emphasis added). (Field notes *Riverside*—playground)

Not only did teachers attach such negative attributes to general categories like 'Turkish' or 'Moroccan' students, they also framed such views within a discourse of 'us against them' in which the ethnic out-group was expected but deliberately failed to adapt to the dominant in-group culture:

RESEARCHER: "And why don't they want to learn Dutch?"
MR. AGGER: "They just want to be Belgian to take advantage of the benefits of living in Belgium. That's why they want to be Belgian, but apart from that? That's it, the rest doesn't matter, they don't need that. They just need Belgium for the money, for luxury, and they think 'we are not going to adapt to you, you just adapt to us', and it starts to turn that way, slowly, we will have to adapt (. . .)."
(Teacher interview: White, male, Flemish senior teacher *Riverside*)

Teachers in *Riverside* not only criticized Turkish students for not *wanting* to speak Dutch and for being arrogant to (Flemish) teachers, they also criticized these students for somehow taking advantage of Flemish people and society. During fieldwork the researcher talked to at least 50 percent of all staff in *Riverside* and the vast majority explicitly subscribed to such views, with the other members of staff usually refraining from expressing their opinion. Although most members of staff expressed such views to the researcher in confidence or in a safe 'backstage' area where no ethnic minority students or less familiar colleagues were present, some teachers also expressed such views in the classroom in front of Turkish students:

Context: Mr. Gerrard is irritated because some Turkish pupils communicate in Turkish and ask the teacher to go slower, and to translate words in Dutch.

MR. GERRARD: 'If you think that Europe will become like Turkey . . . it won't happen!'

HAGI: 'Yes, but I want to copy . . . '

PEPSI: 'Yes, why do you always have to talk about Turkey!?!'

MR. GERRARD: 'Hagi is a Turk, isn't he?!'

HAGI: '(serious) No, I am Belgian!'

MR. GERRARD: 'You don't behave like a Belgian!'

HAGI: (Keeps on talking about his map and that he cannot follow the teacher.)

CIMI: (Says something in Turkish to Hagi.)

MR. GERRARD: (Angry because Cimi talks in Turkish.) 'Cimi, I've got a job for you . . . they need monkeys in the zoo of Antwerp!' (Field notes *Riverside*—5VC during theory lessons auto-mechanics in workshop)

While considerable research in education aims to identify if and how teachers or schools are racist to minority students, this study aims to develop explanations for observed racism of teachers. The following sections discuss the potential influence of various embedded, social contexts on the development of teachers' stereotypes of their Turkish students. In explaining teachers' stereotypes the analysis will adopt a top-down approach, starting with the influence of characteristics of the national (Flemish) educational system, and continuing with particular school characteristics and finally interactions between teachers and students.

Explaining Teachers' Attitudes to Turkish Minority Students

National Education Context

Teachers' Power to Evaluate Students

Secondary school teachers in Flanders have considerable power over students' educational careers as they are responsible for developing, administering and marking the final exams of their students, which have to be taken twice a year for every subject. Students in Flanders have to pass a 'deliberation meeting' each year in order to progress to the subsequent year group in the following school year. During this meeting, teachers, support staff and the head teacher decide whether students are allowed to progress to the following year group, a decision that is heavily influenced by students' performance on exams.

Such a teacher-centered system stands in sharp contrast to the educational-market centered approach, characteristic of countries like the UK and the US. The latter puts much more emphasis on the accountability of schools (and other public institutions) and, related to this, the public assessment of schools through the publication of achievement-related data based on students' standardized tests. In such a system, teachers have less power over students' educational careers compared to their colleagues in Flanders, as they are not responsible for marking their students' standardized tests and making decisions on whether they should fail their school year. Recent research in the UK and US show that in response to pressures to 'raise achievement', school management and staff implement a form of 'educational triage'. Such processes relate to the allocation of scarce educational resources (such as additional in-class support for students) not to the lowest achieving students but to those students who are expected to meet the standards of achievement imposed by governing agencies after benefiting from such additional resources. This study builds on existing research on the importance of nationally specific evaluation systems by exploring how a more teacher-centered system influences interactions between ethnic minority students and their teachers.

In *Riverside* school and Flanders more generally, Turkish ethnic minority students belonged to the lowest achieving groups and are allocated to lower status educational sets or streams. Teachers in *Riverside* often experienced a dilemma in that they perceived Turkish students as lacking basic knowledge and attitudes considered necessary to obtain educational qualifications, but on the other hand they felt pressured to ensure that all students obtained educational qualifications. Teachers in *Riverside* responded to these challenges by lowering their educational standards to a point where 'passing the year' was not so much a function of their perceived ability, but more of students' perceived willingness or motivation to succeed:

MR. AGGER: "When is a student successful? (. . .) I want them to demonstrate a positive motivation, they have to be polite, show respect, be on time and have their school material with them, (. . .) they have to show that they want to do something."
                (. . .)
RESEARCHER: "What kinds of criteria are taken into account during the deliberations? How important is it that a student is considered motivated?"
MR. AGGER: "300 percent! That student is almost certain to obtain an A-certificate and allowed to pass the year, even if his marks are poor!" (Teacher interview: White, male, Flemish senior teacher *Riverside*)

As a result, the Flemish teachers in *Riverside* were more likely to *blame* Turkish students for not reaching appropriate standards imposed by their teachers, as the standards were lowered to a point where 'success' was not a question of ability, but of willingness or effort to do well. Hence, whilst the particular student-evaluation system in Flanders allows teachers to lower standards so that they were perceived to match the ability of their students, 'blame' for educational failure was more likely attributed to students' unwillingness to be successful. This can in turn help to explain why teachers in *Riverside* appeared to express considerable negative views of Turkish minority students and particularly why they blamed those students for not *wanting* to adapt to Flemish society.

Valuation of the Language and Needs of Ethnic Minority Students

Although immigration of Turkish migrants (and other so called '*guestwork-ers*') to Flanders started to increase after World War II, and especially during the 1960s and 1970s, Flanders only started to implement a comprehensive policy to improve educational outcomes of ethnic minorities in 1991. However, this policy largely reduced the educational problems experienced by ethnic minorities to their lower socioeconomic position.[3] Although schools were encouraged to recognize specific minority needs by allocating extra resources to 'Intercultural Education' and 'Teaching in Own Language and Culture', in practice very few schools implemented such measures and instead adopted an assimilation perspective by focusing almost exclusively on 'Dutch Language Development'. Furthermore, teachers who took responsibility for these particular courses in school often lacked experience, were given a lower status by the teaching staff, and even experienced overt resistance from other members of staff . Finally, in part because of the historical tension between the Dutch (Flanders) and French (Wallonia) speaking communities in Belgium, Flemish legislation does not allow teachers in Flanders or schools to communicate with parents in any other language than Dutch. All this suggests that the Flemish Government adopts a policy of assimilation in relationship to ethnic and cultural diversity in education.

Given such particular policies related to multiculturalism in the Flemish educational system, it is perhaps not surprising that teachers in *Riverside* showed little interest, knowledge and sensitivity to the particular needs of ethnic minority students and felt quite unrestrained to express criticism to ethnic minority students. One area in which the influence of such educational policies appeared very strong concerns the language policies adopted in *Riverside* school. In *Riverside* school students were only allowed to communicate in Dutch and expressions of ethnic minority languages were generally regarded by teaching staff as inappropriate at best and offensive at worst. Finally, school staff in *Riverside* was not allowed to communicate formally with parents in any other language than Dutch. A recent study conducted in three inner-city multicultural primary schools in Flanders suggests that such views on ethnic minority languages are not restricted to *Riverside* school. The Flemish teachers interviewed in these three schools considered students only as 'literate' when they spoke standard Dutch, or possessed the specific literacy skills associated with Dutch orthography. Students who could not attain these skills were defined as language-less and illiterate, even if they were proficient multilingual individuals.

In sum, Flemish educational policy shows little recognition and awareness of linguistic and cultural diversity and does not put a lot of emphasis on anti-racism and discrimination. As a result, it should perhaps not surprise us that the teachers interviewed and observed in *Riverside* had quite negative views and poor knowledge of Turkish minority students and perceived expressions of ethnic minority cultural capital (particularly their native language) as contra-productive at best and offensive at worst.

School Context

School Composition in Terms of Ethnicity

While *Riverside* is a multicultural school, ethnic minority students only make up a small proportion of the student population (only 28 percent non-native and 15 percent Turkish). It is likely that the cultural capital of ethnic minorities is more visible, expressed and valued in schools with a higher proportion of ethnic minority students. For example, recent research suggests that the ethnic composition of a school is important in understanding how schools manage ethnic diversity. In analyzing questionnaire data administered from a sample of primary and secondary schools in England, Whiteman concludes that while ethnically heterogeneous schools appeared more likely to adopt a multicultural approach, ethnically homogeneous schools seemed more inclined to apply an integrationist approach. Similarly, it could be argued that the relatively low proportion of ethnic minority students in *Riverside* decreased the availability, activation and the need to value particular forms of ethnic minority cultural capital in *Riverside*.

Furthermore, *Riverside* school counted only one ethnic minority (part-time) teacher, who was responsible for teaching Islam. The lack of availability of ethnic minority teachers in school reduces the availability of people in school with knowledge of ethnic minority languages and culture to assist in the process of teaching, to communicate with parents and/or solve disputes with Turkish speaking students; which can in turn have an effect on how (Flemish) teachers evaluate and treat ethnic minority students.

School Management and Inclusive Policies

A final institutional characteristic that appeared important in explaining teachers' ethnic stereotypes in *Riverside* concerns the support given to multicultural policies by the senior school management. While schools can be discouraged by the larger educational system to value particular characteristics of ethnic minority cultures (such as minority languages), and fail to have the resources (e.g., ethnic minority teaching staff) to value ethnic minority cultural capital, the development of a multicultural school ethos seems to depend in part on the senior's management willingness and ability to make this a priority. Although *Riverside* school organized lessons in Dutch language for foreign students, events and initiatives aimed at valuing the cultural and religious diversity in school were non-existent. Students who failed to attend Dutch language classes were perceived by staff as 'not willing to integrate'. Furthermore, only two teachers in *Riverside* openly criticized the head teacher's lack of interest in ethnic minority issues and the racist attitudes expressed by some colleagues and they felt frustrated that their concerns were not supported by colleagues or members of the senior management team. This suggests the widespread support of assimilation policies in *Riverside* by both staff and the school's senior management, which reinforce each other and can help to explain why teachers in *Riverside* expressed less knowledge and more negative views of Turkish minority students.

Finally, these findings illustrate the interrelated nature of different institutional characteristics in influencing teachers' knowledge and attitudes of Turkish students, as school characteristics interact with each other and with characteristics of the broader national educational system. While case-study research is particularly strong in identifying and illustrating possible causal mechanisms, future, large-scale quantitative research is needed to investigate the inter-relations between these factors and processes and the direction and strength of their relationship to teachers' (expressions of) ethnic stereotypes.

Teacher and Student Interactions

Teachers' Strategies to Avoid Accusations of Racism

The above suggests that teachers' negative stereotypes of Turkish minority students appear to be influenced by characteristics of the school and wider educational contexts in which they operate. However, at the same time ethnographic observations and teacher interviews suggest that teachers were careful not to behave in a way that was considered racist:

RESEARCHER: 'And what is the attitude of foreign pupils towards you?'
MR. GERRARD: 'I don't have any problems with them. They know that from me. I tell you: sometimes we are not allowed to use the words but I use them some now and then, because that, because I have to put myself on the same level as them according to my inspector from twenty years ago. So, I put myself on their level and use their language.' (Teacher interview, February 2002 *Riverside*—Mr. Gerrard: teacher theory and practice car-mechanics subjects in 5VC)

This teacher acknowledges that 'they are not allowed to use the words' in interaction with foreign students. Teachers either considered such behavior as immoral, or they feared that it would result in harmful responses from racial/ethnic minority students or challenge their status as 'good professionals'. Teachers employed different strategies to ensure that they would not be perceived as racist. Sometimes they appeared to confine behavior that could be indicative of racism to a more backstage arena. Another strategy involved behaving in a way that contradicts any possible implication of racism:

	(Tatu's mobile telephone starts ringing)
MR. WHITEBREAD:	'One more time and I will take it away from you, and you can collect it at the Reception!'
	(5 minutes later: Tatu's mobile telephone starts ringing again)
MR. WHITEBREAD:	'Yeah, but I mean it you know, normally I would take it away from you right now . . . you can call me then a racist, but I warned you . . . and besides, you're not allowed to have a mobile in the classroom!'
THE LEGEND:	'No Sir, you're not a racist, you're the best teacher!' (Field notes January 24, 2002, *Riverside*—5VC during Electricity)

Mr. Whitebread is afraid that his punishing of a Turkish student could be interpreted as him being racist. In response to such potential accusations he involves in 'reverse discrimination' by deliberately offering these students more room for deviance, or by treating them better in order not to be perceived as a racist or someone who treats Turkish students worse.

This example suggests that teachers can manage the extent to which they are perceived as racist, as teachers can employ specific strategies to inform how students interpret the teacher's behavior, and related to this, the status of a teacher as a racist. It also suggests that teachers have little to gain from being considered racist and can therefore be expected, for moral, pragmatic and/or professional reasons to behave in a way that cannot be interpreted as racism by their students. This can in turn explain why researchers and students might not find strong evidence for the existence of teacher racism in schools, as strong norms against 'being racist' will encourage teachers not to express stereotypical views and/or engage in discriminatory behavior.

The above analysis of strategies employed by members of the dominant racial/ethnic group to maintain a 'non-racist' status link very well with the key focus of Critical Race Theory and Whiteness Studies. While such analyses is strong in considering members of dominant groups as active agents that can effectively influence their image as 'racists' and therefore the perception of racism by racial/ethnic minorities, the analysis above suggests that such perceptions are also influenced by the students' contextual interpretations of teachers' social actions. Furthermore, the analysis below will suggest that in order to understand the development of racism in school it is not only important to focus on the strategies of racial/ethnic elites, but also on the strategies of ethnic minorities' in response to potential experiences of teacher racism.

Students' Strategies in Response to Teacher Racism

The analysis above suggests that teachers' strategies to prevent or deny students' accusations of teacher racism can influence students' interpretations of teachers' social actions and as a result their (and researchers') perceptions of teacher racism. At the same time the data suggests that students respond differently to potential experiences of teacher racism, which can in turn influence their perceptions of such events; and (if researcher rely on students accounts to study racism) the actual measurement of racism by researchers.

In several interviews students discussed spontaneously how they would respond to teacher racism if they would experience this at first hand. Students' strategies in response to racism seemed to vary, ranging from overt hostility, to calculated resistance, teacher avoidance, exemplary conformity and rationalizing or minimalizing the importance of racism. The kind of strategies adopted by students seemed in turn influenced by their sensitivity or moral objection to racism, their perceived access to resources to respond to racism, their school related goals and the extent to which they perceived racism as a barrier in realizing their goals in life.

Shakur from 5VC did not seem to consider Mr. Gerrard as a racist and instead argued that some students experience a less favorable treatment from teachers because they have a problem with the teacher and not because the teacher is necessarily racist:

SHAKUR: 'There are foreigners who are very quick in saying 'you are a racist, you are a racist'. There are like some teachers or pupils who insult you sometimes, who laugh with you, yeah, foreigners are quick to say that they are racist, but it can just be that they, you know, hate you, but not ALL the foreigners [. . .]'. (Pupil group interview 5VC—*Riverside* January 2002: three Moroccan boys and one Bosnian boy)

Shakur was similar to other students interviewed who did not claim to have experienced (a lot of) teacher racism in that he rationalized the occurrence of racism, did not find it morally very offensive and did not necessarily considered it as a barrier to realizing his goals:

SHAKUR: "I think it is a bit normal that some Belgians and teachers are racist, because a foreigner from Morocco or Turkey comes to Belgium, starts to work, drives a beautiful car and is dressed nicely. And some Belgians who have lived here for their whole life cannot afford those things and start to think of how all that is possible, in their own country . . . and that's how they become racist. But there is not a lot you can do when someone is racist. There is no point in saying 'why are you racist?' to someone who's racist, because someone who's racist will always hate foreigners. (. . .) So yeah . . . it really doesn't interest me who's racist, they can be racist if they want to, as long as they don't touch my wallet (others laugh)". (Pupil group interview 5VC—*Riverside* January 2002, p. 8: three Moroccan boys and one Bosnian boy)

In contrast, those students who appeared more morally opposed to racism and considered racism a barrier to realizing their goals were more likely to observe racism and to respond to it by confronting the teacher (the latter of which was also influenced by students' perceived availability of resources to respond to teacher racism. These findings suggest that students' interpretations of teachers' social actions as racist depend in part on the extent to which they consider such actions as morally wrong and/or problematic in realizing their goals. However, at the same time the data indicates that students' perceptions of teacher racism are also influenced by the (related) strategies that students employ in response to teacher racism, with students 'downplaying' or 'rationalizing' teacher racism as being less likely to interpret teachers' social actions as racist.

CONCLUSION

While considerable research in education focuses on racism in schools, there have been few attempts to integrate existing research in this area into one theoretical framework. Furthermore, most of the studies in this area seem to focus on social-psychological theories and micro-interactions between actors in explaining racism in schools and neglect the influence of characteristics and processes situated at higher levels of analysis, such as school characteristics and characteristics of national educational systems.

In reviewing research on racism and discrimination in educational settings this study suggests the usefulness of adopting an ecological or embedded context approach in studying expressions and perceptions of (teachers') ethnic stereotypes in schools. Such an approach considers teachers particular (racist) values, norms, perceptions, evaluative criteria and judgments for actions as developing from the multilayered social reality in which they operate, including proximal processes (face-to-face interactions between teachers, students and other actors), characteristics of organizations and social groups (e.g., school composition in terms of ethnicity, school policies) and characteristics of larger social contexts, such as the neighborhood, and national educational regulations and policies. Data from naturalistic observations and interviews in one Flemish secondary, multicultural school with Turkish minority students show that the Flemish teachers in our study express quite negative views and limited knowledge of Turkish minority students. The analysis suggests that the particular way in which Flemish educational system evaluates students (in which teachers are encouraged to blame students for educational failure) and their treatment of multiculturalism (which limits the opportunities for multicultural policies in schools) influences teachers' stereotypes of Turkish minority students. Furthermore, the observed differences between Flemish and English teachers in this case-study also seem to be informed by the ethnic composition of the student and staff population in school and the senior management's implementation of multicultural policies. Finally, the findings also suggest the importance of student–teacher interactions, as teachers were perceived to implement particular strategies to avoid being perceived as racist. Similarly, students were perceived to downplay or rationalize incidents of racism, which can in turn influence their perception of such events (and researchers' measurement of racism if they rely on students' perceptions). More generally, this study illustrates the complexity of how racism develops in natural settings and the usefulness of adopting an ecological approach in making sense of variability in (perceived) racism in schools.

In terms of social policy, this study suggests that a 'teacher-centered' system, in which teachers are given considerable power over the educational career of their students will stimulate teachers to adapt their standards of achievement more to the level of their students (and lower their expectations for disadvantaged students) but at the same time assign more responsibility to students in relationship to their educational achievement. If such a system is combined with a comprehensive support package to students with particular disadvantages, and a recognition and valuation of their needs and cultural background (e.g., by introducing ethnic minority languages as part of the curriculum), ethnic minority students could not only be empowered by taking more responsibility on their own educational careers but also have the resources to be equally competitive.

However, since the social processes that were identified in this study relate to the experiences of a small group of teachers in one Flemish school, the findings of this study cannot be generalized beyond the cases studied in this research. Furthermore, although case-study research is particularly strong in exploring, identifying and illustrating complex processes and interactions that appear important to the development of ethnic stereotypes (and as a result help to develop hypotheses regarding the development of such phenomena), it cannot estimate the effects of such processes on the development of ethnic stereotypes controlling for each other and other relevant characteristics and processes.

As a result, large-scale quantitative studies have an important role to play in this field by testing the effects of various embedded institutional contexts through multilevel and longitudinal analysis. The findings of this study suggest the importance of future large-scale nationally comparative studies using similar research designs, measurement instruments and underlying theoretical assumptions and hypotheses.

NOTES

1. Belgium is divided in two main language and political regions that are responsible for organizing their educational system: a Dutch speaking region in the north (Flanders) and a French speaking region in the South (Wallonia). Turkish immigrants constitute are the largest, non-European migrant group in Belgium. The Turkish migrant community in Flanders is quite homogeneous in terms of religion and area of migration and settlement. Compared to native Flemish students, Turkish students generally underachieve in education, with more students having to repeat their school-year, dropping out or enrolling in lower-status tracks.
2. No real names are employed in this chapter. All pupils invented their own pseudonyms; names of teachers and the school are invented by the researcher.
3. The Flemish 'Educational Priority Policy' (*onderwijsvoorangsbeleid*) contained five different dimensions: prevention and support, parental involvement, intercultural education, education in own language and culture and (Dutch) language improvement.

REFERENCES

Allport, Gordon W. 1954. *The Nature of Prejudice*. Cambridge, MA: Addison-Wesley.
Connolly, Paul. 1995. "Racism, Masculine Peer-Group Relations and the Schooling of African/Caribbean Infant Boys". *British Journal of Sociology of Education* 16(1): 75–92.
Connolly, Paul. 2000a. "Racism and Young Girls' Peer-Group Relations: The Experience of South Asian Girls". *Sociology* 34(4): 499–519.
Connolly, Paul. 2000b. "What Now for the Contact Hypothesis? Towards a New Research Agenda". *Race, Ethnicity and Education* 3(2): 169–191.
Foster, Peter. 1990. *Policy and Practice in Multicultural and Anti-Racist Education*. London and New York: Routledge.
Foster, Peter, Roger Gomm, and Martyn Hammersley. 1996. *Constructing Educational Inequality: An Assessment of Research on School Processes*. London: Falmer.
Glaser, Barney G. 1992. *Emergence vs. Forcing: Basics of Grounded Theory Analysis*. Mill Valley, CA: Sociology Press.
Glaser, Barney G., and A. L. Strauss. 1967. *The Discovery of Grounded Theory: Strategies for Qualitative Research*. New York: Aldine.
Whiteman, Ruth. 2005. "Welcoming the Stranger: A Qualitative Analysis of Teachers' Views Regarding the Integration of Refugee Pupils into Schools in Newcastle Upon Tyne". *Educational Studies* 31(4): 375–391.

FURTHER READINGS

Agidar, Orhan. 2010. "Exploring Bilingualism in a Monolingual School System: Insights from Turkish and Native Students from Belgian Schools". *British Journal of Sociology of Education* 31(3): 307–321.

Blommaert, Jan, Lies Creve, and Evita Willeart. 2006. "On Being Declared Illiterate: Language-Ideological Disqualification in Dutch Classes for Immigrants in Belgium". *Language & Communication* 26: 34–54.

Blommaert, Jan, and Jef Verschueren. 1998. *Debating Diversity: Analysing the Discourse of Tolerance.* London: Routledge.

Booher-Jennings, Jennifer. 2005. "Educational Triage' and the Texas Accountability System". *American Educational Research Journal* 42: 231–268.

Bronfenbrenner, Urie. 1979. *The Ecology of Human Development.* Cambridge, MA: Harvard University Press.

Brown, Rupert J., and John C. Turner. 1981. "Interpersonal and Intergroup Behaviour". In *Intergroup Behaviour*, edited by J. C. Turner and H. Giles, 33–65. Chicago: University of Chicago Press.

De Wit, Kurt, and Peter Van Petegem. 2000. *Gelijke Kansen in Het Vlaamse Onderwijs. Het Beleid Inzake Kansengelijkheid.* Leuven/Apeldoorn: Garant.

Dovidio, John F., Peter Glick, and Laurie Rudman. Eds. 2005. *On the Nature of Prejudice. Fifty Years after Allport.* Oxford: Blackwell Publishers.

Enneli, Pinar, Tariq Modood, and Harriet Bradley. 2005. "Young Turks and Kurds: A Set of 'Invisible' Disadvantaged Groups". York: York Publishing Services: Joseph Rowntree Foundation.

Esses, Victoria M., Lynne M. Jackson, John F. Dovidio, and Hodson Gordon. 2005. "Instrumental Relations Amongst Groups: Group Competition, Conflict and Prejudice". In *On the Nature of Prejudice. Fifty Years after Allport*, edited by John F. Dovidio, Porter Glick and Laurie Rudman, 223–243. Oxford: Blackwell Publishers.

Faas, Daniel. 2008. "Constructing Identities: The Ethno-National and Nationalistic Identities of White and Turkish Students in Two English Secondary Schools". *British Journal of Sociology of Education* 29(1): 37–48.

Feinstein, Leon, Kathryn Duckworth, and Ricardo Sabates. 2004. "A Model of Inter-Generational Transmission of Educational Success". London: Centre for Research on the Wider Benefits of Learning.

Ferguson, Ronald F. 1998. "Teachers' Perceptions and Expectations and the Black–White Test Score Gap". In *The Black–White Test Score Gap*, edited by C. Jenks and Meredith Phillips, 273–317. Washington, DC: Brookings Institution Press.

Flick, Uwe. 2002. *An Introduction to Qualitative Research.* 2nd ed. London: Sage Publications.

Gillborn, David. 2008. *Racism and Education. Coincidence or Conspiracy?* London: Routledge.

Gillborn, David, and Caroline Gipps. 1996. *Recent Research on the Achievements of Ethnic Minority Pupils.* London: Institute of Education and Office for Standards in Education.

Gillborn, David, and Deborah Youdell. 2000. *Rationing Education: Policy, Practice, Reform and Equity.* Buckingham: Open University Press.

Gold, Raymond L. 1969. "Roles in Sociological Field Observations". In *Issues in Participant Observation: A Text and Reader*, edited by George J. McCall and J. L. Simmons, 217–223. Addison-Wesley Publishing Company.

Kailin, Julie 1999. "How White Teachers Perceive the Problem of Racism in Their Schools: A Case Study In 'Liberal' Lakeview". *Teachers' College Records* 100(4): 724–750.

Rogers, Ronald W., and Steven Prentice-Dunn. 1981. "Deindividuation and Anger-Mediated Interracial Aggression: Unmasking Regressive Racism". *Journal of Personality and Social Psychology* 35: 677–688.

Smith, Shannon T., and Lisa T. Ross. 2006. "Environmental and Family Associations with Racism". *Journal of Applied Social Psychology* 36(11): 2750–2765.

Spruyt, Bram. 2008. "Ongelijkheid En Segregatie in Het Onderwijslandschap: Effecten Op Etnocentrisme". *Tijdschrift Voor Sociologie* 29(1): 60–87.

Spyrou, Spyros. 2002. "Images of 'the Other': 'the Turk' in Greek Cypriot Children's Imaginations ". *Race, Ethnicity and Education* 5(3): 255–272.

Stevens, Peter A. J. 2006. "An Ethnography of Teacher Racism and Discrimination in Flemish and English Classrooms with Turkish Secondary School Pupils". Doctoral Dissertation, Warwick University.

Stevens, Peter A. J. "Researching Race/Ethnicity and Educational Inequality in English Secondary Schools: A Critical Review of the Research Literature between 1980 and 2005". *Review of Educational Research* 77(2): 147–185.

Stevens, Peter A. J. "Exploring Pupils' Perceptions of Teacher Racism in Their Context: A Case Study of Turkish and Belgian Vocational Education Pupils in a Belgian School". *British Journal of Sociology of Education* 29(2): 175–187.

Strauss, Anselm L., and Juliet Corbin. 1990. *Basics of Qualitative Research. Grounded Theory Procedures and Techniques.* Newbury Park, CA: Sage.

Timmerman, Christiane. 1999. *Onderwijs Maakt Het Verschil.* Leuven/Amersfoort: Acco.

Verkuyten, Maykel, and Jochem Thijs. 2002. "Racist Victimisation among Children in the Netherlands: The Effect of Ethnic Group and School". *Ethnic and Racial Studies* 25(2): 310–331.

11 Conclusion

Christos Kassimeris and Marios Vryonides

Upon reading the preceding chapters one concludes, perhaps prematurely, that one issue common to all countries examined here is that the educational achievements of minority pupils usually lag behind that of the majority. Taking into account the poor performance of migrant children at school, one may also assume that their employment opportunities too are limited, as is the likelihood of improving their living standards, thus the need to assess the state response to education inequalities. The factors accounting for this trend, nevertheless, appear far more complex. That many Western states have long-established ethnic communities, for example, may suggest that they are experienced enough to look after their communities but not necessarily well equipped to actually meet their needs. In spite of the multitude of measures available to address inequality, such as new curricula intended to foster cultural diversity, the instruction of the native language as well as second language courses and anti-discrimination legislation, what each chapter makes evident is that the end result of such attempts is not integration and neither is it incomplete or even failed integration. Rather, it is segregation and social exclusion. The presentation of the various ways with which many countries approach the issue of multiculturalism reveals interesting issues that need to be examined in a comparative fashion. First we will attempt to provide a typology of the various approaches that the authors of the various chapters have presented.

There are at least three different kinds of relationships between politics and education in the countries that are presented in the preceding chapters. One which includes the North American model (US and Canada); secondly, European countries, where the main issues in the way politics intertwine with education has to do with challenges brought about by migration (Britain, Germany, Belgium, the Netherlands); and a third one, where challenges in this relationship are the product of the demographic composition of the indigenous population (Spain, Greece, although the case of Greece fits in the second category as well). First, we will begin by a close examination of the political framework within which policies are being formulated to deal with the issue of multiculturalism. We will then move to an examination of the educational aspects of this relationship.

THE POLITICAL DIMENSION OF MULTICULTURALISM

Britain

Central to the analysis of the school system in Britain is the dominance of the White, middle-class culture and the reproduction of the ideology it expresses. Even though both the Race Relations Amendment Act and the McPherson Report helped highlight the significance of tackling racial discrimination through education, the notion of White superiority/hegemony in Britain is still filtered through society. Immigration policies demonstrating that migrants are unwelcome and stereotypical images portraying Muslims as terrorists and Blacks as criminal elements have left little room for education to spawn a multicultural environment representative enough of Britain's cultural and ethnic diversity. Considering the poor performance of Black and Minority Ethnic pupils, too, education in Britain was clearly in need of reform, thus the initiatives designed by the Department of Education for the purpose of supporting disadvantaged groups while also enhancing the skills of instructors. Despite the positive nature of these developments, the growing concerns about international terrorism together with the increase in immigration controls and the relative radicalization of a section of young British Muslims have only contributed to the rise of Islamophobia, therefore, hindering any attempts towards multiculturalism through education. Attributing the 2005 London bombings to the alienation of ethnic communities serves no purpose other than suggesting that integration in Britain has failed. The existence of schools that have a predominantly Black, Asian and Muslim population are often considered as further evidence of failed integration. Not only had multiculturalism failed to bring the various communities closer together, it was also considered by the media as the main reason for the kind of extremism that London witnessed in 2005. Naturally, the need to address those issues with effect was of paramount significance. Citizenship education was determined as the remedy, however, what is compulsory for secondary education, is only optional for other age groups, and, perhaps, as undemanding as an English language test for those aiming to gain Britain citizenship. Whether the revised curriculum will facilitate nation-building depends much on how Britishness and Whiteness compensate for the race inequalities that continue to characterize society in Britain.

The Netherlands

The socioeconomic background was always considered an important enough factor when formulating educational policies in the Netherlands. When the influx of migrants grew considerably during the 1980s, therefore, the Dutch government already had in place some instruments capable of dealing with the learning difficulties of migrant children given that their families usually became part of the lower social class. Although those educational policies were inadequate for addressing the problems that migrant pupils encountered in school, the perception that immigrants were expected to return to their country of origin before long deemed any revision unnecessary. The Cultural Minority Policy, for instance, was such an instrument that achieved nothing more than making additional learning resources available to migrant children. The fact that Dutch pupils from a working-class background experienced the same problems with immigrant pupils at school prompted the Dutch government to adopt an intercultural approach to education so as to teach both minority and Dutch pupils the values and principles of ethnic and cultural diversity. The end result was the merging of the Educational Stimulation Policy and the Cultural Minority Policy into the Educational Priority Policy. With the support of the National Policy Framework, the Educational Priority Policy focused more on the problems of migrant children given that by the early 1990s little had changed in terms of their performance at school. Other than improving their language achievements, the Educational Priority Policy made provisions for migrant pupils to receive Mother Tongue Instruction in their parents' native language aiming at facilitating their return and integration to their country of origin. When the Dutch government acknowledged that those immigrants were there to stay, the Mother Tongue Instruction policy was reformed in order to both promote interculturalism and help bridge the gap between school and home environment. The merits of this policy notwithstanding, the Mother Tongue Instruction was once more revised in the aftermath of 9/11 when cultural diversity was subjected to assimilation before it was discontinued in 2004. According to the Ministry of Education, migrant pupils made no improvement in terms of their mother tongue nor in Dutch, thus compelling the government to shift its attention to learning Dutch alone. The integration of immigrants became imperative and so did the notion of citizenship, thus the significance of proficiency in the Dutch language, with respect for Dutch values and society also deemed important. Actually, as of 2006, the sheer significance of the Dutch language and social values transpired into a civic integration examination that immigrants from non-Western countries have to take in their native country before migrating to the Netherlands. As one would expect, those that fail are simply not allowed to immigrate to the Netherlands. The following year the same test applied to certain immigrants that already reside in the Netherlands. The level of difficulty of the very same examination was raised in 2009 in what was the government's attempt to make tighter the entry criteria for migrants.

The United States

The same Cold War conditions that affected the national interests and political agendas of the two superpowers of the time influenced much education in the United States early on. The year after the Soviets launched the first satellite, Sputnik, the US Congress passed the National Defense Education Act (1958) in order to better promote the instruction of science, math and foreign languages at ever school level. Yet 'race' relations were only later addressed through the Civil Rights Act (1964), the Title IX of the Education Amendments (1972) and Section 504 of the Rehabilitation Act (1973), thus changing the role of the federal government in education. Despite those efforts designed to reach disadvantaged groups, the main obstacle to revising the educational system, so as to provide equal opportunities to all pupils regardless of their socioeconomic or ethnic background, was the perception that migrant children affected the academic performance of the entire school population, thus rendering the future US labor force less competitive.

The history of the US indicates that it is a nation of immigrants, based on the influx of migrants over the last two centuries, with migrants playing an admittedly important role in the economy of the country, therefore, their needs for better education and equal opportunities should not be neglected perhaps. Even though the US population is expected to grow by 142 million by 2050, with some 82 percent of this increase comprised of immigrants and their offspring, education in the US has almost never been racist-free. In fact, it was as early as Woodrow Wilson's administration that a legislative act was passed that required immigrants to take a literacy test. Immigrant access to educational opportunities has generally been a highly contested issue. When the Supreme Court decided (457 US 202, 1982) that immigrant children had a Constitutional right to free public education, supported by legislative acts such as the Bilingual Education Act and the Emergency Immigrant Education Act, additional funds were allocated for their proper instruction considering these children as an integral part of the future US labor force. Interestingly, education for immigrant children did not coincide with securing employment, since the Immigration Reform and Control Act (1986) still requires that they first return to their country of origin before applying to reenter the US. Even then migrant graduates must produce evidence of employment or financial support prior to returning to the US. The fact that "not being able to apply for jobs after graduation means that they will have difficulty meeting the requirement for reentry into the country," as the authors of the relevant chapter point out, clearly indicated how tight migration policies in the US have become. Of course, should the US Congress decide to pass the Dream Act, graduating from a public school or joining the armed forces would automatically grant immigrants resident status, thus paving the way for naturalized citizenship too.

Spain

The case of Spain is quite special, for the Iberian country was for most of the twentieth century organized in a manner that served Francisco Franco's fascist regime. Clearly serving the regime's agenda, the school system under

Franco was dominated by a sense of military monarchism and relevant activities so as to construct a uniform, Catholic identity. During Franco's years, Spanish was the only language employed in schools, even though the historical nationalities, Catalonia, the Basque Country and Galicia to name a few, opposed the dictator's language standardization and demanded that the mother tongue was used instead. Today, the language of instruction for all subjects in Catalonia is Catalan, except for language courses. Considering the magnitude of the July 2010 demonstrations in Barcelona, when thousands of Catalans demanded greater autonomy (some not even hesitating to call for independence), it is obvious that Catalan nationalism is nowadays at its peak. Naturally, to replace Catalan with Spanish is no option or else the sheer essence of Catalanism would merely cease to exist. The Basque Country, on the other hand, employs quite a peculiar system that separates education into three different models of schooling whereby: (A) Spanish is the main language of instruction, bar the Basque language and literature classes; (B) both the Spanish and Basque languages are used concurrently; and (D) Basque is the principal language of instruction, except for the Spanish language and literature courses, and the instruction of foreign languages. The element of language is so strong in the Basque Country as to render option C non-existent, for the letter C is not to be found in the Basque alphabet. What's more, the sheer absence of any kind of similarity between Basque and any other language around the world throughout history certainly justifies all attempts of the Basque people to safeguard their legacy.

Germany

School curricula in Germany emphasize the significance of citizenship; however, in the aftermath of World War II, European identity clearly presided over the concept of nationhood. Ever since the inception of the European Coal and Steel Community and the European Economic Community, German politicians—clearly influenced by the key role that their country played in setting up the two communities—continue to focus on all things European, even when contemplating national political identity in schools. First published in 1990 and then in 2008, the *Europe at School* publication of the Standing Conference of the Ministers of Education reiterates that education should underline the essence of European identity and the significance of producing good and responsible citizens of the European Union, therefore, revised its role accordingly so as to further Europeanize German identity. Despite the influx of immigrants during the 1960s and 1970s, German education adopted an intercultural approach as late as the 1990s, when it was eventually clear that those immigrants and their children had no intention to return to their country of origin, a false perception based on which was the policy that enabled immigrant children to learn the language of their parents' country of origin so as to facilitate their return there.

Within this context, it is hardly surprising that Germany, too, has adopted an intercultural approach to education that includes anti-racism initiatives in order to better respond to the needs of migrants. While integration is, indeed, the dominant feature of German education nowadays, emphasizing the need for immigrant children to learn the German language at the expense of their mother tongue does not necessarily secure their smooth integration to society. Equally controversial, of course, was the decision of Germany's highest constitutional court to first condemn the federal state of Baden-Württemberg for wrong-doing in the case of Fereshta Ludin and then allow states to legislate on such issues, thus triggering the banning of teachers wearing headscarves in a considerable number of federal states, at the same time as maintaining the predominance of Christian religious symbols at school. Integration is nowadays a critical issue in Germany, particularly after Angela Merkel recently admitted in public that multiculturalism had failed, despite efforts and initiatives such as the integration summits for the opposite. The migrants' willingness to integrate notwithstanding, it is certain that the mistakes of the past need to be rectified or else integration will hardly succeed, particularly if confused with naturalization, as the agendas of the Christian Democratic Union and that of the Social Democratic Party currently dictate.

Canada

Language has been an issue in Canada since 1774 when the Quebec Act, passed by the British some fifteen years after the defeat of the French, was implemented to protect all things French in the province of Quebec. Given that the British maintained control over the remaining area of what is present-day Canada, recognizing the country's bilingual and bicultural setting obviously defined the country's future to a great extent. Little reference was made to the natives' culture and language, not to mention their limited land access, thus allowing the British the opportunity to adopt a rather fervent assimilationist policy that was safeguarded by relevant legislation, thus subjecting all other ethnic and cultural communities to British domination. Power politics between the British and French communities reached a climax in the 1960s with the rising Québécois separatist nationalism. That Canada is a unique case, considering that educational policies are not formulated at national level or within a federal context, is definitely worthy of note for better comprehending inequalities in education. Interestingly, even in the case of the federally controlled education of the First Nations, there are demands for educational autonomy. The lack of clarity over the kind of authority that provincial and federal agencies maintain over education was best illustrated in 2006 when the Supreme Court ruled that Sikh students had a constitutional right to carry religious symbols, after a school board had decided the exact opposite. Equally confusing, evidently, is the nature and scope of the Multiculturalism Act, for it fails to address issues pertaining to inequality with effect, just as it ignores the very origins of Canada (both its European roots, as well as the First Nations). On the whole, multiculturalism in Canada has only succeeded in masking racial inequalities with a disturbed sense of cultural diversity. School textbooks, for instance, maintain stereotypes regarding the various ethnic groups that altogether make up Canada's population. Apart from asking authors to adopt a more inclusive approach in their writing, textbooks are nowadays reviewed by both publishers and related government institutions. But even if the content of textbooks alters significantly enough to portray ethnic groups in a more appropriate manner, the underrepresentation of Canada's minority population in the population of school instructors is yet another serious impediment in delivering intercultural education and while this problem could be resolved with little effort by hiring teachers from abroad, it becomes apparent that the politics of education are once again in operation for their teaching credentials are not recognized.

Greece

In the case of Greece, education is not just dominated by politics, but has acquired a somewhat international dimension, too. Even though the Morning Prayer before classes commence and the dominant position of religious symbols inside classrooms both adhere to the core principles of Orthodoxy, education in Greece has acquired a far more political dimension. The case of the 132nd elementary school, in particular, speaks volumes for the impact of politics upon education. What was initially considered as an exemplary model of intercultural education was later targeted by extreme right elements that perceived any such interculturalism as a serious threat to national identity and social homogeneity. In the same context, it is crystal clear that international politics dictate educational policies in Thrace where the needs of the local Muslim minority are usually determined by the state of affairs between Greece and Turkey and, therefore, overlooked so as to deny any claims for greater autonomy. In this respect, minority pupils may either enroll in a minority school where some courses are taught in the Greek language and others in the Turkish language, or Greek schools where all courses are, naturally, taught in Greek. Although the Muslim minority in Thrace remains the only officially recognized minority in Greece, it appears that deconstructing their identity forms part and parcel with serving Greek national interests in the area. Even when specially designed textbooks were delivered for the purpose of properly educating minority pupils in Thrace, the Greek state's initiatives were far from serving intercultural education, for the teachers often did not speak the same language with minority children, thus suggesting that the main aim was, perhaps, nothing more than marinating political control of the minority. Likewise, the introduction of a new history textbook produced by a team of experts, yet condemned to obscurity, is another clear example of the impact politics has on education.

The kind of criticism that emanated from the educational community, the Greek Orthodox Church and the extreme right rendered the new history textbook treacherous. Needless to say, the new history textbook never saw the inside of a classroom; its content shall be determined by a new team of academics while, in the meantime, the old textbook is still in use.

Belgium

Despite immigration to Flanders reaching new heights in the 1960s and 1970s, it was not before 1991 that education was employed as an instrument of integration of the ethnic communities. While schools were encouraged to address the needs of ethnic minority pupils, however, most concentrated on the Dutch Language Development initiative that aimed at assimilating the ethnic communities and only a few schools decided to allocate considerable resources to promote intercultural education. While the choice of the former cannot possibly be attributed to racial discrimination, the inferior status given to those instructors that taught minority pupils was certainly racist. Then again, language plays a rather dominant role in Flanders considering that Flemish legislation prohibits teachers in Flemish schools to use any language other than Dutch, even when discussing the pupils' performance or relevant issues with their parents. Education in Flanders, therefore, has become a vehicle of assimilation. Unsurprisingly, perhaps, the conduct of teachers at the Riverside school neared discrimination, whether making reference to meeting the needs of minority pupils or the language employed for teaching and, generally, communication purposes. Simply enough, the Flemish education system suffers from a lack of awareness of different forms of diversity, just as it has failed to combat racial discrimination. Of course, instructors and school management alike failing to organize cultural activities that would help immigrants integrate to the Flemish society are also to blame.

THE EDUCATIONAL PERSPECTIVES
OF THE POLITICS OF EDUCATION

The North American Model

The educational systems of the US and Canada share many common elements and differences as well. However, the most interesting common element is the fact that due to their federal system of governance, central government has no direct control over educational policies. Instead educational policy making lies at the state level (in the US) or the provincial level (in Canada).

In the US, public education is at the hands of individual states, local communities and school boards and any attempt of involvement by the federal government in state and local education has been met with resistance at the state and local levels. According to Dworkin and Tobe (Chapter 5), the increasing role of the federal government in education can be traced to concerns regarding the challenges of globalization and immigration. In terms of the first challenge it appears that the federal administration seeks to impose an agenda that meets the perceived needs of the economy regarding the competitiveness of the American labor force against more competitive nations in an environment of economic globalization. Under policies like *No Child Left Behind*, federal guidelines impose mandated standards for student passage rates with severe sanctions for failures to meet such standards. The current US administration's *Race to the Top* (2009), as part of the *American Recovery and Reinvestment Act of 2009*, maintains many of the elements of the *No Child Left Behind Act of 2001*. In this program federal funds are competitive and states have to adopt successful standards and assessments, create and maintain data systems that measure student achievement and inform teachers and principals on how to improve instruction, recruit and reward effective teachers and principals, and raise the achievement in low-performing schools. The expansion of educational opportunities to previously disadvantaged groups and immigrant populations has unintended consequences for the native-born middle class who seem to believe that public schools are no longer creating educational and career advantages for their children. In fact, immigration to the US from developing nations and internal migration of ethnic minorities groups has been blamed as a source of declining academic performance and declines in achievement across the nation and has challenged the school systems.

As with the US, in Canada the education system is politically decentralized because education is a provincial rather than a federal responsibility. This structure influences the political processes through which federal government initiatives, such as multiculturalism, are integrated into educational mandates across the nation. Federal involvement in education is indirect as provinces are in charge of school districts, curricula, approval of textbooks, funding grants and teacher certification.

Guppy (Chapter 8) argues that much like multiculturalism itself, multicultural education is necessarily an imperfect and ongoing process. Its meaning is constantly renegotiated within the nation's collective consciousness through legal battles, public protests and media debates. For example Ontario and British Columbia are more advanced in their institutionalization of multiculturalism, mainly because of their large immigrant populations, while Quebec, the only officially French province, has a particularly unique multicultural policy which encourages recognition of and contact between culturally diverse groups.

In Canada, multicultural education is criticized on four grounds. Firstly, rather than starting from scratch and infusing multicultural issues into a novel curriculum, multiculturalism appears to be added at the margins, worked into the old approach where opportunities permit. A second criticism of multicultural education is that it celebrates rather than challenges diversity. By celebrating cultural diversity multicultural education is thus accused of fomenting the containment and marginalization of essentialized ethnic identity. Third, multicultural education is also accused of either forgetting the foundational origins of Canada, in its European, and especially British and French, heritage, or of neglecting the diversity of new Canadians and ignoring the First Nations peoples who were colonized by the French and British. A fourth criticism of multicultural education is that only the knowledge of privileged groups is found in the curriculum.

Two interrelated issues, however, reveal interesting political issues in Canadian education. Looking at the content of current Canadian textbooks, they appear to represent ethnic groups in a much less stereotypical manner than they did decades earlier and issues of diversity are featured in a much less prejudicial and negative manner. Also, in terms of measures of academic achievement, they suggest that the education system is performing well in its quest to provide visible minority students equal access to skills in core subjects and to promote post-secondary education. In this case, however, inequalities *among* visible minority groups remain significant, especially the disadvantages experienced by First Nations peoples.

The European Experience of Multiculturalism and Education

In the European context politics of education in relation to multiculturalism has been influenced by trends in migration particularly after World War II.

Britain, with influences from its colonial past, has a history of "multiculturalism" since the end of World War II. What appears to be the case is that the multicultural project seems to be failing as the educational policies that have been introduced over the years have not smoothed the tensions between races, but rather, following a number of political events, have led to polarizing effects.

Crozier (Chapter 3) describes as "soft" the options taken in Educational Studies in Britain. While Britain has been recognized as a multiethnic and multicultural society, educational studies according to Grozier, "acted as a diversion to the crucial task of dismantling racism and challenging White hegemony". The 'multicultural project' in Britain is seen to have increased the distance between communities rather than brought them together. A major challenge facing Britain at the moment there is growing concern about the radicalisation of young British Muslims which fuels, what Grozier characterizes, as an unintended consequence, Islamophobia. Multiculturalism had been more of a focus on culture and values rather than equality of opportunity and challenging discrimination. Thus British Bangladeshi and Pakistani heritage children continue to be failed by the education system as do the children of African-Caribbean heritage, especially boys. Research has shown that British Bangladeshi and

Pakistani children experience, at times daily, racist harassment either verbally and/or physically. Diversity politics and multiculturalism have done little to avert these stereotypical and taken-for-granted assumptions. The Citizenship Curriculum, which is compulsory only for lower secondary education (11–14 years), highlights the desire for the strengthening and development of a sense of a 'British identity'.

In a similar fashion with that of Britain, the Netherlands has been confronted with an influx of various categories of immigrants since World War II. According to Driessen (Chapter 4), immigration from non-Western countries has increasingly been viewed as a problem in the Netherlands as a result of increasing numbers, external characteristics (e.g., color of skin, language and dress code) and behavior (e.g., overrepresentation in crime statistics).

A number of targeted educational policies have been introduced to address the realities posed by the presence of migrant children in Dutch schools. A very interesting element of these policies is that schools and welfare institutions worked together in preschool activities, reading promotion, homework assistance and guidance projects for truant students often by providing additional teachers when the needs arose. A major emphasis in the 1990s had been to improve students' language and mathematics achievements. More recently, transition classes were re-introduced with a focus on proficiency in the Dutch language of immigrant children and for extra resources to go to schools in deprived, low-income neighborhoods. Also, citizenship education is a topic that has been introduced into the Dutch educational system recently (law in 2006), though because of the decentralized Dutch educational system, schools are free to put this policy into action any way they see fit. The overall goal of improving the position of immigrants remained constant over the years, although there was a shift in scope from ethnic disadvantage to disadvantage in general. As Driessen (Chapter 4) remarks, however, in practice, a strong focus on ethnicity has remained because most ethnic minority parents have little education and they still remain the policy's main target group.

In Belgium and in particular in the Flemish educational system the way students are evaluated and the way multiculturalism is being treated influences teachers' stereotypes of minority students, according to Stevens (Chapter 10). Specifically, in a 'teacher-centered' system, in which teachers are given considerable power over the educational career of their students, teachers adapt their standards of achievement more to the level of their students and at the same time assign more responsibility to students in relationship to their educational achievement. According to Stevens, the Flemish educational policy shows little recognition and awareness of linguistic and cultural diversity and does not put a lot of emphasis on anti-racism and discrimination. As a result, teachers often had negative views and poor knowledge of minority students and perceived expressions of ethnic minority cultural capital (particularly their native language) and also considered students as 'literate' only when they spoke standard Dutch. Students who could not attain these skills were defined as language-less and illiterate, even if they were proficient multilingual individuals.

In Germany, according to Faas (Chapter 7) there is an effort to leave behind the image of the third-generation 'foreigner' or 'foreign citizen'. History curricula generally promote national and European values whereas geography curricula indicate Germany's recent attempts to add more multicultural values to the prevailing European ideology. Also, in a similar fashion, as with the countries presented above, there is emphasis on the need for better German language skills and on the need for immigrants to do well in school amidst evidence that the children of immigrants on the whole underachieve.

Germany straggled with migrants' citizenship status for a long time. A controversial issue raised by migration to Germany was the provision of mother-tongue education, and the perceived value of the linguistic and cultural capital that migrants bring into schools. This was done because it was thought that migrants will at some point leave Germany for their parents' homelands. Later it became evident, however, that the labor migrants of the 1960s and 1970s, and their German-born children, had settled in Germany permanently. Thus, according to Faas the children of immigrants were no longer obliged to learn the languages of their parents and instead were expected to integrate into German society.

Greece and Spain

The case of these two Mediterranean societies is indeed a very interesting one. These two countries share similarities into the way politics are being played in education but have some very distinct differences as well. Here we will only focus on their similarities and particularly those which tend to focus on internal ethnic communities and the way central governments have attempted to promote national goals of nationalistic identity.

An ethnocentric discourse has falsely argued for a long time that Greece was a homogeneous society until an influx of immigrants and refugees from Asia and Africa, when the Greek State, under the pressure of EU guidelines, introduced policies to deal with the education of both repatriate children (of Greek migrants) as well as migrant children from third countries. The biggest challenge for politics in Greek education comes from the minority in Thrace, which according to Kontogiannopoulou-Polydorides (Chapter 9), constitutes the most unique example of the influence of politics on education in the Greek social and educational context. More specifically, education for the minority was influenced by Greek–Turkish relations and Greek governments over time have considered the minority as a "national threat". This inevitably led to the decision to marginalize the minority as a control policy. Thus, the political dimension was the main issue that drove the educational agenda, and not the actual educational needs of the minority education, with the Greek side trying to limit the Turkish influence and the threat they thought it represented. The other two examples presented in Chapter 9 also reveal attempts, mostly unsuccessful, by the political classes under populist pressure to safeguard a nationalistic identity amidst "dangers" posed by multiculturalism and the loss of what was previously regarded as ethnic purity.

In some respects the modern history of Spain resembles that of Greece but in a quite different fashion. The Spanish case, according to Mariano (Chapter 6), is one of a failed nation-building where there was a collapse of the legitimacy of Spanish nationalism creating conditions for peripheral nationalisms. These peripheral nationalisms used the school system to promote their goals in the same way nationalist governments did previously. Spanish language, under the dictatorship, was the single, uniform language at school, but later, however, there was a demand for mother-tongue education to be enforced in several territories. In the same way as with other countries present in this book, textbooks and language are fields where politics come into play. Mariano reports that, in general, there is a tendency in the educational books of many communities, and much more in these, to give prime attention to their own territory, adding nationalist elements such as pan-nationalist and irredentist definitions of their while Spain is being represented as separate and parallel entity. Similarly, there is often distortion of history in favor of an alleged independent sovereign past of the nationality in question against the existence of the Spanish nation.

All in all, what the present book has, we hope, vividly demonstrated is that educational phenomena reflect and inevitably serve political agendas. What the examination of the previously-mentioned countries has revealed is that the political aspects of education and educational policy in the era of multiculturalism are shaping more than ever the context of educational processes and the content of what is being taught in many European countries and North America and will likely continue to do so in the short- to medium-term future.

Contributors

Gill Crozier is Professor of Education in the Department of Education, Roehampton University, London, and a Sociologist of Education. Her work has focused on 'race' and its intersection with social class and gender. She has researched extensively issues relating to parents and schools, and young people and schooling, students' experience of higher education and is also concerned with education policy and the sociocultural influences upon identity formation and learner experiences. Her books include: *Parents and Schools: Partners or Protagonists?* (2000, Stylus Publishing: Trentham Books); editor, with Diane Reay, of *Activating Participation: Mothers, Fathers and Teachers Working Towards Partnership* (2005, Stylus Publishing: Trentham Books); contributor with Mirian David (editor), Ann-Marie Bathmaker, et al. in *Widening Participation Through Improving Learning* (2009, Routledge); *White Middle Class Identities and Urban Schooling*, with Diane Reay and David James (2011, Palgrave).

Geert Driessen received a teacher's degree before continuing on to study educational and pedagogical theory. He is a senior educational researcher at ITS (Institute for Applied Social Sciences) of the Radboud University Nijmegen, the Netherlands. He was involved in several large-scale cohort studies in primary and secondary education. Those studies were initiated to monitor the Dutch education system in general and to evaluate policies such as the Educational Priority Policy. He also performed policy evaluations with regard to bilingual education programs, early childhood education programs, and community schools. In addition, he has served as a project manager of dozens of quantitative and qualitative research projects. His major research interests include education in relation to ethnicity, social milieu and gender; other themes are: parental participation; school choice; Islamic schools; integration, participation and segregation; citizenship; preschool and early school education; bilingual education; dialects and regional languages; educational policy; compositional and peer group effects.

A. Gary Dworkin is Professor of Sociology and Director of the Sociology of Education Research Group (SERG) at the University of Houston. He received his A.B. degree in sociology and psychology from Occidental College and M.A. and Ph.D. degrees in sociology from Northwestern University. He was a Woodrow Wilson Fellow and has been a senior research fellow in sociology at the Australian National University, Canberra. He has held National Science Foundation and US Department of Education grants. Dworkin is currently President of the Sociology of Education Research Committee (RC04) of the International Sociological Association (2010–2014). The majority of his publications have been in the areas of the sociology of education and race, ethnic and gender relations. Many of his publications address the linkage between school accountability and teacher burnout, while others focus on the unintended consequences of standards-based school accountability, including high-stakes testing. The Brookings Institution in Washington, DC, has published some of his work on accountability and testing. His most recent books include *The International Handbook of Research on Teachers and Teaching* (published with Lawrence J. Saha of the Australian National University; 2009, Springer Publishers) and *The Palgrave Handbook of Race and Ethnic Inequalities in Education* (in preparation with Peter Stevens of the University of Ghent; forthcoming, Palgrave Macmillan Publishers).

Mariano Fernández Enguita studied Economics, graduated and obtained a Ph.D. in political sciences and sociology and later graduated in law. Professor in Sociology (associate since 1883, full since 1994), he has been Head of the Department of Sociology and Communication and Director of the Spanish-Japanese Cultural Centre at the U. of Salamanca, where he leaded the Centro de Análisis Sociales (Centre for Social Analisys, CASUS, casus.usal.es) and the Observatorio Social de Castilla y León (a regional social watch). Now he teaches at the U. Complutense of Madrid, being also head of the Education Section of the Department of Sociology VI, where he leads the Barómetro del Profesorado (Teachers' Barometer) and the Barómetro de Opinión Hispano-Luso (Spanish-Portuguese Opinion Poll). He has researched and published widely on social inequality, organizations and education. He's been visiting scholar at the universities of Stanford, Berkeley, Wisconsin (Madison), SUNY (Binghamton), LSE (London), IOE (London), Lumière-LyonII (Lyon) and Sophia (Tokyo), and has lectured in tens of Spanish and Latin American universities and institutions. Among his more than twenty books and two hundred book chapters and journal articles, some recent publications are: *Educar en tiempos inciertos*, published in Spain, Brazil and Portugal, and *¿Es pública la escuela pública?*; and, in English language, *School Failure and Dropouts in Spain, Barcelona*, Fundación La Caixa, 2010; "Ethnic Group, Class and Gender in Education: Paradoxes in the Schooling of Moroccan and Roma Students", in C. McCarthy, Editor, *Transnational Perspectives on Popular Culture and Public Policy*, NY, Peter Lang, 2009; "Get to Know Yourself or Better Not: The

Multidimensionality of Power and the Pseudoradicalism of Intellectuals and Teachers", *The International Journal Of Interdisciplinary Social Sciences,* vol. II, 2008; "Professionalism, Accountability and Innovation in Teaching", *Education et Societés* 25, 2010.

Daniel Faas is Lecturer in Sociology at Trinity College Dublin and Visiting Fellow with the University of Aarhus. His research interests focus on migration and education, citizenship and identity politics, multiculturalism and social cohesion, ethnicity and racism, curriculum and policy developments, and comparative research within and between Europe and North America. Daniel Faas was Fulbright-Schuman Fellow in the Department of Sociology at the University of California at Berkeley (2009), and Marie Curie Research Fellow at the Hellenic Foundation for European and Foreign Policy (2006–2008). He is winner of the 2009 European Sociological Association award for best article and author of *Negotiating Political Identities: Multiethnic Schools and Youth in Europe* (Ashgate, 2010).

Neil Guppy is Professor and Head of Sociology at the University of British Columbia. He was Associate Dean (Students) from 1996 to 1999 and Associate Vice-President (Academic Programs) at UBC from 1999 to 2004. He is a graduate of Queen's University (BA/BPHE) and the University of Waterloo (M.Sc./Ph.D., 1981). He has published several books, including *Education in Canada* (Statistics Canada, 1998, with Scott Davies), *The Schooled Society* (Oxford University Press, 2010, 2nd edition; with Scott Davies), and *Successful Surveys* (4th edition, Thomson Nelson, 2008, with George Gray). He is the lead author on a recent national report produced by the Society for the Advancement of Excellence in Education: *Parent and Teacher Views on Education: A Policymaker's Guide*. Recently he has published work in the *American Sociological Review* and *International Migration Review* on public opinion and immigration, in the *Canadian Review of Anthropology and Sociology* on occupational prestige judgments, and in *Sociological Forum* on cultural capital and job search/attainment. His research interests include social inequality (especially class, ethnicity and gender), work and occupations and education. At UBC he has received both a University Killam Teaching Prize and a University Killam Research Prize. He is a member of the UBC Faculty Pension Plan Board of Trustees and the Board of UBC Press.

Christos Kassimeris heads the Department of Social and Behavioral Sciences at European University Cyprus and is coordinator of the B.A. in European Studies. Before joining European University Cyprus, he was teaching European integration politics and international relations of the Mediterranean for three years at the University of Reading. He is the author of *European Football in Black and White: Tackling Racism in Football* and *Greece and the American Embrace: Greek Foreign Policy Towards Turkey, the US and the Western Alliance,* has several publications in the field of international relations and is Visiting Research Fellow at the University of De Montfort.

Gitsa Kontogiannopoulou-Polydorides was appointed Professor of Sociology of Education and Research Methodology at the Faculty of Mathematics, University of Patras in 1985. In 1989 she was appointed Professor. In 1995 she was appointed by special invitation Professor at the University of Athens, where she serves today. She has served in a number of academic posts as: Dean of the School of Humanities and Social Science (1990–1995), Director of Postgraduate studies (through 1995), Head of the Unit of Sociology of Education and Social Policy and the Adjunct Laboratory (1992–1995). She is currently the Director of the Joint Post-graduate Programme in Education and Human Rights (University of Athens and University of London, Institute of Education). She is also the Director of the Center of the International Association for the Evaluation of Educational Achievement (IEA) and Policy Research. She has participated in a number of international research and development projects in education and has a number of publications.

Katherine Lyon received her M.A. in Sociology and the Collaborative Program in Women's and Gender Studies from the University of Toronto and her B.A. in Honours Sociology from the University of British Columbia. Her M.A. thesis explored how common-law gay and lesbian couples in Toronto, Ontario, negotiate and experience their access to the institution of marriage (legal in the province since 2003). At U of T Katherine was a junior fellow of Massey College and a recipient of the C.B. McPherson Graduate Admissions Award, the Dean's Students Initiative Fund and the Ontario Graduate Scholarship. As a research assistant for the UBC Department of Sociology, Katherine currently works with Dr. Neil Guppy analyzing British Columbia secondary school sex education curricula from 1875 to 2010. Her research interests include gender, sexuality, education and inequality. She applies her feminist sociological perspective in a community setting by volunteering with local organizations committed to ending violence against women in Vancouver's Downtown Eastside. Katherine is also a member of the Board of Directors for The Downtown Eastside Studio Society, a support and micro-entrepreneurship organization for people facing multiple social barriers.

Peter A. J. Stevens has an M.A. in sociology (Ghent University, Belgium), an M.A. in race and ethnic relations (Warwick University, UK) and a Ph.D. in sociology (Warwick University). Stevens's research interests cover the areas of sociology of education, race/ethnic relations and mixed methods research. His past and current research focuses on: race/ethnicity and educational inequality, processes of tracking/streaming in schools and the contextual development, management and consequences of experiences of racism. Stevens was research assistant at the Department of Sociology, Ghent University, post-doctoral research officer at the London Institute of Education (UK), post-doctoral Fellow of the Scientific Research Foundation Flanders (FWO) and part-time lecturer at the European University of Cyprus and the University of Nicosia. Dr. Stevens is currently doing research on the development of ethnic stereotypes and experiences of discrimination in particular school settings in divided communities (Belgium and Cyprus).

Pamela Tobe is Senior Research Associate and Co-PI with the Sociology of Education Research Group (SERG), and Senior Research Associate for the Institute for Urban Education, both at the University of Houston. She received her B.A. in Cultural Anthropology, B.S.W. (Social Work), and M.B.A. (Marketing and Human Resources Management) degrees from the University of British Columbia, Canada and her Ed.D. degree from the University of Houston, Texas. She currently works as a grant and program evaluator in addition to assisting urban school districts and non-profit organizations in understanding student academic achievement, school and teacher effectiveness, teacher work attitudes, school climate and professional development. Her recent publications include "Teacher Value-Added Models" in *The International Handbook on Teachers and Teaching* (2009), edited by Lawrence Saha and Gary Dworkin, and "Teacher Burnout in Light of School Safety, Student Misbehavior, and Changing Accountability Standards" published with Gary Dworkin, in *Schools in Society* (2011), edited by Jeanne Ballantine and Joan Spade.

Marios Vryonides is assistant professor of sociology at the European University Cyprus and scientific collaborator at the University of the Aegean, Greece. He got his B.A. in sociology from Panteion University Athens, his M.A. in sociology from the University of Essex and his Ph.D. from Institute of Education—University of London. From 2004 until 2009 he was visiting lecturer at the Institute of Education—University of London. He has taught at Anglia Polytechnic University (2001–2003) and the University of the Aegean (2004–2007). Since 2008 he has been Cyprus's national coordinator of the European Social Survey. He is currently the secretary of the Research Committee on Sociology of Education (RC04) of the International Sociological Association. His research interests are focused in contemporary sociological theory, sociology of education, in the theories of cultural and social capital and in the processes of educational choice-making.

Index